Wild Boy

MY LIFE IN
DURAN DURAN

ANDY TAYLOR

GRAND CENTRAL
PUBLISHING

NEW YORK   BOSTON

The names and identifying characteristics of some incidental characters [persons] in this book have been changed.

Grand Central Publishing
Hachette Book Group USA
237 Park Avenue
New York, NY 10017

Visit our Web site at www.HachetteBookGroupUSA.com.

Printed in the United States of America

First Edition: September 2008
10 9 8 7 6 5 4 3 2 1

Grand Central Publishing is a division of Hachette Book Group USA, Inc. The Grand Central Publishing name and logo is a trademark of Hachette Book Group USA, Inc.

Library of Congress Cataloging-in-Publication Data

Taylor, Andy.
    Wild boy : my life in Duran Duran / Andy Taylor.—1st ed.
        p.   cm.
    ISBN-13: 978-0-446-50930-5
    ISBN-10: 0-446-50930-2
    1. Taylor, Andy.   2. Rock musicians—England—Biography.
3. Duran Duran (Musical group)   I. Title.
    ML420.T25A3   2008
782.42166092—dc22
    [B]

                                                        2008022270

CONTENTS

PROLOGUE

Philadelphia—July 13, 1985

WELCOME *to Live Aid. It's a boiling hot summer afternoon, and I'm about to perform with Duran Duran at the biggest gig on the planet. I'm standing backstage, from where I can hear the roaring audience reverberating throughout JFK Stadium. The noise is deafening, and I've been told that steam is rising off the crowd because the crew have been hosing people down, just to try to keep them cool and from passing out in the searing heat. The sweet, pungent smell of marijuana is wafting in on warm, moist waves of air coming from outside, where hundreds of people are smoking weed, drinking beer, eating pizza, and having the time of their lives. Officially, there are supposed to be 90,000 rock fans in the stadium; however, the turnstiles have been swamped and there's maybe upward of 120,000 bodies, could be even higher. Nobody really knows for sure, but it's stacked to the rafters.*

The scale of the event is mind-blowing. The lineup is a quintessential Who's Who of rock and roll: Led Zeppelin, members of the Rolling Stones, Bob Dylan, Madonna, Eric Clapton, Tina Turner—everybody is here. I've somehow managed to drink at least a liter of iced white wine, and I look on from the side of the stage as Jimmy Page and Robert Plant

1

from Led Zeppelin perform with drummers Phil Collins and Tony Thompson—"the black John Bonham" from the Power Station. There's so much adrenaline pumping because of the Zeppelin performance that the alcohol doesn't affect me at all. I guess with this many legendary artists on the bill, Live Aid is unquestionably going to be the biggest show in history. Two billion people, almost half the population of the world, will have tuned in to watch on TV as we rally to make a stand against poverty in Africa, the first time the Western world has witnessed the horror of these images through TV. I think to myself that as one half of the Earth is eating and watching, the other half is starving.

The Hollywood A-list is out in force and Jack Nicholson, Bette Midler, and Don Johnson have been introducing the acts. Now Chevy Chase is out there with the microphone and it's our turn to be announced.

"Are you ready?" Chevy shouts to the crowd. "Here they are . . . Duran Duran!"

The audience goes wild. Only a US crowd can make that sound of whooping, and we are at number one in America with "A View to a Kill," which we plan to open with, so they are delighted to see us, even after Led Zeppelin. Suddenly I am onstage, and the sheer size of the stadium stuns me as I look straight out at almost 120,000 people. They look like ants, and because of the low, wide, endless stadium the haze of people fades into the humid air. I can't see individual faces—it's just a blur of color and noise, although my "hazy" viewpoint has got nothing to do with the booze. I should be staggering around like an English drunk by now, but at twenty-four years old just give me a crowd and some loud gear and I'll keep standing. The wall of sound created by the audience reaches 121 decibels, above the limit at which noise begins to distort the human ear. As per usual, we'll need to crank it up to at least 123 decibels, and, not for the first time, we probably can't be heard. This is not your average show; there's a lot more energy to control, and it's not just "our show"—although for the next twenty minutes it has to be ours. For twenty minutes we have to own the audience, liquid diet included. So here I stand, guitar in hands, and I'm pretty fired up. Usually I don't think about it, but today I mustn't fuck up. Get it right, son! Some shows have a cup final feel around them. I try not to think about it as the adrenaline and the urgency will take me to a different level. I wonder if this is what it is like in a football game—if we don't score, the crowd will turn against us. Part of my brain cuts to autopilot, and the muscle memory acquired from playing so many gigs kicks in.

Simon Le Bon is to my right, there's a stack of amps behind me, and I can hear the band through a side monitor to my left. It all sounds a little ropey at first, but at this point I'm just glad to be plugged in with six strings and a working amplifier, because earlier in the day my equipment fucked up when I was onstage with the Power Station (another dark omen). I can feel Nick Rhodes on keyboards behind me; Roger Taylor is poised nervously on his drums in the middle, and I can see my partner in crime, John Taylor, on the far side of the stage with his bass guitar bouncing on his hip. The bass looks huge because he is so bloody thin. The scale of the event doesn't appear to be fazing the band at all . . . Then, just as everything seems to be coming together fine, I notice Simon's voice is getting a tad croaky. He looks great, but it's been a while since we were last onstage together, and one gig isn't enough to get the voice back into shape. I can tell he is straining to hit the notes and there's still that note to come as the song reaches crescendo. I hope he isn't thinking about hitting that note . . . "Thinking" is a bad thing when you perform, I muse. Then, shit! His voice suddenly gives way . . .

"With a vie-yoo-ow to a kill!!!" he screeches right at the end of the song, with no time to recover. All bloody live . . . Well, at least he ain't swimming with the fishes. I grimace and the cameras capture everything—again all live, but so what? It doesn't matter and it was sort of inevitable. We carry on playing, and the number ends to rapturous applause.

Now it's Simon's turn to speak to the audience:

"Hello. Good evening to Philadelphia, to the whole world that is watching," he says triumphantly as the crowd settles. "Tonight, we are here to celebrate something which has worked so far . . . This is a song called 'The Union of the Snake.'"

Then we slow things down a bit with "Save a Prayer," before Simon gees up the crowd one last time.

"If you've got any energy left, we'd like to see you dancing," he tells them, and we finish with "The Reflex," another recent US number one, which wins the audience over big-time, and they go nuts. As we leave the stage the cheers are still deafening—not bad after Zeppelin, *I think to myself,* but which bastard put them on before us? . . .

AT that moment, everything should have been perfect, but privately we were screwed and in turmoil. When we came offstage in Philadelphia there were no congratulatory hugs or friendly smiles. It was like we were completely foreign to each other, and it would be the last time we played together for almost two decades. Unbeknownst to the rest of the world, we had quietly (in our ever-so-English way) been falling apart at the seams for many months prior to Live Aid.

In truth, we could barely stand to be in the same room. Frustrated by the constant bickering and hostility within Duran Duran, John and I had formed the Power Station with Tony Thompson and Robert Palmer, which had been hugely successful. Simon and Nick had formed their own spin-off group, Arcadia.

The rehearsal in Philadelphia had been an absolute nightmare. The air was acrid with tension. Nick and I barely exchanged a single word, save sorting out the set list, which probably suited us both fine. Roger looked like Death warmed up, almost as if he wasn't there, and you could see the strain of our spirit-sapping lifestyle etched across his face. I was lucid, but only on a level that would confound most scientists. Even Simon was getting ragged around the edges and looking decidedly "sailor faced"—still forever the optimist, but of late preferring to go sailing on his yacht than be with the band.

John and I were in a dark place. We might have looked lean and hungry from constant touring with Duran and the Power Station, but we were dying inside. We were tired of twenty-four-hour attention, tired of drinking and taking drugs, haggard from the lifestyle we had once aspired to.

Live Aid was the first time all five members of Duran Duran had been together for months, and we had just one day to try and make ourselves sound half-decent before going onstage. Not surprisingly, the rehearsals were a disaster and I ended up ordering everyone who wasn't in the band or essential crew to leave—where had all these people come from? "Bloody rubbernecks" was Roger's affectionate term for them. Two people who were not present at this point were the Berrows, my now-former managers . . .

I spent the morning of the show in my hotel suite watching Status Quo live from the UK—they opened up the day's proceedings across the Atlantic in London. But not even the Quo and a huge American breakfast could brighten up our day, and things continued to get darker during the ride to JFK Stadium. At least there was no sound check. We were being hailed by the press as the Fab Five, the most successful British band since the Beatles, but instead of celebrating any of this, we just got on the bus and sat in silence.

We'd reached rock bottom and we had absolutely nothing to say to each other. We drove to the venue through streets packed with excited rock fans, but inside the bus the atmosphere was as if we were on our way to a funeral. (Little did we realize that we were on the way to a funeral—it was ours.) The only people who spoke were Tony, who was due to play with both the Power Station and Led Zeppelin, and Danny Goldberg, who had previously been Led Zeppelin's PR man. I'd met Danny through Michael Des Barres, who'd agreed to sing with the Power Station after Robert Palmer had dropped out. Danny was a powerful character, and behind the scenes he had been rather clandestine in attempting to prize me away from the madness of Duran Duran. He was a clever guy, but he never seemed to be far away from troubled musicians. Years later he became Nirvana and Kurt Cobain's manager, staying with them till the singer's death, then he went on to become chairman of Warner Bros. Records.

Philadelphia—July 13, 1985   5

As our bus approached the grand old JFK Stadium, which has long since been demolished, we might have been regarded as the hottest band in the world, but there were so many great acts on the bill that it felt as if we went down somewhat in the rankings. Later, when I came offstage with Duran Duran, I could feel exhaustion begin to take effect. Live Aid had been a long show day; in addition to going onstage with Duran Duran, both John and I had performed a set with the Power Station. Despite being tired, I stayed around to watch Bob Dylan onstage with Ronnie Wood and Keith Richards. Woody and Keith were so off their nuts that their performance was a shambles, but nobody gave a toss—I guess people were just happy to see them at all. I'd watched them arrive together in a stretch limo earlier that afternoon, and they'd been so legless that they had literally fallen out of the car, Woody laughing hysterically. When they made a mess of the songs onstage it seemed to give everybody else license to get roaring drunk, and it's still one of the most memorable moments for me. So when the time came to go back to my hotel I was slightly the worse for wear, but my hair was still looking good. For some bizarre reason I found myself sitting in a big cardboard box being dragged across the car park to the artists' bus by Eric Clapton. "You seemed like you might need help," he later told me . . .

Back at the hotel there was a bigger-than-usual party; I'd never seen a bar with so many people in it who I loved. Michael Des Barres introduced me to Jimmy Page (what a sweet man, you'd never guess he was so fascinated by Aleister Crowley) and at one point I was sitting on a sofa with Jimmy, Ronnie Wood, and Keith Richards. I had Michael snap a photo; he knew all these guys from the seventies and he had a friendly, endearing charm, even with Keith. Later, when I saw the shot, I couldn't help but laugh. Their legendary craggy faces reminded me of the heads carved on Mount Rushmore, with me sandwiched in the middle, trying to do my best "rock" look. Yet despite all the mirth, my heart just wasn't in the mood to party, and shortly before midnight, as the booze slowed down, I retired to my suite.

I crashed into bed and reflected that Live Aid should have been one

Prologue

of our biggest highs, but it wasn't—although I suppose I had anticipated that. To the rest of the world, we were the best-selling band in the UK and America and we could do no wrong. We were five close friends who mixed with royalty, and we had enjoyed a level of success that most bands could only dream of. But behind all the glamour, the smoke and mirrors, everything tasted sour, and the medication was no longer working. I lay there alone in the darkness of my hotel room, lit a blunt joint, and tried to inhale deeply, slowly, and ignore the constant whining in my left ear caused by the volume of the stage audio monitors.

Ahw no . . .

Suddenly there was a knock on the door. It was a member of our road crew.

"Super T"—that was my nickname—"we've booked a table. Meet by the elevator in ten."

Bollocks, *I thought.* Super T? All I want is a cup of tea.

So there I was, Andy Taylor of Duran Duran. The UK press had recently accused me of being the "wildest of the Wild Boys," but I just couldn't consume any more booze or drugs. Worse still, there was no twenty-four-hour room service tonight.

"Fuck off and leave me alone" was all I could muster.

I'd had enough. I needed a rest from this Groundhog Day *coke-fueled lifestyle. I realized that the consumption had to stop for the madness to begin to subside. For a while, success had brought us happiness and wealth beyond our wildest dreams. But the lifestyle we had aspired to, and for which we had worked so hard, became the very cancer that was starting to destroy us. Little did I realize how long it was going to take to repair some of the lives damaged as a consequence of our excess. For sure, we paraded around in our fast cars, with beautiful models on yachts in the south of France and the Caribbean, without needing to pay the bill at times (that came later). But it begs the question: Was it all worth it? Not too many people knew about our incendiary arguments or my fights with our management—and the dark depression and bitter resentments that these confrontations created. Neither did they know about the blood and the exhaustion, all from being constantly on the road, or about the mad cocaine binges, or the paranoia and insanity that was caused by being in the spotlight for what amounts to twenty-four hours a day.*

We were hanging on by our fingernails.

We were called Duran Duran. This is the story of how we came to rule the world and nearly threw it all away. Brace yourself—it's a roller-coaster ride . . .

CHAPTER ONE

The North East—1972

FOR most kids, the first day at grammar school is a big occasion. For me, it changed my life forever because it was the day my mother chose to abandon me and my brother. I was eleven years old. When I came home from school on the bus in my brand-new uniform, I discovered that she had just disappeared and taken all her things with her. Everything she owned was gone: her clothes, her ornaments, everything—there wasn't even a note to say good-bye. Nothing was left but a very dark feeling in a place that was supposed to be safe. It was like a heavy guillotine had suddenly come rushing down with great force and sliced everything apart without any explanation as to why I was guilty.

IT would be four very long years before I would see her again, but I didn't cry at the time (that would come a lot later). You see, the way I've always thought about life is that you can either choose to give someone a friendly slap to say, "Hello, stop being such a fucking idiot," or you can just hit them with a bat. If you give them a slap you might wake them up a bit, but if you hit them with a bat you proverbially risk killing them. So no, this wasn't just a little slap, this

9

was from the middle of the bat, the part that hurts the most. The irony was that up until about the age of ten I had enjoyed a relatively normal childhood. But once you've been hit by the bat, life will never be the same . . .

I was born on the sixteenth of February 1961 at Tynemouth Jubilee Infirmary, the first child of Ronnie and Blanche Taylor. My mum and dad had grown up in a small fishing village called Cullercoats, which is just up the coast from Whitley Bay and Newcastle upon Tyne, so it was only natural that they would eventually set up their own marital home in the same village. Three years after I was born my little brother Ronnie arrived, and for a while life must have seemed perfect for my parents. We lived in a beautiful little bay close to the seafront, in a crowded fisherman's terrace that we shared with my dad's family, who were spread out over three or four floors. We lived downstairs, my grandma and grandfather on my father's side of the family lived in the middle, and an aunty and uncle lived on the top floor.

In those days, as everyone got older and began to get on their feet, they moved out and got their own houses, but it wasn't necessarily the case that when you got married you moved out straightaway—you had to work hard and save first, which was the position my parents found themselves in. Our little terrace lay behind the workingmen's club (the CIU) and close to the Fisherman's Institute. We always referred to the CIU affectionately as "the club," because it had been founded in part thanks to my family's efforts. Close by on the bay there was a fish-and-chips shop and an amusement arcade. My earliest memories are of standing on a beer crate in the arcade and playing pinball at the age of five, and I was quite good at it, like a little pinball wizard.

We literally grew up on the beach, and we would have endless games of football on the sand, during which all the kids in the neighborhood would turn out in great numbers. There were no fearful parents with four-by-fours; you just had to be home when your dad said so. There wasn't a hidden cove that we didn't know about or a cave that we hadn't explored. On Guy Fawkes Night we'd build huge fires on the beach and let off fireworks and feast on baked potatoes. In those days there were no health-and-safety experts or prying council officials to order us around, so we were pretty much left to our own devices when it came to creating our own fun. We had our own set of social rules, because people rarely traveled in those days. I think the farthest any of my family had been was a day trip to Blackpool with the club. Life belonged to an earlier age, and it was before the big housing redevelopments of the late sixties and seventies, so we still had an outside toilet, which was next to the coal bunker and the air-raid shelter. It would be freezing and dark if you had to get up in the middle of the night for a number two, so I used to wake my dad up and ask him to stand by the door. Otherwise it was a pee in the pot.

Apart from mining and farming, the only other industry was fishing. My grandfather and all my uncles had boats, so most days I used to get up at 4 or 5 a.m. when they went out to sea. They would come back with fishing pots brimming with lobsters, and we used to kill them in the kitchen. My grandfather was a lifeboat man, and my great-grandfather was on the same boat before him. A loud cannon used to boom in the middle of the night to signal its launch, and the whole family would all get up to gather on the bank while the sons and husbands went off to sea. The explosion was really loud. To a child, it was incredibly exciting to watch the drama unfold. There could be a full-scale gale going down over the North Sea but they would still get up in the night and get the boat out; it was amazing nobody ever died. Most people's lives in our community were linked to the sea in some way. During World War II, most of my dad's family had been in the Royal Navy or the merchant navy. At home we had an old framed photograph of a corrugated-iron bomb shelter that still stood in the backyard. My dad grew up during the war, so he was obsessed with it and spoke about it constantly. We used to joke that he kept the photograph up on the wall just to remind everybody, lest we forget.

Early on, there was no hint of the trouble with my mum that lay ahead. I've still got lots of family photographs that show us all looking normal and happy. Christmas was always a grand affair. We used to do all the traditional different bits and pieces, and all my grandmother's extended family, who lived miles away in a distant rural area, would descend upon us in a big group. So there were always a lot of people around at Christmas, sometimes so many people that I don't actually know where they all managed to sleep. In the summer, all the folks would come over again and our family would spend hours singing together, belting out northern folk songs and all the old classic numbers by Bing Crosby and Jim Reeves, my grandmother's favorite.

The musicians of the family were definitely all on my father's side. My grandmother used to sing a lot in the workingmen's clubs, and one of her brothers was a brilliant trumpet player. Whenever her family came from the countryside to stay with us on the coast, we used to have huge get-togethers that would basically involve drinking and singing while my dad would play some fantastic tunes on the harmonica. We used to go to church a lot, and all the family would come and sing there, too, so music was part of my childhood from the beginning. My cousin Marjorie had bought a copy of *Sgt. Pepper's Lonely Hearts Club Band* by the Beatles on the day it came out, and she would come round so that we could play it together. Later she gave it to me, and I still have that original copy of *Sgt. Pepper* from forty-odd years ago with her name on it. We also used to play all the great singles that came out during that period, which were all stacked up in the corner of the room, and I have lots of little memories of my family being together around the record player. We used to play the Beatles, the Hollies, the Kinks, and lots of sixties bands. Around this time I was very excited to discover that my dad had a guitar hidden away in the cupboard, which with hindsight turned out to be a very important find. There was a guitar tuition program on BBC Two at the time called *Hold Down a Chord*, and I was hooked. I managed to get the instruction book that accompanied the show, and I spent hours practicing until I could play the chords by heart.

SO for a while, we functioned like a normal family. I used to help my mother in the garden doing greenhouse work in order to get the tomato plants to grow and we had lots of rosebushes that needed constant attention. I remember sitting with her, looking at all the blossoms in the trees and listening to the birds sing. But if I'm honest, I was always closer to my father, even back then. I was quite a stroppy kid, and I had a lot of confrontations with my mother because she was obsessive about tidiness and would order me not to go in and out of certain rooms, which I used to hate. She would have her favorite things that I wasn't allowed to touch, and this often led to friction between us. I was always much more comfortable with my grandmother on my dad's side of the family. She was a lovely, kind woman. After my mum's parents passed on while I was quite young, she would become the main matriarch in my life.

A few months before I was due to go to senior school we moved to a new house of our own, a bright little cottage on a corner plot about a mile or two away. My dad worked as a foreman for a building firm, and his speciality was carpentry. He soon put in a new electric fireplace with some timber borrowed from the joiner's shop, and he went on to do the place up. To outsiders everything must have looked idyllic, but secretly my parents' marriage was already in a lot of trouble. They would argue late at night, and sometimes I'd end up trying to break them up. It had been going on since I was about nine, and I was spending more and more time with my grandmother, particularly on weekends—which I guess must have been my old man wanting to get me out of the way because they were fighting so much.

There was a strike in the construction industry that summer, so there was a lot of upheaval because he had to break a picket line in order to get into work. My dad was a Tory, but nearly everybody else in the North East was a Labour voter, so he and my uncle Bob had to arrange to get people into work round the back entrance in a pickup truck, and it could get very violent.

The world was a very different place back then. Breaking a picket line was a big deal, but my father had just bought a house and taken on a big mortgage, and he probably felt he didn't really have any choice. Putting a kid through grammar school wasn't going to be cheap; there might not have been any fees to worry about, but if you factored in all the uniforms and the extra school materials that you needed, along with the cost of numerous school trips and outings, it was much more expensive than comprehensive school, and my dad had to shell out a lot to afford it all.

MONEY had always been tight, so my mother had taken a waitressing job in a club during the evenings to help make ends meet. But in many ways her waitressing job turned out to be the root of all evil, because that was when the trouble began.

The change was almost instant. A few weeks after taking the job, she dyed her hair blond instead of its normal brown color, and she started dressing differently. I remember sitting on a bus with her one particular morning and looking at her outfit.

Bloody hell, your miniskirt is short, I thought to myself.

She would stay out late waiting on tables, and often she would not return until the early hours. It wasn't long before I started seeing my mother do things that I shouldn't have seen her do. The first time was when I was about ten. I wandered back from school one morning, maybe because I'd forgotten something or didn't feel well. It was about ten past nine, and I saw a red car that had suddenly parked outside the house. I don't know why, maybe it was childhood intuition, but I decided to watch instead of going inside. I'd seen men drop her off a couple of times in the past, so maybe there was a part of me that was already suspicious that something unhealthy was going on. Even as a ten-year-old kid you start putting two and two together.

I used to have places all over where I could hide, so I climbed up onto the garage roof. From there I could see the house without being spotted, because it had a brick front that was a little bit higher than the slope of the roof. She came out with a strange man and they were physically all over each other. I had a sick feeling in my stomach, because I just knew it was wrong and I was terrified they'd be spotted.

"What if the neighbors see them?" I whispered to myself.

Then I wondered if perhaps everybody did that sort of thing at a certain age. Maybe they were *all* at it! I wanted to convince myself that everything would be okay, but deep down I knew that what I had just seen threatened everything that we had, because I understood how hard it had been for my parents to get a mortgage and afford a home together, and I knew this could tear us apart.

I kept things bottled up and hoped it would go away, but soon similar things started to happen again. I couldn't believe it and at first I didn't know what to do, but eventually I plucked up the courage to tell my dad. I thought he wouldn't believe me, so I started keeping a record of what I saw by speaking into a cassette recorder. But when I told my dad it turned out he knew full well what was going on. He tried to explain it to me as best he could and said that things would be all right. It was the reason they'd been having all the arguments at night. I used to stay up late in bed to listen to Radio Luxembourg through a little earpiece and wait to hear what time she would come in. It would get later and later and later. I could hear the car pull up outside, and I would hold my breath and listen with a sick feeling inside as she came into the house. Then my dad would get up and I would hear their arguments. I was completely aware of it all. When you are a kid, you can't sleep when something like that is going on, because it fascinates you as much as it upsets you. Their arguments got worse and worse until sometimes, as I said, I would get out of bed and try to break it up.

I think my dad forgave her several times. They were still trying to make a go of things when we all went off for a family holiday together at Butlins holiday camp near Scarborough before she left. I had passed my 11-plus exams and earned a place at Whitley Bay

Grammar School, which was a big step up socially from the local comprehensive school. So as my first day at grammar school approached I was very chuffed and excited, and I certainly had no idea how suddenly my parents' problems would come to a head. My dad saw getting into grammar school as a big achievement, too, and when we went into Newcastle to buy my new uniform it felt as if a whole new life was about to start all over again. I was right about that, although not for the reasons I'd imagined . . .

SHORTLY before my mother left I found a silver ring hidden in the bathroom. I was looking for something else when I discovered it tucked away in the corner of a cabinet. It was a shiny little band, and I assumed it was something that someone had bought for my mother, but I soon had other ideas for it.

I'd left junior school over the summer, but I was in touch with a girl called Claire, and I wanted to pluck up the courage to ask her to be my girlfriend.

"Take the ring and give it to Claire," a little voice said.

I knew it was wrong, but part of me was angry with my mother because the ring was almost certainly a piece of jewelry given to her by a man other than my father. I found a little box and put the ring in it with some cotton wool. But I never got to give it to Claire or go out with her because when my mother discovered it was missing, she summoned me to the bathroom to confront me, and it led to a terrible fight between us.

"How dare you take it?" she raged, after I confessed.

"Why not? You don't care about us," I shouted back.

Soon we were screaming at each other at the tops of our voices as she continued to discipline me for meddling in her stuff. I stepped backward, lost my footing, and suddenly found myself tumbling down the stairs. I landed in a heap at the bottom and hurt my back.

Just then, the front door opened and my dad walked in from work, his tool bag over his shoulder, to discover us amid the mayhem.

"What the hell is happening?" he demanded.

My tumble down the stairs had been an accident, but I think my father harbored suspicions that she'd pushed me. When I was a very small child, I'd fallen over and suffered a cut above my left eye while I was alone with her. The wound had needed eleven stitches and my father gave me the impression that he felt the circumstances in which I'd fallen had never fully been explained.

Eventually we all calmed down and the row diffused, but the tension didn't go away.

MEANWHILE, I knew a couple of other local lads who had won places at grammar school. When our first day arrived, we all got onto the bus together with our kit, each of us with a cap and satchel.

No matter how hard I try, I can't remember what my mother's last words were to me that morning. (Maybe there's a part of me that doesn't want to.) But I do know that I didn't suspect anything. As I recall, she just treated everything normally, making sure I was in my new uniform, that I had all the things I needed, and that I got down to the bus stop on time. One of the other lads knocked for me and we were on our way, full of excitement. The grammar school itself was great; it had a big new sports hall and lots of impressive walkways that were all raised above ground level. There were language labs and cricket fields and almost every facility you could possibly wish for. Even the teachers were fantastic. So coming back on the bus that day as a kid I felt as though I had been given so much.

Then when I got back there was nobody at home, which had never happened before. I didn't even have a key, so at first I went round the back to investigate, but I still couldn't get in.

In a certain sort of way, I think I knew what had happened because there was no electric heater on inside, there was no sound from the telly, and there were no lights on. It wasn't exactly as if a bomb had gone off, but it was so different from what I would have normally encountered at 4:30 p.m. in the afternoon that I knew something was up. Bewildered, I went and phoned my dad at work. He didn't have any idea where my mum had gone, so he told me to go to my aunty's house, which was about a mile away.

What happened next is a bit of a haze, but I must have gone and picked my little brother up from his school on the way because I remember we arrived together. My dad met us at my aunty's place and it was then that we went home and went into the house, all three of us together, and we discovered it was empty and all the suitcases were gone. The missing cases were the first thing I noticed, because that morning they had still been on top of the wardrobe from when we'd been to Butlins. Even the mantelpiece, where she used to have bits and pieces of china, was just bare now. All the little things about which she'd been excessively tidy, and which we'd argued about so much, were gone.

To say my dad didn't take it very well would be an understatement. It was as if life had kicked him in the nuts after he'd worked so hard for everything. We had just had a new kitchen extension built, and he went in there for a bit on his own, just to pull himself together for a little while. My brother and I sat in the living room in silence. I assume my father was in the other room weeping, alone. I don't think my brother really had a clue what was going on because he was only about seven, but later on it would hit him very hard, much harder than it hit me.

My dad came back after he'd composed himself, and he was very calm when he spoke to us.

"Well, what we have to do now is get your gran to come up, because she would want to be here," he told us. His words were practical, not emotional. It was his male Northern dignity that kept him going.

Soon another aunty and an uncle drove up to the house with my nan, and she made some dinner. I'm pretty sure she cooked mince and dumplings, because she always used to make that for my dad when he was miserable, and we tried to put a brave face on things while we ate. All of his family were kind of aware and had come that

WILD BOY

night to show support, but the next day I knew I would be expected to go to school as if nothing had happened.

"It's my second day at school and I am not missing it," I said.

"You're right, you can't miss it," replied my dad.

It was the timing of everything that hurt the most, because I couldn't believe my mother cared so little for me that she'd chosen to vanish on my first day at school. You feel physically painful when something like that happens to you. My dad knew that I had a good insight into it all, although at the time I was still clinging to the thought that she'd come back after a few days. I think I talked to him about it that night, but we were both very tired and we didn't discuss it in much depth. We didn't need to; I understood. I knew exactly what had gone on, but it was much more difficult for my little brother.

The next morning I got my thruppence for the school bus, and off I went. My father went to work as normal, as well. I guess it was a cultural thing that had been learned during the war: "They might drop bombs on us, but we'll keep going no matter what."

After four or five days went by, I realized my mother wasn't going to return. It was as if she had been swallowed by a black hole. That's when my dad and my grandmother had to explain things to my brother, Ronnie. I somehow managed to find this funny little Off switch that allowed me to cope. I suppose it was a defense mechanism, although I would often run through things in my mind to see if I'd done anything that played a part in her decision to leave us.

"Why did she do it? What did I do? Am I to blame?" I'd ask myself.

Sometimes at night I would also worry about something happening to my dad; then my brother and I would be left on our own with nobody to look out for us. But in a strange way, despite all the pain, I was glad it was finally all over, because it meant we wouldn't have to keep shutting our eyes and pretending it was going to work out with my mother. I know for a fact my father forgave her for her behavior a couple of times, and he just kept saying that maybe things would be all right.

But things were not all right, at least not in that sense. It was eight months before I heard from my mother again. Later on in life, as an adult, I found one of the things I grew to hate about being on the road with a band was being apart from my own children; after seven or eight weeks of not seeing your kids it feels unbearable. So I often wonder how my own mother could have gone so many months without getting in touch. For me it seemed an eternity, because when you are a child the days seem longer and eight months seems like eight years.

You can process a lot at that age without knowing it. Suddenly I was interested in a whole new world filled with girls and guitars and football and all the things boys are crazy about when they're setting off on that whole teenage ride that lies ahead. It's probably no coincidence that the Christmas after my mother left, my dad bought me my first electric guitar. I used to spend every Saturday going up to Newcastle in order to go around all the music shops just looking at the guitars and thinking *if only*. They were replicas of the ones I'd seen rock stars use, and they cost £19.95. Sometimes the shop owners would let you have a go on them. By now I'd really got to grips with the guitar book, so it was my dream to own one. My dad must have seen this, and maybe he wanted to make things up a bit for the fact that Mum had left us, so he gave me £20 for my Christmas present. We went up to town, and I belted out "Smoke on the Water" by Deep Purple in the shop while my dad watched and listened. He asked the assistant if I was any good, and I was flattered by the answer.

"Good? He can play better than most of the grown-up blokes who we get in here!" said the shop assistant.

I suppose I'd just passed my first audition. My gran gave me £10 on top of the money I had from my dad, so I managed to get a little amp to go with the guitar, and that Christmas became known in the family as the "Electric Guitar Christmas."

We were obviously still very raw over my mum's departure. I used to discuss it a lot with my dad. He was furious and angry and hurt, but he would talk about it in a controlled way, not in a violent or an aggressive way, and I never saw him react angrily or do anything like throw stuff around the room. In a way I think that helped me, because he could articulate his frustrations and anger and I could relate to that and agree with him. It was as if he was speaking for both of us. I channeled a lot of my own anger into playing guitar. I would really thrash it for hours on end, and I became completely obsessed with it. I must have driven everybody mad with the noise, but my father never said a word. I think he was glad I'd found something I could focus on, and I doubt I would have had that sort of freedom had my mother been around.

IT was inevitable that my parents would divorce, which was something people just didn't do in the early seventies. We grew up watching *Coronation Street*, a cozy English TV soap opera and people in the fictitious Northern town where it was set just didn't do things like that, it was a complete taboo. Cullercoats was like *Coronation Street* with fish.

It was difficult at school because I didn't know whom to confide in, but when I did I soon found out that plenty of my mates came from families with similar problems.

But the truth is that by the time my mother contacted us again, I wasn't exactly missing her. Life had improved because there was no more tension. When she finally got in touch, it came in the form of a handwritten letter, which my father showed me one morning out of the blue. I remember being struck by how matter-of-fact the tone of her note was. She simply told us where she was living and said it was our choice if we wished to get in touch. There was no explanation of why she had abandoned us, but what really shocked me was the fact she'd been staying just a few hundred yards away from my grammar school. I wondered whether or not she'd watched me getting off the bus on all those winter mornings, and I questioned how it was that I'd never spotted her myself. She must have seen me coming and going; it would have been impossible not to. I was angry with her, too, for trying to put the responsibility about whether or not to see her again onto my shoulders.

"So I've got a choice now, have I? I don't remember having any choice in the matter last September," I said to myself.

I guess it must have taken a lot for her to have written that note after such a long time, and I understand that for any parent it can be difficult when you make a mess of things. But it was too late. I didn't want to see her.

LATER on, when I got to about thirteen or fourteen, sometimes I used to think that maybe I should do something about the fact my mother was no longer part of my life, but then I'd think, *Actually, you know what? As it stands there isn't much wrong with the way things are.* To go back and try to integrate everything again would have been almost impossible without causing everyone a whole lot of new pain. To this day I still don't know the full facts, and there are questions that I will never get an answer to, but as far as I know she moved in with another man. And I now know I have a half brother who was born later on, so I guess she had to make some difficult decisions of her own.

My father and I were going to church during the time that he was having troubles with my mum. He used the church as a means to help him through it all, but he knew he would be eventually excommunicated if he were to divorce, and so he faced a horrible dilemma. At one point he sat me down and asked me if I felt he should try and give things another chance with my mum. I had to be honest and I simply asked him how many more chances he would have to take before he knew it would never work. The fact that we were forced to discuss a lot of adult issues together meant I learned to communicate with him on an adult level at a very early age, and I guess it brought us a lot closer together. We used to sit together for hours on end at night talking, and he explained politics and all his views about the world to me.

Church certainly played an important part in our lives. Our

vicar, the Reverend Eric Zachau, helped me a lot when it was time to study for my confirmation exams. My dad used to do little carpentry jobs for him, and at one point when I was an altar boy I would carry a wooden cross that my dad had made. I had to kneel at the altar for an hour and ten minutes through the full Church of England service, which was a real killer on my legs. Then I had to set the wine and bread, and follow the priest around the congregation.

We would go there every Sunday. Once a month they would have morning tea after the service, and I was always struck by how nice the people were. The church had an enormous cemetery, and we used to cycle there if we were staying at my grandmother's house; or if we were at home it was close enough to walk. But despite the fact it was such a comfort to us, the whole experience would eventually leave me with a terrible contempt for authority, because of the way the church finally treated my dad. He got confirmed knowing full well that he would eventually get excommunicated because of his divorce, which was a crushing blow for him. He did it because it was just something that he felt he had to do, but it absolutely shattered him, and as far as I could see none of what happened had been his fault.

Ironically, once he got himself back together within a couple of years he went out socializing a lot and had a good time, but initially it must have seemed like life was constantly trying to cut him down. As soon as they excommunicated him I stopped going to church as well, and not long afterward I started drinking alcohol. The experience was another point of anger as a child, and I would think to myself: *Well, if you don't want my dad, I'm not coming either.*

I couldn't understand how, if they had taught us that Jesus loved everyone, they could suddenly say Jesus didn't love my dad! But it wasn't religion I had a problem with, it was the church. I didn't stop believing in Jesus as a good person, and I still find all the teachings of the Bible fascinating. But I realized there could be a very dark side to religion, and I lost my respect for authority because of it.

Not surprisingly, things quickly went downhill at school. I started hanging around with the sort of kids who would always be sat at the back of the class. My disciplinary record wasn't great and my attendance suffered. Suddenly we had found ourselves as a one-parent family, and despite all the overtime my dad worked we missed the money from my mother's income, and we were forced to move to a smaller place. The grammar school claimed I now lived outside their catchment area, so I had to drop out and go to the local comprehensive instead. As far as I could see, nobody else who moved house had ever been asked to leave, so I think secretly they were just glad to have an excuse to see the back of me. But by then I wasn't too bothered, because I was starting to get seriously interested in bands and drinking and girls, which meant I was more than happy to hang out with the kids I knew from the local comprehensive who were into similar things.

I threw a lot of my frustration into sports activities, and some days after school I would throw a javelin for hours on end. But like every other kid in the North East, my favorite sport was playing football. I played left back and used to charge up the wing. I soon won the captaincy of the school team and went on to play at county level. I enjoyed it so much that at one point I had dreams of turning professional. One Sunday afternoon, when my dad and I were walking along a country lane together, I asked him what he thought would pay more, being in a band or being a footballer. The one thing I was sure of at the time was I didn't want to end up like him, working his nuts off only to be slapped down all the time. He thought about it a bit before giving me his advice.

"Son, you might find if you are a musician that your career will last longer than if you are a footballer," he told me.

My father was very musical himself, and I suppose it had always been something he'd wished he could make a go of himself but never got the opportunity, so I think he was glad I'd found a focus in life.

As well as my dad, the other really important person in my life throughout most of my childhood was my grandmother on his side of the family. I still used to see some of my mother's family around the village, but by now her own parents had passed on and we didn't have much contact with her other relatives. But my paternal grandmother became the matriarch in my life and she later moved in with us. She looked after us in every respect. She was a kind, decent lady whom we all adored, and despite all the upheaval I never once went wanting for any care or love. She filled our lives with it.

She believed in that Northern family thing that you had to have your dinner every night and you never went off to school without eating breakfast or wearing clean socks. And I never did. I never, ever had to suffer any indignity and the fact I was okay was because of her and the fundamental care that she gave us. I always went to the cinema and had a new pair of football boots at Christmas. My dad had two sisters, my aunty Meta and my aunty Pat, and together with my grandmother (whom we called Mam) all three of them had old-fashioned blue rinse hairdos. They were traditional, strong Geordie women. My brother and I would never dare to disobey our grandmother, but she used to cut me a lot of slack, presumably because she'd been so horrified by what my mother had done. As I got older, she'd let me keep my dinner money for a packet of cigarettes and then cook me a beautiful meal in the evening to make sure I didn't go hungry. In the end we had to force her to stop working so hard, because she was basically looking after all of us right into her old age.

IT was against the background of my parents' breakup that music became the main focus of my life. I don't know where I would have ended up without it. Throughout my teenage years I was jamming three or four nights a week, practicing guitar at home and playing records. It filled a lot of hours when I would otherwise have been getting in trouble. That's not to say I still didn't manage to find time to get up to no good. I had a pretty bad behavioral record, and I had the worst attendance in school by the time I was fourteen or fifteen. I had a mate called Tommy, and we just used to go and get our attendance marks in the morning and then bunk off from school together for the rest of the day. Tommy had been through similar experiences at home, so we were both in the same boat.

We had every cave up the northeast coast covered, and we would go there with a can of cider and do daft things like attempt to smoke dried banana skins, because we'd heard rumors they could get you high (trust me, they don't!). There was one little bay where amorous couples would go to have sex and we knew about a cave up above, so we'd go up there and throw things at them for a laugh. There were lots of fabulous beaches and big rural areas to explore in Northumberland; and we used to go on bike rides and set fields on fire, then ride off. At night we'd build fires on the beach and sit around drinking snakebite and eating potatoes.

When I actually did bother to go to school, I think the shock of my mother leaving gave me a sort of rabid determination to do well, so when I played football I'd tackle too hard or I'd go in too hard at judo. Perhaps without knowing it, I was trying to prove myself by trying to kick someone. I was always clashing with two sports teachers, Mr. Denham and Mr. Chambers, whom we nicknamed Dodgy Denham and Choppy Chambers. They'd pull me up for my tackling and bellow, "Taylor—off for a minute." My mates and I used to get into a lot of fights, and if you saw some of the kids that went to my school at the time you'd know why. They would go into pubs at fifteen or sixteen and look for trouble. They used to like picking fights at that age.

Thankfully, if I was angry as a kid I used to take it out mainly on music. I soon discovered that music allows you to break the rules, change the rules, and make up your own rules as you go along. It allows you to thrash the hell out of a guitar and use up all your energy and frustration. The first band I was in as a young teenager was called the Haze. As I got older I started going to concerts at Newcastle City Hall and Newcastle Mayfair Ballroom on a Friday night. We'd catch a bus there along the coastal road, but we often ended up having to walk home at the end of the evening because we'd blown all our money on beer.

Virtually every act on the planet played in Newcastle over that period—David Bowie, Roxy Music, and all the great metal bands like AC/DC and Van Halen. Concert tickets cost about 75p or £1 in those days, so I got a milk round to pay for them. I worked six mornings a week, and I had to be up at 5 a.m. in all weather, but fortunately my family had a large supply of old fishing clothes that I could wear. The milkman had big Eric Morecambe–style glasses, and he nicknamed me Elvis because I was so mad about rock and roll. Every day he would greet me by saying, "Morning, Elvis—made any progress yet?" It was tough work, but it meant I could go to two or three gigs a week and also afford to keep up the payments on a new electric guitar I'd bought.

I was fifteen when I saw my mother again for the first time since she'd left us. I had a cousin on my mother's side of the family whom I used to see out and about around town, and occasionally we'd stop and chat. One day he told me one of my aunts on his side of the family, who lived down South, was having a sixtieth birthday party at the same time that an uncle was due to retire. They were planning a joint celebration in Kent. I thought, great, a trip to London!

I was starting to get inquisitive about my mum, and something inside of me just wanted to go to the party. I suppose it was curiosity. The only problem was my dad, as I didn't want to upset or hurt him. He'd moved on by now; he was a good-looking bloke and he was having a great time, having met a new partner named Sandra. But even so, I didn't think he'd be very agreeable to opening up old wounds, so I told him a bit of a story about going to see a band and I went down on the train. I thought it would be nice to see all the other members of the family whom I hadn't seen for so long, but of course inside I was a bit apprehensive about seeing my mother. By now, I was a teenager in a band, with a regular girlfriend, and I was confident about what I wanted to do. But the last time I had seen her I was an eleven-year-old schoolboy, and a bit of that child was still within me.

When it finally happened, it wasn't a big emotional reunion like you might see in a movie. We didn't throw our arms around each other and burst into tears. I just walked in and she was there and we said a polite hello. She was never very tactile, at least not with me, and we didn't cuddle and we certainly didn't discuss anything about what had happened. We just spoke about trivia—I can't even remember what, but I know that it was completely nonemotional. I suppose in some ways we'd become strangers and it was very sad, but at least we were both at a stage where we could move on. I don't blame her, but when I looked back at it as I got older, the one thing that stood out as thoughtless was her timing. She was never there to support us through certain achievements, and I'd wonder why she chose such a significant day to leave. You couldn't pick a worse day to do it to a kid.

We tried to keep in touch as the years went by, but it was very difficult because she never gave me an explanation for what happened. Years later, after I got married, my wife, Tracey, contacted her and urged her to explain things but my mother just wouldn't do it. She was proud of what I later achieved in Duran Duran but she did not throw any real light on what happened. I daresay it has left me with a few scars, and to this day I don't like saying good-bye to people, maybe because inside I fear I won't see them again. But I don't bear her any animosity. Why should I? In a way she did me a favor because all the trouble that had been going on before she left just went away. So that was it. Our meeting was over, and I got the train back to Newcastle and got on with my life.

I'D had enough of school by now, and I didn't bother staying around to take most of my exams. Looking back, school turned out to be one of the most negative experiences of my childhood. I may have had a lot of adult conversations with my dad, but when I tried to do the same with the teachers they would talk to me as if I was an idiot. I had a real taste for kicking authority by then, so I guess they just found me too hard to handle.

I was playing a few pub gigs with my band but it wasn't enough to make ends meet, so my dad got me a job on his building site. It was hard, physical work, but I was used to that from the milk round. Every morning we'd get the same bus together, and we'd try to arrange things so that we could work in the joiner's shop, because that was a slightly easier shift than on the main site. The building trade is a tough knockabout business, and there were plenty of would-be comedians working on the site who loved nothing more than to wind up the foreman's son! But overall it was good fun. I didn't even have to go for an interview, because my dad was held in such high regard by his employers. Most of the time we were treated very well, but I was really just filling time. Rock and roll was what I really wanted to do.

I'd been working on the site for about six months when I got my first big break. One of my neighbors, who lived across the road from us, was a guitar player named Dave Black. He had played in all the workingmen's clubs and had a band called Goldie, who were very successful locally and who later had a hit with a song called "Making Up Again." Dave had given me about half a dozen guitar lessons when I was in my early teens, and I used to go and watch him play quite regularly. Anyway, one day he came to see me and said he knew someone who was looking for a guitar player in a band.

"They are very professional, and you'll be expected to play everything that they ask you to," he warned me.

I couldn't wait to give them a call, and so I played a few numbers to them and that was it, I was in. So I was sixteen and a half, I'd spent a few months "on the buildings"—and then I was suddenly on £35 a week in a band, and from that point on I never did anything different. The money was double what I'd been getting on the site, and I was doing the one thing I loved in life more than anything else. We were called the Gigolos, and we used to play all over the North East, touring up and down the motorway, doing covers of other people's songs.

We used to play in the workingmen's clubs a lot, and every Sunday afternoon they used to put on strippers. They paraded in front of a men-only audience, who all wore flat caps and pretended to be disinterested and read their papers. The lady would come on, and if you were in the group backing her you would have to play something like "Devil Woman" by Cliff Richard. The strangest act was in Sunderland, where in one of the clubs the lunchtime highlight on Sunday was a fire-eating stripper with the glorious stage name of Singed Minge. I'll leave the rest to your imagination.

The Gigolos were a new wave band and we performed our own songs. At one point we even secured a deal with A&M to cut a single called "Teenage Girls," but it wasn't a hit. The lineup of the band and the name would change from time to time, but I'd nearly always find myself on the road in a transit van of some shape or description, and I lost count of how many times I slept in one. Later on, when I was in another band we had a van that we called the Streak, which was painted red with some paint we'd managed to get on the cheap from the Post Office. We used to call it the Streak because when we were coming back from gigs late at night we used to streak it up against a parked car and the red paint would come off. It was a pretty dangerous game, not to mention illegal, but at the time we didn't care.

MY guitar playing was going from strength to strength, and I managed to win a contract with a covers band to play a series of gigs at military bases in Germany. Looking back, it was another really important break in a formative sense, because it meant we had to learn a huge repertoire. It was also in Germany that I really learned how to party!

By now it was 1979. Maggie Thatcher had just become prime minister, the cold war was at its height, and Germany was stacked to the rafters with American troops. The country had been heavily militarized ever since World War II, and the whole place had to be prepared to go to war again at any minute, this time against the Russians. My dad had done his National Service there when he was eighteen, so he could relate to it, and he taught me a few phrases before we loaded up the Streak and headed off to the ferry down to mainland Europe.

The biggest base we played at was Ramstein Air Base, near Frankfurt. The sheer scale of it was staggering; it was like a small city in its own right. They would drive us around it and we'd see missile transporters and endless rows of fighter planes. To an eighteen-year-old from near Newcastle, the American culture was like a whole new world. Back in England all we had were Wimpy Bars, but on the base they had a vast array of American catering. Believe it or not, short-order food like hamburgers seemed very exotic at the time. You could eat as much as you wanted, and there were delicious things to try like pumpkin pie. The military was superorganized, but when you arrived at the base all you had to do was show your passport so they could check it briefly, and then they would give you a pass for the month. Terrorism was a threat even then, what with the IRA and the Baader-Meinhof supporters, but somehow the security didn't seem to reflect that—I suppose they were more worried about the Russians.

We obviously had to play things that would appeal to an American audience, so we'd do covers of numbers by Stevie Wonder and Aerosmith. I also used to play a fifteen-minute solo of Lynyrd Skynyrd's "Free Bird" and all the GIs would go nuts. If you got them going they would be really noisy on a Friday and a Saturday night, so the colonels who ran all the shows would sometimes intervene.

"Don't play that, don't whip them up. They got too drunk last night," they'd warn us.

We'd often be told off if we went too far, especially if we did too much AC/DC. I used to put on a kilt and do an Angus Young impression until they eventually banned us from doing it—because it caused too much of a frenzy! If we played in the officer's mess we had to be a bit more reserved and maybe do some jazz or something smooth, but it had to have an American flavor, so we'd also do the Eagles. I started to sing a bit, too, and I was sharing lead vocals in the band, so I had to learn all the great American songs and harmonies.

The Americans themselves were fantastic, because they were so open and confident. I had come from an area that was depressed at the time and falling apart by comparison, and then suddenly I was eating and drinking with the American military, who are the most confident bunch of people you are ever going to meet. They were all massively interested in me because I was still so young and no one does anything before they are twenty-one in America, unless they're in the military.

So I met a lot of people who were the same age as me. They'd sit there and hold out a joint and ask me, "Have you ever smoked one of these?" They'd get high on American weed on the weekend and have big parties in the barracks. It was a real eye-opener, like something out of *Animal House*. They were like fraternity brothers who lived in these big barracks, which were just bedrooms linked by corridors. They would all put their speakers out in the hall and link them up, and it was just like you see in movies such as *Hamburger Hill*. They used to have these talent shows, for which we provided the backing music, and it was a great bit of relief for them to do a little show. They'd shout, "Come and party with us, dude," and then someone would belt out "Gimme Some Loving" before the black GIs would get up and sing "Papa Was a Rolling Stone." It was great fun but I used to think, *Shit! If the Russians attack now we'll all be partying!* Aside from the talent shows, we used to play six hours a night as part of our contract, which was exhausting, but it strengthened my voice when I was young.

The pilots were the most impressive people on the base. I remember standing in a queue in the officer's mess and some pilots came in wearing their flight uniforms with their names on them, like in *Top Gun*. They exuded aggression; it was as if they were saying they were ready at any moment to go up in the sky and shoot Commies. The European front line was obviously prepared to go to war at any time. You didn't really get a sense of it off the GIs, but you knew the pilots were ready for it. They all had to be under twenty-four and ready to kill the moment the order was given, and they were a bit of an exclusive club. Some of the officers also had a certain air about them, too, that seemed to say, *I can kill anyone if I am ordered to. I have the authority to kill.*

The colonels were much more approachable. There was one

colonel and his wife who befriended me, and I used to regularly go and eat with them. They had a video player, which was something almost unheard of in the North East, and I remember I was blown away when we sat down to watch the latest *Star Wars* movie on it.

It was easy to forget that the whole place was one big war machine. However, there was no animosity between the Germans and the Americans. We used to stay in the local gasthaus, and it was okay to walk down the road doing Adolf impressions, à la John Cleese in *Fawlty Towers*. In those days the locals thought it was quite funny, and we weren't so fearful about political correctness as we are now. The Germans were just like us and liked to get drunk on their beer. All the towns around the bases would have loads of great bars filled with German girls, American GIs, and the British bands that came to entertain them. It was a lot of fun, but all good things come to an end, and eventually so did our contract. I had to return home, but it had opened up my eyes to the world.

THEY say traveling is the only way you ever learn anything, apart from what's handed down to you, and it was true for me. By the time I got back to England, I knew it was time to move on and join a bigger band. I started checking *Melody Maker* every week, because it used to carry adverts seeking musicians for bands. It wasn't long before I spotted one seeking a "Live Wire Guitarist." It cited Mick Ronson of the Spiders From Mars and Steve Jones of the Sex Pistols as musical influences, so I thought it looked worth a call, but what I didn't know as I went down to the call box was that it would change my life once again.

Looking back, I suppose you could say that all the great things that lay ahead in my life began with that phone call (even though I am now notoriously difficult to get on the phone). All the money and the record sales, all the fast cars, the drugs, the champagne and five-star hotels, all the meetings with royalty and the visit to the White House; all the exotic video shoots in Sri Lanka and all the wild parties with the likes of the Rolling Stones and rock's royalty, all started from a call box outside a sleepy newsagent in Cullercoats.

I dialed the number and explained that I was replying to the advert for a guitarist.

"What's the name of the band going to be?" I asked the girl who answered at the other end.

I listened as she replied in a broad Brummie accent: "Oh, the name of the band is Duran Duran."

CHAPTER TWO

The Rum Runner—1980

SO here I am, I've just turned nineteen and I'm sitting on a train to Birmingham on my way to my first audition with Duran Duran. Not that there was much of a band to audition for, as I would soon discover. There was no singer, no lyrics, no record deal, and very little by way of repertoire—but I was about to enter a ready-made world of fashion and hedonism in the form of a nightclub called the Rum Runner, and it would quickly drive us to the top of the music business.

Blondie were at number one in the charts with "Call Me," and within two years we would be appearing on the same bill as them in America. But for now Britain was in the grips of its worst economic recession since the early seventies, and I was down to my last few quid left over from what I'd earned playing at US military bases. Touring in Germany had been enormous fun, but after I got back to the UK the money soon started to run out, and it left me hungry to make a living from rock and roll.

I remembered my grandmother telling me, "If ever you get the chance, leave this place." When I was younger, she had seen a medium who had predicted that one day I would travel. I knew that my grandmother always had my best interests at heart, so it was time to follow her good advice. Despite the gloom that seemed to hang over large parts of the country in early 1980, I was feeling pretty positive when I arranged over the telephone to meet the fledgling members of Duran Duran at the Rum Runner.

"It's close to the City Centre. You can't miss it," they told me.

I packed my electric guitar and little portable amplifier, and I passed time during the four-hour train ride down from Newcastle by flicking through a copy of a newspaper that I had found on a seat. The headlines at this time would soon be dominated by the Iranian Embassy siege in London, during which terrorists took twenty-six people hostage for several days and threatened to execute them. The papers still found room to report on the fact that Prince Charles had fallen off his polo horse. Later that summer, the world would watch breathlessly as an attractive young girl, Lady Diana Spencer, fell in love with the heir to the Throne. She would become the most iconic woman of her time, somebody who loved music and who embodied the aspirations of a generation. I had no way of knowing it as I sat on the train, but I was about to join a band that would eventually become Princess Diana's favorite rock act.

I'd already done a lot of touring with various bands, but travelling wasn't something you took for granted in those days, so as the train pulled into Birmingham New Street just after lunchtime it felt as if I'd been on a long and epic journey. In a way I had, because culturally Birmingham was at least a million miles away from Newcastle. I had come from a region that was heavily depressed due to the economic downturn of the seventies, and the area was starting to suffer terribly due to the first cold blasts of Thatcherism. By comparison, Birmingham was rocking: it had its own arts college and lots of great cafés and little fashion shops that had a real buzz about them. The Midlands were also thriving musically: Dexys Midnight Runners were based there and they had just released *Geno,* and UB40 and the Specials were all emerging there around the same time.

The first thing I noticed when I got off the train was that everybody was speaking in a funny Black County accent. When I'd called to arrange the audition, the girl on the phone had a Brummie drawl that was so rich that I actually had trouble understanding some of the things she said. Brummie accents in the UK are like a long drawn-out drawl, and they are regarded with similar affection to the way some southern accents are in the States. When I got to Birmingham, the other thing I noticed was how trendy everybody looked. There was a big North/South divide in the UK in those days, and everybody I spoke to assumed that I was Scottish.

Birmingham wasn't as big then as it is now, and I didn't have any money for a cab from the station, so I decided to walk the rest of the way to the club. I bumped into a group of guys who all had big floppy hair and pointed shoes, and they told me they were in a local band called Fashion. I had trouble understanding what they were saying because of their accents, but I managed to get directions to the Rum Runner, which, from what I could gather, was located down an alley in an old Victorian building near a canal.

The Rum Runner had previously been a casino in the sixties, and it had its own boxing gym on the same site. From the outside it had an air of faded grandeur about it. Inside, it was not what you expected it to be at all, because it had been fitted out as a brand-new chic club, complete with mirrors everywhere, plush dark carpets, and its own triangular champagne bar, plus a DJ booth and a dance floor. It had big, wide seats made out of old rum barrels. There were also rum barrels set into the walls, which dated from the times when rum had been shipped up the canal, hence the name of the club.

The first person to greet me after I was shown inside was John Taylor. He was a very different-looking bloke than the handsome pop pinup whose photo would eventually be pinned on the bedroom walls of thousands of teenagers. He also went by a different name.

"Hello, my name is Nigel," he said, holding out his hand in a friendly if slightly awkward manner. (His full name is Nigel John Taylor, and it was only later that he became known as John.) He was a tall, skinny kid who was well styled, but he wore these little round glasses that made him seem a bit of a geek. In hindsight, he looked a bit like Harry Potter! In truth, he was an incredibly good-looking bloke, and at first I thought he was deliberately doing the geeky glasses thing just to be cool. It turned out that he wanted contact lenses but he couldn't afford them. One of the first things I noticed about him was that he was wearing a ridiculous pair of enormous winkle picker shoes. I remember thinking, *Christ, I hope I don't have to wear a pair of them!* That aside, John was very friendly and confident, and we clicked immediately. He struck me as a straightforward and easygoing person who didn't hold back. I later found he would always be the first to come and introduce himself whenever there was someone he wanted to talk to, and he was very good at making people feel at ease. It turned out that we had plenty in common, because John had played lead guitar for a while before coming off it to play bass. He was a few months older than me, although he hadn't quite turned twenty. He had just been through art college, so he was basically still an art student at heart.

Roger Taylor, who'd previously been a drummer in a couple of punk bands, was also there when I arrived at the club, and the three of us had a good laugh about the fact that by coincidence we all shared the same surname. It turned out to be a good omen because we got on well despite our different backgrounds. They had long, floppy hair and were into David Bowie and Bryan Ferry and the whole new fashion trend that had started to gain currency ever since punk had died away. They were in on the beginning of what became known as the New Romantic movement, with its emphasis on frilly shirts and baggy trousers, whereas I was much more from a rock background and I had arrived wearing jeans and a scruffy old pair of training shoes. Later on, the rest of the band would spend a lot of time taking the piss out of my cheap shoes! (Nick's dad still has a pair of my shoes as a souvenir, which I had bought for £2 out of a bargain bin.)

Musically, we found we shared a lot of ground straightaway. The advert that the band had placed in *Melody Maker* had cited certain guitar influences whom I admired, such as Steve Jones of the Sex Pistols and Mick Ronson of Bowie's Ziggy Stardust and the Spiders From Mars band. John also confided that he was a fan of the American bass guitarist Bernard Edwards. I admired Bernard, too, so I thought, *Oh, great, we've got something in common.* John was a bit of a traditionalist when it came to guitar, because he wanted to hear a rock-and-roll sound in the mold of Steve Jones, so later that afternoon I played him the Pistols track "Pretty Vacant," and thankfully it blew him away.

There was a strong punk influence in the Midlands and there was an old punk club there called Barbarella's, where all the top bands used to go to play. Just as New Romanticism grew out of punk, I discovered that Duran Duran were named after Milo O'Shea's character, Durand-Durand, in *Barbarella*, the sixties movie starring Jane Fonda. I got the impression that the name had mainly been John's idea, and it was an example of his art-school mind working at its best. He didn't realize how good he was as a bass player; he was a complete natural at it and he could play effortlessly.

He was very particular about getting the look and feel of everything right, but you got the feeling that, at the heart of it, what he wanted most of all was to form a great rock-and-roll band.

Meanwhile, my first impression of Roger, who was also age nineteen, was that he was very much the quiet one. His dad ran a small business near Castle Bromwich, so, like John, Roger was another local boy. Roger had done a few dead-end jobs since leaving school, but he was only really interested in playing drums. He'd previously been in a punk band called the Scent Organs, who'd reportedly been banned from practicing at the local church hall. But I soon sussed out that Roger wasn't the sort of person who liked confrontation. In fact he was quite shy and definitely not one to be pushing his views into your face all the time. He didn't say much, he just went over and started banging the drums. Roger had a classic James Dean look; he was quite muscular and he reminded me a bit of the Fonz in *Happy Days* (except instead of saying "Hey" all the time, Roger would go "All right" in a Brummie accent). One thing Roger definitely had was fantastic ability as a drummer. He was coming out of a punk phase, and he was beginning to approach things in a slightly different way, which was influenced by disco, and it sounded really interesting. A drummer needs a lot of mental discipline, because if his timing is out then the rest of the band will lose it, too, and I could see that Roger's concentration was very impressive.

Nick Rhodes was the next person to arrive. He turned up about an hour or so later than arranged, and I would soon discover that was Nick all over, because he was always late.

"If there's one bad thing I've learned," he once told an interviewer, "it's that if you absolutely have to be somewhere by six a.m., you don't have to get out of bed until at least eleven."

My other enduring first impression of Nick, to this day, is that he carried all his personal possessions around with him in a plastic bag. It would always be a "decent" carrier bag, maybe from Marks & Spencer rather than a flimsy one from the corner shop, but he simply refused to put his personal stuff in a briefcase or a satchel. Nick's dad was quite wealthy and owned a toy shop. Nick was the youngest member of the band and he hadn't quite turned eighteen, but he'd been childhood friends with John. Nick was naturally androgynous even without makeup; he had a sort of boy/girl look about him that was to become one of the hallmarks of being a New Romantic. His voice was slightly flat and nasal, and his real surname was Bates. (I used to call him Master Bates and he later changed his name to Rhodes for "aesthetic reasons.") As a keyboard player he was a bit of a genius in the sense that he had the ability to see some things in a completely different way from anyone else. Having said that, he didn't seem to want to understand the traditional structure of music, and he didn't care about knowing the difference between a major and a minor scale. Musical scales are a bit like male and female. One is minor and dark, the other is major and uplifting, and you have to be careful how you cross them. When Nick played I noticed that he was just using the black notes on his keyboard, which was something that Kate Bush was famous for doing at the time.

"You're only playing the black keys?" I said.

"Yeah, so?" he replied.

"Well, that means you are just doing one key."

WILD BOY

"Really?"

"Yeah, like Kate Bush," I said.

"Oh, yeah, like Kate Bush," he replied, but I wasn't quite sure if he knew what I meant.

Nick's interpretation of doing music was very obviously going to be different to mine. *Playing* seemed to be the last thing on his mind, but he wanted to make keyboard *sounds* and *textures* and *layers* of sound—and in that sense he wanted to do something different that had never been done before. He could certainly make beautiful sounds, but in those days he couldn't sing or dance (in fact, I used to joke to myself that his voice sounded a bit like a robot with a Brummie accent!). In terms of music, John and Nick had grown up watching *Top of the Pops* on BBC One, just as I had. There were no Internet or satellite music channels, so *Top of the Pops* was a huge event that the whole nation would tune into. In that way we all shared a common background, and we spent most of the afternoon jamming and playing together.

It was obvious that they wanted someone who could really play in lots of different styles and genres. But I soon discovered that they didn't really have anything by way of their own repertoire. They didn't have any lyrics or finished musical numbers, but they did have one little diamond, which was the chorus to "Girls on Film," and Nick had a little wisp of a keyboard sequence to go with it. You could hear immediately that it was something special. John and Roger had obviously practiced together a lot, because they were using many different techniques to let the sound come through from Nick.

I remember Nick telling me, "This is one of the songs that we have got and we really think it is going to be a hit."

Then he sang the line "Girls on film, girls on film," and I knew he was right. I thought: *Fuck me! That's cool—I wonder who wrote that?* But it turned out none of them had, because it had been written by their previous singer, Andy Wickett, whom they told me was on holiday. In fact, Andy had already quit the band, and what they didn't mention at first was that they didn't have any singer at all. That small piece of chorus from "Girls on Film" was the only thing that had survived from their earlier lineup, but to be fair to Andy Wickett it was quite significant, and later on we had to do a deal with him when we released the song commercially. It was a very good chorus for a song, and I am pretty sure that we came up with the basics for the rest of it when we first jammed together that afternoon. They were impressed by all the different styles I could do. Playing rock and blues was my standard thing, but I could also do funky stuff, and I'd learned all the different chords that go with R & B as well as pop. My time in cover bands had served me well, and I could do things by bands like the Beatles, the Rolling Stones, and Thin Lizzy.

I knew I had won them over, because while we were playing together all the secretaries and the staff from the rest of the nightclub stopped work and came down from upstairs in order to listen to us and watch us play together. By the time we had finished the club was due to open for the night, and they invited me to stay on for the evening. I had to get the late train back up to Newcastle, but before I left I could see that the Rum Runner had a fantastic buzz about it. There were people starting to queue up outside, and you could see it was going to be packed.

The whole nightclub scene was going through a period of change in those days, and places like the Rum Runner were at the forefront of it. The old-style cabaret establishments that were famous for serving chicken in a basket were being replaced by disco clubs. Then off the back of disco came a new breed of ultraslick clubs like the Rum Runner, where people went to drink champagne and have a great time. I guess it was a kind of counterculture that allowed people to get away from all the gloom and unemployment in the real world. Whatever it was, I could see the Rum Runner was like a little fun palace where it was party time every night. It also turned out to be packed with Page 3 girls, who were at the top of the showbiz A-list. In those days topless models were regarded by the press a bit like the way newspapers today regard footballers' wives who the headline writers in the UK are fascinated with and now refer to as WAGs

WILD BOY

(which stands for Wives and Girlfriends). The Page 3 girls were the WAGs of their generation, but instead of dating footballers they were desperate to be seen with pop stars.

By the time one of the club's managers offered to drive me back to the station I'd already seen enough of the Rum Runner to know that I wanted to be part of it. The club was owned by two brothers, Mike and Paul Berrow, who were in their late twenties and part of an established Birmingham family who had business interests in the rag trade and property. Their father, Roy, had run three or four casinos in the city during the sixties and seventies. If you run casinos you inevitably get the odd member of the underworld frequenting your establishments, and it turned out that an associate of the Kray twins had once been arrested while coming out of the Rum Runner.

The Berrows themselves were straight, but some of the gangster chic rubbed off on them and people used to wrongly assume they were into all sorts of shady dealings—and I suppose it was an image that didn't do them any harm. They were actually sharp-minded businessmen, and it had already been agreed they were going to be the management of Duran Duran. It was obvious the club's party scene and the band were going to complement each other perfectly. As Mike dropped me off at the station, I noted the fact that he had a flash BMW and I remember thinking, *This is perfect—even the managers have got plenty of money!*

They'd told me that they had a few more people to try out and I went back to Newcastle, but it was all very positive. Sure enough, a few days later I got a phone call asking me to go back down. I borrowed £30 off my dad, packed the rest of my gear and that was it—my new life began.

The Rum Runner was an ideal base because I could crash there and use the facilities in the old boxing gym to shower each morning before work. We'd spend our days practicing and jamming, then we'd party every evening in the club. We were soon running up an enormous champagne tab every night, and in order to pay it off I did a bit of cooking in the kitchen and a few odd jobs around the club.

Roger, who was dating one of the cloakroom girls, Giovanna Cantone, also collected glasses and did a bit of painting here and there to pay his share. I daresay the odd rump steak used to get wolfed down by us on the quiet, but we never took advantage of the hospitality.

TUESDAY was the big night of the week at the Rum Runner, when the New Romantic crowd would turn up. All the guys dressed in frilly shirts and wore makeup, and there would be scores of gorgeous female models, some of whom were very famous. Mike Berrow was dating Carole Dwyer, a Page 3 girl. Her sister Joanne was also a regular at the club, along with another model, Joanne Latham. They all had big, blond, back-combed hairdos, and they wore skintight Lycra leggings or miniskirts, just like Hot Gossip, the sexy dance troupe from *The Kenny Everett Show*. Giovanna caused a stir by shaving her head bald like a character from *Star Trek*, which was a very bold thing for a girl to do in the eighties. The Rum Runner was very exclusive—the doormen would make customers line up outside the entrance, and then they would deliberately turn away anyone who didn't look cool enough to be let in. This just made everybody else all the more desperate to come inside! Nick was a great DJ. He used to work in the club, and he really knew how to get people onto the dance floor.

I soon discovered that lots of local celebrities liked to party at the Rum Runner, including the footballer Frank Worthington, who played for Leicester City and who lived in a Holiday Inn, which was considered the height of luxury at the time. We'd sometimes go off to the Holiday Inn for late-night boozing sessions. Roy Wood from Wizard was another regular at the Rum Runner, and all the characters from Black Sabbath would hang out there, too—so there used to be some pretty full-on partying.

We would stay up until six in the morning in a little drinking posse at the back of the club after it closed. It didn't take much to encourage us. I was known for being very loud and for having hollow legs when it came to drinking. Nick could drink copious amounts of champagne (which meant Roger and I had to collect even more glasses). John, in contrast, used to get drunk on two pints of beer, and he'd lose his spectacles and walk into walls!

SO my first memories of life in Birmingham aren't just about the band but everything that went with it. It was like walking into this ready-made rock-and-roll world that was filled with excitement. What we desperately needed, however, was a front man, so for our first big task we auditioned a singer named Guy Oliver Watts. He was a lovely bloke and stayed around for a couple of weeks, but we just didn't click. I was flattered when the other guys asked me what I thought of him— because I was still very much the new boy myself and it showed they valued my opinion—but I told them I didn't think Guy was right for us. We sent him packing, which seemed a bit brutal at the time, but it was part of the process of elimination that we needed to go through in order to form a perfect band. We did some demo material on which John wrote some lyrics and I sung some vocals, just to have some singing on our music, but it wasn't very productive.

Then one of the barmaids told Mike Berrow that she shared a flat with a guy who had sung in a band and he had written a lot of songs.

"He could be just what you are looking for," she said, so Mike arranged for him to come down to the club one afternoon.

So there we all were, in the Rum Runner, when in walked this tall, good-looking guy with long legs and lots of confidence.

"Hello, I'm Simon Le Bon," he said in a Southern accent.

The first thing I thought was, *Fuck me—he looks just like Elvis!*

He reminded everyone of a young Presley because he still had a lot of boyish puppy fat around his face . . . You knew straightaway that he would be a hit with the girls. The only slightly unfortunate thing was that he was wearing skintight pink leopard-print trousers! The flashy pants had been Simon's way of making a grand entrance, and I can assure you that all the stories that have been repeated over the years about how outrageous he looked are true. He was perfect, our own ready-made Elvis (albeit one who looked like he'd been to the chip shop a few times)!

Simon explained that he'd been in a punk band called Dog Days when he was seventeen. He'd also done a bit of singing with seventies pub bands. He sang us a few numbers and we were impressed. But most important of all, we discovered he could write lyrics. Simon brought along an A5-sized book with a paisley pattern on the cover, which was packed with his own handwritten poems. The book turned out to be a real Aladdin's lamp because it contained all the lyrics we could ever wish for. Looking back, I believe that was our Ground Zero —for me, the defining moment in the history of Duran Duran was when Simon pulled out that little book of lyrics. There was even one poem that he brought along on that first day, called "Sound of Thunder," that fitted perfectly to one of the tunes we had already been rehearsing. We tried it out straightaway that afternoon and it worked; eventually it became a track on our first album. We were in business.

Simon is a much better songwriter than people realize. He's very deep and thoughtful, and he was just like that when he was young. It was obvious that he was very well read, and I was very impressed by him. His lyrics and his tone fitted our music perfectly, and he always managed to find a vocal melody that worked with the music that I had already created. He also had a commercial ear, which appealed to all of us.

"I really like the new Simple Minds album," he told us in conversation, which impressed both John and Nick, who had both just bought the same album.

"Good, you're in," said John. "We've got a gig in four weeks."

And that was it, he was hired! That was the day the band was formed. Everything before that moment seemed to suddenly lose importance. As well as the lyrics, Simon had a decent voice, maybe not the best, but he had an *original* voice and, more important, it was a *pop* voice. We never needed a rock singer; we needed someone like

Bryan Ferry who could cruise over the top of our music—and that was exactly what Simon could do brilliantly.

Simon and I bonded straightaway. We had something in common—unlike the others, who all grew up locally, we were both from outside Birmingham. Simon was a drama student at the University of Birmingham, but he came from a suburban family down in Bushey, just outside of North London. His family were descended from French Huguenots, and his father, John, was a civil servant. His mum, Anne, ran small businesses in antiques and catering. Simon was the eldest of three brothers . . . and he loved attention. In fact, he was totally up himself—but I mean that in a nice way, because the one thing you need in a good front man is for him to be self-obsessed in a theatrical manner.

SO with Simon Le Bon on board, we were flying before we knew it. There were now five of us and we each brought something special to the mix. A good band is made up of people with different strengths and weaknesses, and the sum is always greater than any one part. In Duran Duran we were each good at something different, and the strength of each person's individual contribution was important. For example, Nick's contribution was very different from mine, but every member of the band was equally vital. I developed a knack for being able to hear something and pick out the bones in order to work out how every part fit together. I had done all the basic work of learning music while I was out on the road, and I'd figured out how all the guys before me had done things. It meant that I could take an idea and help translate it into something original, so I hoped that what I gave the band was a kind of musical cohesion that they had previously been lacking.

Until now, no one seemed to fully grasp some of the things Nick was trying to do on keyboards. Nick might have lacked some of the traditional musical skills that I possessed, but it was our juxtaposition of different approaches that helped to make us so successful.

Technology was starting to change keyboards in a big way and suddenly there was a whole raft of new equipment available, mainly from Japan. Whereas in the past bands used to have big banks of wires and stuff, the equipment suddenly all became solid-state, much smaller, and a lot more user-friendly. Technology was always Nick's thing—he was obsessive about being the first to have a new piece of kit in order to create a certain type of sound before anybody else could do it.

Years later, when Simon wrote the lyrics to "The Reflex," there was a lot of speculation that the song was about Nick. According to the song, "The Reflex is in charge of finding treasure in the dark." That's what Nick would do: he was a genius at finding little bits of treasure in a song. (Nick's also an only child like in "The Reflex," although Simon denies the lyrics are about him.)

My own little piece of genius was working out how to reinvent the way I played guitar in order to integrate it with all the new technology. We formed at a time when most bands were removing guitars in favor of synthesizers, so I had to change the way I played to work alongside the new type of sound.

I'd been around enough musicians in the past to know it's not easy to get something special going, and I had a sixth sense that I'd just met a bunch of people who were going to make it. I had great respect for them because they all had the ability to think outside the box—and I was convinced that I could help them build that box. There was a certain magnetism around the band. It felt almost like a foregone conclusion that we were going to do well—although it wasn't particularly well thought out to begin with. One thing we all agreed to do very early on was to split any future royalties five ways, because we felt everyone's contribution was strong enough to justify an equal share. We were all young, and to us it didn't matter who wrote which bit; we'd all share the credit.

THE crowd in the Runner loved us from day one, especially the women. Ironically, the fact that we wore makeup turned out to be a

WILD BOY

great chat-up line. We'd end up discussing cosmetics with the girls—I'd been a fan of Bowie, who wore a lot of makeup of his own, so I wasn't at all fazed by the idea of wearing it—and it wasn't long before I was dating a gorgeous model. Mike Berrow came over to me one evening and pointed out a beautiful blonde on the other side of the club.

"There's this girl over there called Janine, who wants to meet you," he said, smiling.

She was a model named Janine Andrews, who at the time was one of the UK's most famous pinup girls. Sexy photographs of her were published in newspapers on almost a daily basis, and the British public were obsessed with her in much the same way as they are in a model called Jordan today. Janine was five foot ten, tall, well over six feet in her heels—a lot taller than me, anyway! At first I didn't believe Mike, but Janine turned out to be a smashing friendly girl and we got on well. It wasn't so long ago that I'd been a penniless nineteen-year-old in the North East and here I was, in a champagne paradise with a model for a girlfriend. I remember thinking, *If the boys could see me now!*

The Rum Runner turned out to be a great setting for the band. We had a ready-made headquarters with its own support base. A similar cultural thing was happening down in London at the Blitz Club, where Spandau Ballet were creating a stir. Certainly for us, being based in a club was a godsend. When you took all the hormonal and creative energy that we had and combined it with all the girls and the socializing and drinking, it brought out the best in us. I guess it had been like that for bands ever since the sixties, with the Beatles and the Cavern Club being the ultimate example.

We were soon belting out new material at our jamming sessions all the time, and within about five or six weeks we had cracked most of the ideas that would eventually form our first album. At the same time we were making plans for our debut performance in front of a proper live audience, and it was only natural that our first gig should be at the Rum Runner. The Berrow brothers were determined to make it a huge success, so much so that Mike suddenly announced that he'd be making a guest appearance onstage.

"I'll be playing saxophone during 'Girls on Film,'" he proudly told us. "Don't worry, I've been practicing. I think you'll be impressed."

When the big day arrived in July, Roger and I were the first people in the Rum Runner. It suddenly struck me that we'd always rehearsed on the main floor of the club, rather than on any type of raised platform.

"What's the matter?" asked Roger, who must have noticed my puzzled look.

"Well . . . where's the effing stage? Where are we actually gonna play?" I asked him.

"Oh, there's these big boxes outside, and we've got to move them all in order to make a stage," he explained.

So much for all the glamour! I have a vivid memory of lifting all these boxes with a terrible hangover at 10:30 in the morning, while John, Nick, and Simon were nowhere to be seen. I thought, *Lazy bastards! I hope it is not always going to be like this!*

That night all the New Romantic crew turned out to support us in great numbers. We played all our new original material, including "Girls on Film," which went down like a storm. We also did a cover version of "I Feel Love," by Donna Summer. I snapped a guitar string during the evening, but the most memorable thing about the night—for all the wrong reasons—was Mike's performance on saxophone. Playing sax might have sounded like a great idea to him, but he was dreadful! Saxophone isn't something you can just pick up overnight, but as far as I could tell Mike had simply gone and bought one and assumed he could play it. It doesn't quite work like that with a sax; you have got to learn it, which takes a long time, and even if you do learn it doesn't guarantee that you'll be any good!

Luckily, we had twigged in rehearsals that he was useless, so we decided to isolate him by putting him on one side near the DJ booth, which was encased in glass. We told him it was for acoustic reasons, and we pretended his sax was being picked up by a microphone, although secretly we had switched it off so the audience would be spared. Nonetheless, when Mike came to do his bit, his girlfriend and all the other models gathered nearby and killed themselves with laughter while he pranced around and made some dreadful noises!

We later met to decide what to do about Mike's awful sax playing, and we decided we'd gently persuade him that his talents lay in management rather than in the band. At one point it got a bit heated, half the band regarded him as an old duffer who couldn't play, but some of the others were more relaxed about it. I was against him playing. The way I saw things, the five us all had something special, whereas Mike just seemed to be there for vanity. In the end he saw sense and stuck to management. To be fair to Mike, he and his brother, Paul, pulled off some great stuff for us in those early days, but we were right to put our collective foot down.

The rest of the year flew by, and pretty soon we had a whole string of gigs across the Midlands under our belts. We'd play trendy wine bars and University shows, and we avoided smoky old pubs or anywhere that didn't come up to scratch. Simon still had a lot of other commitments that we had to work around, and he insisted on pursuing his aspirations as a drama student by going up to the Edinburgh Fringe. He still harbored plans to become an actor, but eventually it became obvious that the band was going to be a full-time occupation. Simon then announced he was dropping out of University. After a while I moved in with him when a room became available in his house. It was a gaudily decorated place with gold taps, which was located near the red-light district in Moseley, so there were always a lot of dope dealers lurking nearby. A lot of the Rum Runner crowd used to smoke dope but Simon never did. I guess he was worried about the effect it might have on his voice. Nonetheless, we used to have some wild times together, and I used the new culinary skills I learned at the Rum Runner to bake some mean-tasting chocolate cakes—with a bit of help from certain resin-based ingredients.

Unlike the other three members of the band, Simon and I didn't have the support network of our families nearby, so we focused on getting a record deal quickly because we needed one to survive financially. A week's shopping for us was two plastic bags filled with potatoes and pasta; that was all we could afford. It was a rough area to live in, and since we wore a lot of makeup we had to stop traveling by bus due to all the stick we got from the locals. But if the going got too tough, there were some hard characters down at the Rum Runner who could look after us, including a security guy named Simon Cook. He was a smashing bloke, and his twin brother was a paratrooper who later served in the Falklands War. They were both regarded as martial arts experts at the local karate club, and eventually they came to work for us.

With Simon Le Bon now permanently on board, it wasn't long before we started to get noticed by the music press as the New Romantic movement gathered pace. Spandau Ballet were always being mentioned in the same breath as us, so we went to see them when they played in Birmingham. We discovered they were a bunch of Cockneys who wore kilts onstage! We invited them back to the Rum Runner, and we were delighted to learn that Simon was taller than Tony Hadley. There was already a friendly rivalry starting to develop between us. Neither band had been signed by a record company at this stage, but I suppose that whenever you get two strong bands emerging at the same time you get a bit of conflict. It had been like that with the Beatles versus the Stones in the sixties, and after us in the nineties it would become Blur versus Oasis. In the eighties, it was Duran Duran versus Spandau Ballet, and we lapped up every minute of it. We also went to see Adam Ant, who was the forerunner of the New Romantic movement, at Birmingham Odeon, and we were very impressed by his live show.

After we'd played a lot of the trendy boutique-style gigs we wanted to turn things up a couple of notches. There was a young agent, Rob Hallett, who became one of the most important young people in helping to form our early career. He was a very nice guy from down South, and before getting into the music game he'd worked with mentally handicapped children. He was a couple of years older than us and he had a slight stammer that used to get more pronounced if he had a drink. It was as if he could think quicker than he could talk, but he was very smart and street-wise. Rob had heard about us, and one Sunday afternoon at three he called us to offer us a cancellation gig that night at the Marquee Club in London after another band had pulled out. We couldn't wait to get down there, but it was a huge rush. We had to borrow a three-ton truck, and we sat in the back all the way to London. We ended up playing a great set. Rob was seriously impressed.

I remember him telling us, "It all sounds so different, but every song is a hit." He loved us and soon afterward he told us, "I've got another great show for you."

He offered us a slot opening up for John Cooper Clarke at Hammersmith Palais, and we were only too happy to oblige. He was obviously lining us up for greater things because he invited along Dave Ambrose, an A & R guy from EMI, the famous record label behind the Beatles. Dave had been a member of a band with Mick Fleetwood before he went on to form Fleetwood Mac, and he had signed the Sex Pistols to EMI, so he had been around musicians a hell of a lot and he knew his stuff. Hammersmith Palais was our first time on a really big stage, and we felt we handled it well. Dave was impressed enough that he decided to take a proper look at us afterward by coming on the road with us. We used to tour around in a big Winnebago, and occasionally we'd all have to sleep in it if we were gigging a long way from Birmingham.

The Berrows must have sensed that things were starting to happen. Mike remortgaged his house to get the cash to book us a place on Hazel O'Connor's Megahype Tour. Hazel had just starred in the punk movie *Breaking Glass,* and she was really big at the time, so we had to pay to get on the same bill as her. I think it cost Mike around £8,000. Hazel had a lot of media currency, which helped create a lot of interest in us, and we started playing to some decent-sized audiences. We liked opening up for a girl band because it meant we didn't have to compete with another male act on the same bill. It was a smart move that we would later repeat when we toured the States with Blondie. Along with the Berrows, who were like a protective bubble for us at this point, we had a strange instinct for making the right decisions, and our androgynous look (which was heavily influenced by Adam Ant) worked well in front of the softer audiences who were attracted by Hazel O'Connor and Blondie.

Thanks to all the fuss of the Megahype Tour, several other record labels became interested in signing us, including EMI's rivals, Phonogram. In those days getting a record deal meant everything; it was a huge step up for a band. When more offers eventually started to come in, Phonogram put more money on the table. We decided to go with EMI, because we knew they had a global network and they could launch bands across America. The company was headed by the legendary music industry figure Bhaskar Menon, who'd presided over EMI during the rise of the Beatles.

By the time December approached—just six months or so after I'd first walked into the Rum Runner—we agreed on terms with EMI, and we were due to go down to London to sign the deal. Things had happened incredibly quickly for us. To tell you the truth, we were all still on an enormous high from all the fun and partying in Birmingham, and we hadn't really paused to take anything in.

We were still on the road, just a few days before going to London, when Nick and I had a huge row in front of Dave Ambrose in the Winnebago. It jokily became known as the Infamous Pork Pie Incident because Nick and I got into a furious bust-up after a few too many drinks, and we ended up throwing pork pies at each other. I can't remember what it was all over, but it caused a lot of mirth.

Eventually we all made it down to London in one piece to sign the deal. We stayed in a little hotel close to Chelsea Football Club's ground. During all negotiations, we had insisted that we wanted to maintain creative control of all our own material, rather than let the record company dictate to us (like some bands do). We were in a position of strength, because we had written all our own tunes and we didn't need the record company to bring in any songwriters. It was an important point, and it meant we retained an awful lot of power for the future. We felt the world was ours for the taking, and we couldn't wait to start the ride.

For Duran Duran it was a bright new beginning, but a terrible tragedy was about to unfold. We stayed overnight in London on December 8, 1980. Everything was set for a huge celebration the following day at EMI, where many of the senior staff were still on first-name terms with the ex-members of the Beatles. But at the very moment we were about to sign our deal, a quirk of fate robbed the record company of one of its most important artists. I found out when I was just about to tuck into a breakfast of bacon and eggs in my hotel room, and I reached up above the bed to turn on the radio.

"And now over to New York where the shocking news overnight is that John Lennon has been assassinated . . ."

The news shocked the whole world—and it caused enormous upset at EMI. Some of the management at the record label had been there since the late fifties, so they personally knew the Beatles. Although none of us in Duran Duran had ever met John Lennon, he was a huge idol to us all, and our surroundings somehow brought the events in New York closer to home.

"John Lennon was the Arch Beatle . . . He never lost his gentleness or his childlike faith in the power of love and goodness," said the tribute to him in the *Sun* the next day.

Despite the turmoil, EMI were a very professional outfit. The news didn't prevent our deal from going ahead, although it obviously cast a pall over things. The label had been itching to sign us ahead of their rivals at Phonogram, mainly due to Dave Ambrose. When things calmed down, EMI gave us a talk about how they would give us the chance to do things in America, just as they'd done for the Beatles a generation earlier. You've got to be my age to remember the Beatles, but they defined the times they lived in, and for me the memory of them was still very real. Our two proudest examples of contemporary culture as a nation were music and football, which were symbolized by a copy of the *Sgt. Pepper* album and a photo of England's 1966 World Cup–winning captain Bobby Moore in a West Ham strip.

EMI were still regarded as the home of the Beatles, and we were contented with our deal at the time. They put up £35,000 in order to fund our first album, plus each of us got a £50-a-week retainer. Crucially, they also agreed to our demands to retain creative control over everything we released. We also hammered out good clauses that guaranteed us a reasonable share of things like radio airplay money from any big hits we would have in the future. It was the Berrows who negotiated most of this deal. The band members also played our part, but this was really what the Berrows were good at—they were strong negotiators (as I've said, they were like a protective bubble). It felt strange and unreal to be at the headquarters of EMI negotiating a new beginning at the same time that John Lennon's death brought to a close a huge chapter in the history of rock and roll.

We didn't know if it was fate or a bad omen.

CHAPTER THREE

Girls on Film . . . and Everywhere Else!

IT'S Christmas Eve, 1980, and I am about to take cocaine for the first time. It's not something that I am proud of, but nor am I going to pretend that it didn't happen. Drug use would eventually play a big part in the story of Duran Duran, and it started here. When we landed our record deal with EMI it seemed like all our dreams had come true, and we were in the mood to party. By the time we arrived back in Birmingham for Christmas we were ready to indulge in our newfound status. Getting a record deal meant everything. We had most of the material we needed for the album from our first few months together at the Rum Runner, and we were confident we'd be in a position to release it early in the new year. "Planet Earth" had been written at the club shortly before we'd gone down to London, and a decision had been made that it would be our first single. "Girls on Film" was always going to be a bigger hit, but the plan was not to release that until we'd established a bit of a profile for ourselves. We already had most of "Planet Earth" recorded, and Nick and I were due to go back down to London together on Boxing Day to finish mixing it.

"In the meantime, we're going to have a great big piss-up," I declared to the rest of the band.

We had a gig booked at the Cedar Club in Birmingham. We were determined to turn it into a real Christmas show, followed by a rip-roaring party at the Rum Runner. There wasn't enough time for me to go back up to Newcastle for Christmas, so I booked into a little bed-and-breakfast hotel near to the station so that I could catch an early train down to the studio on Boxing Day. All our crew came along to the Cedar Club, which was decked out in tinsel and cheap Brummie decor that the Berrows had probably gotten from the local market. The crowd consisted of the usual mix of gorgeous women, outrageous gays, and straight guys wearing makeup. The Hazel O'Connor tour had really sharpened us up as a live band, and at the end of our performance everyone came onstage to join us as we sang a load of old numbers by David Bowie. We were a lot more confident and starting to feel like we were going places, although I got brought down to earth when I popped outside for a smoke and a bouncer refused to let me back in.

"I am actually in the band!" I said, laughing at the idea that I couldn't get into my own gig.

I was in a great mood that night, and cocaine certainly didn't figure into my plans when we all piled back to the Rum Runner. There used to be a short driveway outside the club, which was really just a glorified alley where the bouncers used to line up people in a queue to get inside. A guy called Al Beard was in charge of the door and he was very meticulous. As we arrived that evening I noticed there was a battered old VW camper van pulled up on the curb, right outside the Rum Runner. It struck me as a bit weird, as the only people who were usually allowed to a park there were the Berrows in their flash sports cars. They loved to show off their wealth, and in that respect I guess they were the first of a new breed of entrepreneurs who became known as Yuppies.

There was something about the head doorman, Al Beard, that I didn't quite trust. He was a bodybuilder, not hugely tall, but he was very physical. He was always surrounded by women whom he would attempt to chat up in a posh accent that sounded a bit fake. Al and

WILD BOY

his men had been told to keep a close eye on us in case we needed protection from any of the locals who took exception to all the makeup we used to wear, but in fact there was rarely any trouble inside the club itself. I was more interested in having fun, so I soon forgot all about the camper van and once I was inside the Rum Runner I was downing champagne like there was no tomorrow. Most of the band were there, and we drank late into the night. Everything we wanted was free (although we'd end up paying for it later when the money from the record company started to roll in). We all used to hang out near the ladies' toilets, which had a big walk-in lobby and it was a bit of a meeting place. Some of the girls used to hold hands with each other, and sometimes they'd kiss and get very tactile with one another, so the atmosphere was always very free and easy.

Fantastic! I love this fucking place, I thought to myself.

The party was in full flow, when my attention was caught by a kid who I will call Johnny, who was slightly older than me. Johnny used to hang around with the older brother of one the girls in our circle, so I'd spoken to him a few times and we shared an interest in rock and roll.

"Hey, Andy!" he cried to me above the music. "You gotta come outside. I have something for you."

"Nah, I want to stay here and party," I yelled back, reluctant to leave the girls' kissing show.

"Come on, I've got something very cool you've got to try."

He looked at me conspiratorially, so I assumed he wanted me to go outside and smoke some dope with him. I'd hung out with enough crazy GIs in Germany to recognize an invitation to smoke a spliff, or so I thought, so I followed him to the front of the club and we went into the street together. The dirty old camper van was still there, and Johnny paced straight up to it and beckoned me over. Before I knew it we were inside, where a couple of his mates had already sat down in the vehicle's living area. There was a small amount of white powder on the surface in front of them, and then I realized: *Shit, it's cocaine.*

"Come on," said Johnny. "We're going to have some coke."

I'd done some pretty mad things during my time on the road with various bands, so I wasn't fazed or intimidated—in fact, I was curious to discover what it would feel like. As far as drugs went, I was nineteen and still at the stage where I was willing to try anything once, except heroin, which had killed Sid Vicious and just about everyone else who had meddled with it. Heroin had been heavily demonized by a government awareness campaign, but cocaine had been glamorized by the media. Unlike heroin, cocaine seemed new and exotic, and my attitude to drugs at this point was innocent, experimental, and social. Cocaine had an image of being a rich person's drug and there was a naive belief that it couldn't do you much harm. Nothing could be further from the truth, although I didn't know it at the time.

"Okay, what the fuck do you have to do?" I said eagerly.

I watched as they took part in the simple ceremony of rolling up a crisp banknote and using it to sniff up the powder, each of them gasping and tipping back their heads after they snorted it. It was so quiet in the van that I could hear the distant thumping of the music back in the Rum Runner. When it was my turn to roll up a banknote, it seemed as if my own heart was thumping almost as loudly. I leaned forward, quickly inhaled through one of my nostrils and then . . .

BOOM!

They say the first time you do cocaine is so intense that you'll never experience the same thing again, and it's true. Within seconds your teeth go numb. The second time might still be powerful but it's not quite as heavy. The first time, you just go *bang* and you're immediately overcome with a tidal wave of euphoria and a feeling of overwhelming confidence. I felt as if the whole world had suddenly speeded up and at the same time I'd won the football pools and the lottery. There was very little drug awareness. I just wanted to enjoy the great feeling, which enhanced everything, sexually and socially. Cocaine makes you feel as if nothing can stand in your way, and that was exactly how I felt, like I was riding the crest of an enormous wave at the Christmas party. You feel that everyone is there for you; it's *your* party. Your mind cannot naturally be elevated to that state of euphoria, that's the danger, and there are diminishing returns from day one, so you'll end up paying a heavy price. But it was 1980, we'd won a record deal, and I'd just been watching three girls kissing.

I didn't hang about. I went straight back into the club to get some money to buy some more cocaine. Before I knew it I was in the camper van again and handing over £60 for a whole gram of the stuff. The rest of the night passed in a fantastic blur. I was the life and soul of the party; I felt invincible. Whenever I took cocaine everything went into Technicolor. I didn't think twice about the fact that Al Beard's doormen had witnessed me going back and forth to the camper van.

"Everything okay, Andy?" was all they would have said as I went in and out.

Al Beard would soon discover that I'd taken cocaine, but at the time I didn't care. After all, I thought he was there to protect me. Years later, when we found ourselves at the center of a cocaine scandal, I would realize that life isn't that simple. But that was all still in the distant future, and this was to be the first of many occasions on which I took the drug. Tabloid headlines were the last thing on my mind—all I wanted to do was party. Circumstances tend to dictate the way that cocaine affects your moods, and this was the beginning of a period that consisted of one long party. It was only much later on that my occasional cocaine use turned into regular abuse.

When I got back to the little bed-and-breakfast place that night, I couldn't sleep because of all the booze and coke, but as I lay there tossing and turning and sweating, I didn't care. It had been a great evening and I felt indestructible. Eventually I drifted off into a stupor, unaware that a little time bomb was now ticking away and that one day cocaine would come back to bite me.

I awoke on Christmas Day alone in the little B & B with a raging hangover. What a comedown! John, Roger, and Nick were all spending Christmas locally with their respective families, and Simon always had plenty of friends from University to hang around with. No one had thought to ask me round for Christmas lunch, so I ate a lonely meal and watched a bit of TV on the black-and-white portable set in my room. During the time that Duran Duran were based in Birmingham, we used to take Sundays off, and I would often find myself on my own when everyone else went off to their families. It could get very miserable and lonely. I wasn't dating anyone by this point, and I can remember thinking that I needed to find a decent girlfriend. Still, at least it was never long until the next party.

On Boxing Day, Nick and I caught the train down to London together and we finished mixing "Planet Earth" as planned. It was one of the last songs we wrote for the first album and it was influenced by the Rod Stewart hit "Do Ya Think I'm Sexy." The rhythm is very similar in terms of how it is arranged. Not many people spotted the similarity at the time, but years later I did actually tell Rod. It wasn't a copyright issue because the two songs obviously sound very different, but the style of "Planet Earth" and the way it was put together was similar to Rod's way of doing things.

"It's going to be a hit," said Nick.

Nick and I were probably the two band members who were the most involved in making the commercial decisions at this stage. Nick can be very astute when it comes to money, and his dad had done a bit of research into how things worked on our behalf. I'd also spoken to a lawyer who lived near me back home in Cullercoats, and I'd picked up a lot of advice from older musicians over the years. So even though we were still just kids, we were pretty switched on when it came to the financial side of things. Phonogram had offered us slightly more money, but we were in love with the whole romance of being signed to EMI because it was such an iconic label. The celebrated cover sleeve photograph of the Beatles peering over a stairwell on the fourth floor of the EMI offices in the West End was one of the most famous images in rock. One of the first things we did was lark about on the same stairwell, taking photographs of ourselves in similar poses to our idols. Thankfully the pictures were never released because they would have sent out an arrogant message for a fledgling band, although ironically we were soon to be dubbed the Fab Five by the press.

Surprisingly, the one member of the band who initially struggled a bit when we got into the studio was Simon. Singing on an album is not like simply going into a studio and plugging in an instrument. When you sing into a microphone with headphones on for the first time, you can hear every aspect of your voice and you have to learn how to control it. I knew how difficult it could be, as I'd done vocals in the past and I could see a bit of apprehension creeping into Simon when it was time for him to record. We'd laid the rhythm tracks down on drum and bass at Red Bus Studios in London with a producer called Colin Thurston, who had worked with Bowie and the Human League. We then went to Chipping Norton in Oxfordshire to complete guitars, keyboards, and vocals; and for the first few days it was tough for Simon. The label were really aggressive about wanting to get things moving, and we felt they were putting him under a lot of pressure to do things very quickly. It got to the point where a couple of people at EMI were openly critical, which was stupid because Simon had written all the lyrics in the first place and that made his position unassailable. He hadn't been in a band as long as some of the other members of the group, so to be fair it was no surprise that he was a bit wobbly.

Colin Thurston was a nice man, but he could be a bit pedantic. He was very tough on Simon and kept asking him to redo things. The Berrows were also initially concerned about Simon, and they privately confided that they feared his singing might be too flat. There was even a hint that we might be asked to get rid of Simon if he couldn't learn to sing in tune. In the end Dave Ambrose intervened. Dave had worked with some seriously big bands in the past like Queen and AC/DC, so he'd seen it all before and knew it was nothing to worry about. "You know it's your first album and everyone has got to find their feet," he reassured Simon. "If you've never done it before you just have to take your time—and don't forget, it's all about the songs."

I agreed. "Yeah, and Simon wrote all the fucking songs, so it's not as if anyone else is in a position to tell him what to do," I pointed out.

As far as I was concerned Simon was our vocalist: end of story. Plenty of singers would have taken a lot longer to get it right; he just needed a bit of time to learn his own vocal technique in the studio. I knew from my own experiences that when you put on the headphones and hear your voice in your ears, it feels like your clothes have been ripped off because it sounds totally different to what you expect. But Simon is a very positive person and he never got moody about it; he just took his time to get things right. Simon's character overcame it and I admired his professionalism. Eventually, it all worked fine, and we soon had a good-sounding record that was full of attitude and energy. We all had to learn as we hit the ground and it took us until the *Rio* album to understand exactly how to do it. In Duran Duran, it was always about precision, because it was a very tight, technical electronic sound that had real drums, real guitars, and real keyboards. There were lots of different facets to our music, so we needed a bit of help from someone like Colin, who had worked with avant-garde bands and who had a different set of ears. John called it "punk chic," because we were all heavily influenced by punk, but also because we loved the new disco sound emerging in the States from bands like Chic (hence us being fans of their bassist, Bernard Edwards).

"PLANET Earth" was due to be released early in the new year, but Spandau Ballet's debut single was released before it, in November. At the time we were a bit worried they would steal our thunder as we were still in negotiations with EMI, so we managed to obtain an advance copy of the Spandau record. They were signed to Chrysalis, and they were getting a bigger write-up in the music press than us, mainly because the London scene was slightly more fashionable and people like Steve Strange and Visage were based down there.

We'd done our first press interview with Betty Page of *Sounds* just after she had interviewed Spandau, and she told us, "Oh, yes—

they have been talking about you. What have you got to say about them?"

Their manager, Steve Dagger, had been slagging us off to everybody in London, saying things along the lines of: "Duran can't do it. They are from fucking Birmingham, they are never going to make it."

We were very much perceived as the underdogs, so we couldn't wait to get their single back to the Rum Runner. Nick, as always, was anxious to be first to check out something new.

"Let's see how good they are," he said as he put it on the turntable and blasted it through the big sound system in the club. We knew straightaway that we had much punchier songs than their release, which turned out a bit of a dirge called "To Cut a Long Story Short."

I thought, *Oh yeah—is that it? If that's the best they can do, we're not going to have too much to worry about.*

It was an anticlimax. *If that's London you can keep it,* I thought. Everyone had been saying Tony Hadley had a style similar to Sinatra. He had a good voice, but to me it just sounded corny. The others were all as unimpressed as I was. We felt their song was overtheatrical and very German-sounding, like Kraftwerk. Spandau had been overhyped, and even though it got them to number five, we thought their song had a coldness about it, whereas, later on, "Planet Earth" didn't. I think we had a more original sound and we played better together. We had blasted all our own tracks through the same sound system in the club to check that all the mixing was cool, and we had a hunch we would appeal to a broader base than Spandau. There were five of us and five of them and we were all the same age, but in my view we had very little in common with Spandau musically.

"PLANET Earth" was finally released on February 21, 1981. It got to number twelve, and it stayed on the charts for eleven weeks. More important, it got us a vital slot on *Top of the Pops*. We launched a mini tour just before the single hit the shops, and we were in Liverpool when we got the call from the record company to tell us we'd gone into the top forty. We had to do an interview on Radio One and go down for a recording for *Top of the Pops*.

We all thought, *Fucking yeah! It's happening—this is a dream come true!* I remember phoning my dad in excitement from a call box and saying, "Dad—we got it—*Top of the Pops!*"

"Well done, son—I am proud of you," he said.

I tried to stay in regular contact with my dad whenever I could, although in those days there were no mobile phones (and not all hotel rooms had their own phone either), so sometimes we'd go a while without talking if I was on the road.

As far as the band was concerned, EMI had really fast-tracked us. *Top of the Pops* was the BBC's flagship entertainment show at the time, and it used to get around 18 million viewers, so *everybody* wanted to appear on it. It was an iconic thing to be seen on and your record was guaranteed to do well in the charts afterward. All eyes and ears would focus on Radio One and *Top of the Pops*, because there was nothing else.

There was only one snag. Due to strict union rules in force, every version of a song that was broadcast on *Top of the Pops* had to be a special new recording for the show. It was a rule designed to generate extra money for all the highly paid TV technicians. This was before Maggie Thatcher had ripped apart the unions, so the rules had to be obeyed—at least on paper. The record companies hated it because the last thing they wanted was to risk a bad recording going out on air.

"So what happens is this," explained someone in the know. "The version that goes out on air is *remarkably* similar to the album version."

Someone told me that what happened was there was a clandestine swap of tapes so that the "new" version never got broadcast, which suited everybody. I'd heard about this from an old friend of mine who knew about the music industry. The unions were none the wiser, presumably because they got paid anyway. It would have been a big scandal at the time if anybody had known, and it explains why our lip-synching on the show was a bit more obvious than it would have been otherwise—the version we "sang" had been recorded months earlier.

On the day of filming, we were incredibly excited, although when we got to the studio we all thought, *Is this it?*

It was small, with a tiny, tiny stage, and the dressing rooms were very basic. The BBC were very bossy and were notorious for slinging people off if you were not on time.

"There will be no special treatment for anyone. If you miss your call you are out," they told us.

We discovered we were to be on the same show as the Who, who were obviously regarded as rock gods. They had a *huge* set and a *giant* dressing room.

"Hold on," I said. "I thought everyone was equal!"

The reality was that dealing with the BBC establishment was like going back to school. You had to play by their rules. Record companies were terrified of the BBC because they had the power to make or break bands, unlike today. Every child of every age in the UK watched Saturday TV, *Top of the Pops* and *The Old Grey Whistle Test.*

WE started being recognized almost immediately after *Top of the Pops,* and it gave us a real buzz. Whenever you spoke to anyone you'd want to ask them, "Did you see it, did you see it?" But unlike some of the other New Romantic bands we felt we still had a rock edge, and at first we thought we'd reach a much more rock-based audience than we did. EMI obviously had other ideas, and they had a publicity plan already worked out for each of us.

"We are going to promote John first because he is the most photogenic," they explained. "And we are going to start with him in Japan."

I sensed this strategy would secretly wind up Simon because, as the singer, he was naturally expected to be the front man. It was the shape of things to come, and there were many times when Simon and John would be vying for attention, often with hilarious results. It would irritate Simon that John attracted the most fuss from female fans, but when it came to photo shoots it would irritate John that the photographers always wanted the singer to stand in the center. Sometimes there was a lot of shuffling to see who stood in the middle. The simple fact was that John *was* incredibly photogenic but he *wasn't* the singer, so that caused problems between them straightaway.

Nick, meanwhile, who loved talking about pop art, was obviously going to enjoy doing a lot of interviews, so the record company had plenty of plans for him. As for me, Dave Ambrose had some interesting advice.

"When we get to America, your role will become really important," he told me. "Over there all the attention is always on the lead guitarist, and you will be the one who does all the interviews when we get to the States. You can't break the States without a good guitar player, and the last band who did it were Queen."

It was a lot to live up to, but the record company seemed to have everything worked out, and, as always, what would really make or break us would be the music. "Planet Earth" had done well, but instead of capitalizing on it EMI next released a single called "Careless Memories," which made only number thirty-seven. It was the record company's choice, but everyone else around us said, "Why didn't you release 'Girls on Film' instead?" It was a bit of a wobble that knocked our confidence, and after that we always made sure that we dictated which songs were released. But we needn't have worried; on July 25 we released "Girls on Film," and it really lit the touch paper. It got to number five and stayed on the charts for eleven weeks. Suddenly everyone wanted to meet us—and the female attention started almost immediately. Never mind "Girls on Film"—there were crowds of screaming girls almost *everywhere* we went, and it wasn't long before the press picked up on it. We developed such a big female following largely as the result of a conscious effort on EMI's part. They had a clever marketing plan based around what they learned from promoting the Beatles in the sixties—and the girls loved it.

"It's been so wild that we have even had to be smuggled out of our gigs in a Black Maria," complained Simon in a *Daily Star* interview. "There have been times when I've gone back to my hotel room to find fans sitting on my bed."

Within a few months things had gotten so crazy that some of the venues we visited had to call the police because they were afraid they'd be overrun by marauding teenage girls. The tabloids got to hear about one incident in Sheffield when the cops had a real battle to get us out the stage door and Simon got mobbed.

"Lead singer Simon Le Bon is recovering from almost being throttled when a girl grabbed the scarf around his neck and wouldn't let go," reported the *News of the World,* which also quoted Simon as saying, "I think she wanted to take my head home with her."

Simon got quite badly ruffled, but he loved it. Secretly, we were all loving the attention—and so were the record company, as it looked like their cunning plan was working. They made sure we appealed to the female audience through publicity in publications like *Smash Hits.* "Planet Earth" had got to number one in Australia, so EMI announced we were going on a world tour that would begin Down Under and would include Japan, Europe, and America.

We had a wild stopover in Thailand on the way to Sydney, and the journey was a bit of an experience in itself. Including our road crew, there were about twenty-five of us traveling in a group. The record company booked us economy class with an Indian airline. Air travel was a lot less regulated then, and there were actually people trying to cook up meals in the aisle of the plane using little gas camping stoves. During the brief stay in Thailand we were high on excitement, and there was lots of drinking and wild partying. When we finally got to Sydney we were greeted by a great big bear of an Aussie, who picked us up at the airport in a large American car and acted as our minder.

"G'day, I'm Grant Hilton—pleased to meet you boys," he said, extending his hand like a big paw. He was a six-foot-two-inch stereo-typical Aussie.

We soon found out that the local sheilas were just as mad for us as the English girls were, except they were much noisier and were never afraid to get their kit off! Grant was the manager of a little rock-and-roll hangout called Benny's Bar, where the boys from INXS used to hang out. It was only a tiny venue and it had a little round window set in the front door, which you had to go up to and show your face in order to be let in. We met INXS there on our first night. Simon and Michael Hutchence spent a lot of time together and eventually became good friends. INXS were a young band just like us and they wanted to have fun, so the first thing we decided to do was throw a party out by the beach for our road crew. It was a rock tradition to give them a celebration before the start of a tour.

Someone phoned up a modeling agency, so the beach was crawling with crowds of gorgeous women at the party. There was a trampoline on the sand, and everyone was urging the girls to have a go, shouting, "Come on—it's for the road crew." Before we knew it, the girls took off their bikinis, and they were bouncing up and down, topless, on the trampoline while the crew were all openmouthed. We were fast learning that 80 percent of our audience was female, and that kind of raw female energy followed us everywhere. Some of the fans could be incredibly persistent; they would wait outside our ho-tel and tell us they had never missed a single gig.

We would react by saying, "Fucking hell, how many gigs did you say you had been to? Okay, fifty shows! We'll let you in for an hour."

It was a really young hot female audience, and at that age it was a very difficult thing to manage—at times, impossible. Our fans were—and still are—amazingly warm to us and they'd go to great lengths to do something nice. Once, Simon mentioned in an inter-view that he liked continental chocolates, and suddenly we were sent an avalanche of them. Apart from Roger, who was with Giovanna from the beginning, none of us had serious girlfriends in the very early days, so there used to be a lot of rivalry, particularly between Simon and John, about who got to chat up the best girls.

Being number one in Australia gave things a lot of heat. We were invited onto *Countdown,* the Australian version of *Top of the Pops,* which was presented by a lovable old bloke named Molly Meldrum. He was famous for wearing a big cowboy hat and his catchphrase was "Molly Meldrum loves you lots." He gave us a massive buildup for weeks on end to promote us, and the tour soon sold out. We'd travel from gig to gig under the blazing sun in a dusty convoy of giant cattle trucks with all the gear stowed in the back, which was open sided.

To celebrate, we went to a party at Molly's house in Melbourne, and all the Australian cricket team came along. Molly had lots of expensive Egyptian art all around the place and I was amazed it survived the party. On another occasion we went to the Manzel Room in Sydney, which had a reputation for being the roughest rock-and-roll place on the planet, and we got thrown out for being too rowdy.

We pretty much met everyone we wanted to meet in Australia, and the whole thing was like a big dream. I loved cricket, so it was a big deal to meet Greg Chappell and his boys, as they were people you only normally got to see on the BBC.

LIFE was so much fun that when we got back to the Rum Runner, I remember thinking, *Well, even if we don't make it any bigger, this has all been worth it.* We were surrounded by everything that young men aspire to have, and at times some of us tended to get a bit overindulgent. We had a little private room at the back of the club for "extra activities," which was decked out to have a bit of fun. We had cushions and mattresses and candles in there, and it was a place where you could go to smoke a spliff or be alone with a girl. I jokily called it the "sex offender's room" (things weren't so politically correct then), and it ended up being used quite a lot. The Rum Runner was still very much our base; it had a policy of letting in two girls for every guy, so there was never any shortage of female company.

There was one girl in particular who was absolutely gorgeous, and she just loved sex with any man who would go with her. I won't use her real name here, so let's just call her Miss X instead. I was the first to discover her delights but I found out that afterward she went through quite a few of the males at the club. She was blond and beautiful, with looks that would have made any Hollywood starlet jealous, but she was quite happy to service you in the sex offender's room or anywhere else if need be. Generally the MO of girls like Miss X was that if they went with one of us they'd attempt to go after the others, too, not just the band but those around us.

Sometimes someone would accidentally walk in on people when they were in the sex offender's room. I can remember Al Beard running over on one occasion and spluttering, "Oh chaps! Have you heard about Roger and Giovanna? We've just caught them at it!"

I think most of us had an unexpected walk-in at some point, but we were just doing what young men do when they're single and surrounded by beautiful women, and the choice of females at the Rum Runner was overwhelming and unreal. This was before the scourge of AIDS became a national issue, so things were still very hedonistic.

"That was the whole point in forming a band. Girls, absolutely gorgeous girls," Simon once said in an interview. "We were five heterosexual, good-looking men. We competed against each other for the sexiest girls . . . and I won!"

In fact, it was John who often found himself with the most girls on his arm, sometimes with outrageous consequences. John was very popular, and he just bounced in and out of girlfriends every few weeks. After the album had come out he'd managed to find time to sneak off to Paris for a romantic couple of days with a girl named Roberta. It must have been a passionate time, because a few years later we opened up a copy of the *Daily Mirror* to see Polaroid photos they had taken of each other in bed. John was pictured drinking a cocktail naked in bed, and Roberta was reclining on the sheets dressed only in stockings, suspenders, and high heels, under the headline A HIGH TIME IN PARIS.

"When we went to the Louvre it was closed, so we spent most of our time in bed, eating strawberries, cheese and French bread," she told the paper.

The rest of the band had a bit of a quiet smirk at the article, but to be fair to John it can't have been very nice for him, especially as his parents would have seen it. The article was one of many invasions of privacy he suffered, and it must have been upsetting. When we played in Japan, John had more girls chasing him than anyone, and I think it started to get to him. We knew we would have female attention, but it was hugely difficult to manage on a personal level. The record company had planned it that way and had pushed John into doing lots of interviews with *Smash Hits*, but they didn't realize just quite how big it would become. It started with John, and then it spread to Simon and the rest of the band.

In some ways our hedonism was completely at odds with what was going on in the rest of the country. This was the summer of '81. There were violent riots all across the UK, caused by mass social discontent. In music, as well as in the country generally, it was almost as if there were two cultures running in parallel. There were bands like UB40 and the Specials, who were singing about unemployment and urban decay, and then there were the likes of us, who just wanted to have a good time. I was the same as any other guy on the street—we were working-class escapists who wanted to live out our dreams.

We played one gig at Birmingham Odeon while there was literally a full-scale riot going on outside. The Odeon was in a beautiful old building on New Street, and the rioters were tearing the city apart while the police battled to clear the street. We had allowed a journalist from the *New Musical Express* to accompany us inside, so it was a very strange interview because we could hear the roar of the crowd outside. These were very troubled times in the UK, and it was also the height of the cold war, so the world was living in fear of nuclear disaster, but we took it all in our stride. It was during this interview that Simon came out with the famous line, "We want to be the band to dance to when the bomb drops."

WHEREVER we went, we were determined to export the party atmosphere with us—and America was no exception. Our first jaunt to the USA turned out to be three weeks of mayhem and we nearly got kicked out of the States before we'd made an impression.

Los Angeles was one of our first stops. We'd heard lots of legendary stories about British bands' hell-raising in the past at the famous Hyatt House Hotel on Sunset Strip. It was nicknamed the Riot House because Led Zeppelin's drummer, John Bonham, had ridden a motorcycle through its corridors and Keith Moon of the Who was supposed to have driven his car into the pool there. We'd read a book called *The Diary of a Rock 'n' Roll Star*, by Ian Hunter, which catalogued all the wild behavior of British bands on tour in America, and it became our bible.

"Come on, fellas, we've read the book, now let's do it," I said to the others.

The only trouble was that by 1981, the Hyatt wasn't quite so tolerant. We had been boozing it up all day long, and someone decided it would be a wheeze to put shampoo in the fountain. It was amazing—there were bubbles billowing everywhere. Then we went up to the roof and we could see all these well-heeled guests enjoying a brunch buffet down below. Before long there were cream cakes raining down on them. I think at one point I actually tipped a bucket of water over someone from above on the balcony. We were just being childish rock stars, but it couldn't have been fun for anyone else in the hotel. There were lots of complaints about us during the day, but we didn't really take any notice until about 6:30 p.m., when the stormtroopers finally turned up in the form of the LAPD. One of our crew had gone to the toilet and heard the police talking outside. It gave us thirty seconds to escape.

"Quick, it's the cops—get rid of all the dope!" shouted one of the roadies.

The adrenaline suddenly kicked in. Before we knew it the place was swarming with big, armed cops, who were very tough and aggressive. In my boozed-up state, I was convinced we'd all be deported, so I legged it as fast as I could. I ran up the road to the Roxy club and banged on the door.

"If anyone is in there, let me in," I begged. "We need to call the British Embassy."

I was allowed into the Roxy, but after a stiff drink I decided that maybe calling the embassy wasn't such a good idea after all. Thankfully nobody was nicked, and a member of our entourage managed to smooth things over with the cops. The person who sorted it out had a great sense of humor and he used to get drunk and fall asleep with a briefcase containing all the cash from our gigs chained to his arm. The police agreed to let everyone go on condition that we left the hotel. But the news traveled fast. We discovered no other decent hotel in town would take us, so we had to stay in this grotty little shithouse for the rest of our stay in LA. Nick and I had to share a room, and I can remember the sheer horror on his face when a cockroach crawled over him in the night.

New York turned out to be far more welcoming and we were greeted there as if we were a young Bohemian band whom everyone wanted to be seen with—even the great pop artist Andy Warhol. We could just walk into anywhere and be given a table, which was amazing given the short space of time we'd been together as a band. Capitol Records, who were owned by EMI, were looking after us; when one of their press officers heard that Nick and John were fans of Warhol, she called him up to arrange a meeting.

"There are five good-looking young guys in town from a great band who want to meet you—and they wear makeup," she told him.

Sure enough, we were invited down to Studio 54 on a Sunday night to meet him. There was a huge queue to get in because as an underground club it was still coming to the end of its heyday, but nobody told us that Sunday night was gay night! It was obviously a huge honor to be seen with Warhol and it caused quite a stir. He latched onto us immediately, and I remember him saying to me over and over again, "Oh, Andy, you've got to wear pearls. You gotta wear pearls, Andy!"

Then it was Nick's turn.

"Oh, I like that Nick and I got a photo at home to prove it!" screeched Warhol.

I kept thinking, *Wow! It's Andy Warhol and he knows all our names.* I was flattered because Warhol was an icon and I knew that David Bowie, Lou Reed, and the Velvet Underground had all been heavily influenced by him. I could see the beauty in what he did, but I wasn't really from that school—unlike Nick, for whom Warhol was a real source of creative energy. At times it seemed as if Nick was obsessed with him. The fuss caused by our meeting with Warhol was huge, and the association never really wore off. Studio 54 was amazing with all the lights and the great atmosphere, and I could see that the Berrows had tried to style the Rum Runner on it. But I couldn't really immerse myself in the New York gay scene, and I found all the hunky boys in shorts a bit too much. Having said that, New York would eventually become a great playground for us, particularly John and I—but that was all still in the future.

We did a lot of traveling during 1981, and places would seem to go nuts for us whenever we went there for the first time. Paris was one example of this, when we played a gig there in September 1981, a few weeks before we went to New York. We'd hit upon the idea of taking two coachloads full of fans from the Rum Runner with us to France, just to ensure the party went with a swing. EMI agreed to spend £20,000 to pick up the tab. The plan was to turn the whole evening into a big stunt for the press.

When we got to Paris we held one hell of a party in a club at a grand old Parisian ambassador's residence, which had opulent works of art adorning all the walls. They took one look at our crowd and nearly didn't let them in. We were lucky to even get into France at all, because earlier in the evening the border guards had seen our buses and wanted to put us back on the ferry. Everyone had put on their most outrageous New Romantic gear, which meant the gays all had huge feathers and the girls had virtually nothing on; they were just scantily clad in underwear with a pair of angel wings on their backs. Some of the men wore SS uniforms, which were accepted then as part of the fashion and not meant as a political statement. It was just a way of looking cold and austere. Back then, it wasn't considered as an insult to victims of the war—we'd beaten the Nazis and to us they were figures of fun. You have only to look at the furor caused by Prince Harry wearing a Nazi uniform at a party to realize how much things have changed.

We knew we'd make an impact in France because nothing like that existed in Paris. "Impact" turned out to be an understatement. The party got so wild that we damaged some seats and the toilets were awash with drugs. Worse still, someone drew a funny moustache and comedy glasses in lipstick on one of the oil paintings. It caused a right old stink because it was an expensive work of art and EMI were forced to pay thousands to have it restored.

But the evening served its purpose and the party got loads of media coverage, more even than the gig itself.

The word was starting to spread . . .

CHAPTER FOUR

Rio: Love & War

I danced with a gorgeous blond girl during our trip to Paris and I soon found myself falling in love with her. Her name was Tracey Wilson, and the following year she would become my wife. Tracey was a hairdresser who managed a salon where Duran Duran used to go to blag free haircuts and she was part of the regular crowd at the Rum Runner. Unlike some of the other girls, she didn't drink or take drugs—and at first she wasn't impressed by my advances. In fact, prior to going to France, whenever I approached her she usually made it quite clear she wasn't interested and at one point I was horrified to learn that Simon had started to take an interest in her.

"You can 'eff off, there's plenty more fish in the sea," I told him. "She's mine."

It was almost a year since Duran Duran's first album had come out. Simon and I were still living together in the flat we shared in Moseley. The album had got to number three on the charts and it was still selling well, so we were getting a lot of attention because of it—although strangely in Moseley most people continued to ignore us. Being a red-light district, there were cars crawling everywhere—but they weren't looking for us. There was a curry house if you went in one direction from our flat and a corner shop if you went the other way. It was a funky place to live and we'd walk past chilled-out Rasta-farians with boom boxes in order to get our groceries, but at nighttime we'd avoid the bus and always get a taxicab straight to the door.

When I'd moved to Birmingham to be with Duran Duran, finding a partner hadn't exactly been part of my plans, but those long Sunday afternoons that I used to spend alone while the rest of the band were with their families left me wanting to find a decent girl-friend. The first time I'd seen Tracey had been in the Rum Runner. Her brothers, Sean and Mitchell, ran a string of salons and I was mates with them because they were part of the crew that used to hang out in the club. Mitchell was Tracey's younger brother and he had movie-star looks just like her. He did a bit of photography and took some photos of the band at the salon. Sean, the older brother, was as mad as a fish, but he was also the one with the brains, and together they were a very entrepreneurial family. Tracey was close friends with Giovanna, who was still working in the cloakroom and dating Roger. She was also friends with Nick's girlfriend at the time, Elaine Grif-fiths. The three girls all used to dress dead sexy.

What first attracted me to Tracey was that she had a certain dignity and pride in herself. She was one of those kids who the first time she had one gin and tonic too many she hated it so much that she never really drank again. I was leading a fairly hedonistic lifestyle at the time, so it was appealing to see someone who was so different to me in that respect—plus, of course, the fact she didn't seem inter-ested in me at first just made me all the keener!

"I've seen you. You're in the band with all them lot and all those who party in the club," she told me dismissively in one of our early conversations.

No matter how hard I tried to impress her, I got nowhere for weeks. It was as if she was thinking to herself, *Hmmm. I am not sure if I want to mess about with him. He is always on the road.*

Giovanna, who remains a good friend of mine to this day, didn't help matters to begin with. "Ooh, you want to watch him. He is a right womanizing bastard," she said to Tracey. Thanks, Giovanna—

like most guys in a band I had my fair share of female attention, but it was hardly a fair description! I'd been in bands for several years, including in Germany where I had my share of fräuleins (including one incident where I got caught with a German girl in the back of the Streak by her father!).

A few nights before our gig in Paris, Tracey was in the Rum Runner celebrating her twentieth birthday, so I spent the evening trying to chat her up. It was my way of saying *happy birthday!* Although she was initially quite cool toward me I sensed I was starting to make some progress and we ended up flirting together by squirting each other with a soda siphon. At one point she flung up her arm and it knocked the siphon into my face and chipped one of my front teeth. Ouch! At the end of the night I sidled up to the bar and explained how much I'd enjoyed her company and joked that at least she'd knocked only one of my teeth out—but when I looked round I was talking to someone else who looked a bit like her. I was so drunk that I'd been chatting to the wrong girl for the last ten minutes!

Tracey was part of the group who traveled to France with us and I must have made a good impression on her birthday because she agreed to dance with me in Paris, and this time we really hit it off. Getting a girl to dance with you was significant in those days, and it had a certain charm about it. It counted for something because there was still an air of innocence about the female population. I can't ever remember seeing girls rolling about in the gutter or comatose through booze: frat school behavior for women was still a thing of the future. Somebody took a photograph of Tracey and me while we were dancing and it appeared in the papers in the UK the following day. The picture caused a bit of a stir because the press believed I was loosely seeing another girl back home, and the newspapers kicked up a bit of a fuss. After Paris, Tracey went straight back to Birmingham on the bus, but the band were scheduled to do some more gigs in Europe, so we had to go back on the road. Suddenly I found myself calling her whenever I could from a call box, and when we got back to the UK I asked her to come to dinner.

"Well, come round and we will have something to eat," I said. Then, because I'd had to learn how to cook a bit when I was younger, I added: "I'll cook, or you cook, you know, like out of the way of everybody."

"Oh, that's okay. I'll bring something round to eat," she said.

When Tracey arrived she brought along a homemade spaghetti Bolognese in a Tupperware container. It was delicious, but I later found out her mum had secretly cooked it for her. And that's when I knew she was the one.

I thought, *Oh good—at least she must want to impress me, and if she wants to impress me she must like me.* She couldn't cook very well herself at that time, but she wanted to present something nice. If a girl makes an effort to bribe you like that, it has to be a positive sign. She did that trick a couple of times, and it was deliciously devious because it made her appear very thoughtful.

Tracey loved riding, and her father owned a horse sanctuary on a farm out in Shropshire, where he had a herd of three or four hundred rescued horses. She had two horses of her own, called Bobby and Daniel, and she used to talk about them all the time.

"Why don't you let me come with you the next time you go out to the farm?" I asked.

She agreed and after that we used to go down there every Sunday and whenever else we could. It was nice getting away to the farm in the summer. Tracey was a county champion at Side Saddle. We'd be trotting around and she would gallop off into the distance, but I couldn't even canter. Sometimes I'd even have to hang on to a gatepost to try and stop a horse because I couldn't control it! We'd share funny moments like that, which had nothing to do with my life in rock and roll. It was fantastic and it gave our relationship balance, because it wasn't just about me being in Duran Duran.

I soon discovered that despite our differences, we had a lot more in common than I realized. Like me, Tracey's parents were divorced and she had not had a normal childhood. We'd been at the same age when our respective parents had split up, so she'd also been through some acrimony. Maybe some of Tracey's experiences when she was younger made her think twice about getting involved with me. I think she saw where it could go wrong and knew what it could cost, the same as I did. But she was a very calm person, and she brought stability into my life at a time when I could easily have slipped into a different lifestyle that I would have later regretted.

By the time I was twenty, I'd played hundreds, if not thousands, of gigs in different countries, but for the first time I had something worth sharing in life. The first Duran Duran album and the tour were a success, and we were now on increased retainers from the record company that were worth the equivalent of a couple of grand a week. For the first time, everyone in the band could afford to think about doing things that we couldn't afford to do before, like buying cars and houses. It felt brilliant. I can remember buying a beautiful new BMW—it was a blue 325, and I showed it to my uncle, who was an old car fanatic. I couldn't even drive officially, but I took him out for a spin in it and he was terrified. A lot of girls started to flock to us because they needed what we had, but Tracey didn't need any of it. She had her own business with her brothers, she had her own income, and she had her own car. Tracey had a little Citroen 2CV, and her brother Mitchell had worked his backside off to own a Jag. A few weeks after we started dating I invited her to come to New York, but she was really nervous about the sleeping arrangements.

I was being a gentleman at this point, and I think I did actually say, "You don't have to stay in my room if you don't want to."

Tracey accepted. I flew her out to America with Giovanna, and they came along to Studio 54 when we met Andy Warhol. We stayed in a really nice hotel near Central Park. It was as if I had to pinch myself to make sure I wasn't dreaming, because things were going so well. We played several small shows, which were sold out, and suddenly there were a lot of emotions running through my life.

Music is an emotion, it's a passion that's about being confident and projecting yourself onstage. But the biggest emotion of all is love.

I was beginning to realize that if you don't have a partner to share things with, then everything else seems to have less value.

AFTER we came back from the States, Tracey and I started seeing each other regularly and we became very close before I went down to London with the band to record our second album, *Rio*. Tracey's brother Mitchell had a small house out in the countryside that he wanted to sell. Tracey and I went to see it and we decided to buy it. I think the house cost in the region of £27,000, and I was able to pay for it in one go, which was a nice feeling. One of Tracey's family hair salons was just around the corner, so it was an ideal location for her and it wasn't too far from Birmingham for me. Tracey was officially living with her dad, but she was mostly staying with me in Moseley.

It was while we were discussing buying the house together that I began to think about asking Tracey to marry me. Call me an old traditionalist, but I decided to propose to Tracey on the night of my twenty-first birthday. It was 3 a.m. and I'd been out to celebrate at the Rum Runner while Tracey had stayed at home because she had a cold.

"Wake up, Tracey, I've got something to ask you," I said. "Look, you know it's my twenty-first birthday. I have had a few drinks, which, er . . . you know, has given me the courage to ask you an important question. Will you marry me?"

I paused as I waited for her response, but just as she'd done when I originally pursued her for a date, she kept me holding on for her answer.

Tracey rolled over sleepily. "Okay—I'll tell you in the morning," she said, and went straight back to sleep. Charming!

The next morning Tracey awoke and said yes straightaway . . . and I couldn't wait to share the news with Simon. I went down and saw him in the kitchen, where there was always a big pile of dishes in the sink waiting for someone to clean them, just like you'd find in any other house shared by young people.

"Well, that's it, mate," I said. "I'm getting married."

Simon didn't say a word, apart from "Oh, really?"

I think what he meant was "Are you sure?" It must have all seemed very sudden, but with Tracey I just knew by human instinct that I'd found the right person. Later on that morning I went back downstairs again, and out of courtesy Simon wished us well.

"It's great, if that's what makes you happy," he said.

In those days it was very common to get married by the age of twenty-one. Back in the North East, you were expected to be working by sixteen, you were voting at eighteen, and you were a full-fledged adult by twenty-one. In fact, in Newcastle all my mates were married by twenty-one. I was brought up not to put life on hold and my dad was pleased for me. All our parents had been married by that age, and, after all, having a partner is the most important thing in life. If you find someone whom you love and trust, why wait just because you are young and living in Moseley? It turned out to be the right decision because Tracey and I have now been happily married for over twenty-five years. In media interviews, I've often described Tracey as my soul mate, and part of being in a successful relationship is that there is one person whom you can talk to about anything. Someone who will see things from a unique perspective and who will consider you a little bit more than other people. For me that person is Tracey.

AFTER I proposed, there was a small matter of a Duran Duran tour and a new album to get out of the way before Tracey and I could tie the knot. We'd started writing our *Rio* material in Birmingham. I was in the office at the Rum Runner one morning when I heard Nick playing a little sequence on the keyboards downstairs. It was the opening notes of what was to become "Save a Prayer" and my first reaction was, "Bloody hell—that's good."

Nick didn't have it perfect at this point. Roger and I started working out the notes with him and counting out a beat, and suddenly we had something special. Nick, Simon, and I later finished it off together in the basement at EMI using a drum machine, although Roger was so precise in his playing that it was never as easy when he wasn't around. We had a budget of around £65,000 from the record label to record the *Rio* album, which was about double what we'd had for the first album. It took about eight weeks to record; we rented apartments in London so that we could be close to Air Studios, where we were mixing it.

It was while we were working on the album that we first discovered the delights of the Embassy Club, which was in Old Bond Street. It was owned by Stephen Hayter, the flamboyant party host who socialized with the likes of Princess Margaret and Freddie Mercury. The club itself was very hedonistic and packed with celebrities, and we started hanging out there with Pete Townsend, whom we'd met previously at the Rum Runner. Roger Taylor from Queen was a regular there, as was Lemmy from Motörhead, who would always be downstairs playing on the Space Invaders machine.

We were quite disciplined in our approach to work. We'd written and rehearsed all the songs and we knew exactly what we wanted to do in the studio. It's fair to say, though, that we'd developed a few London habits that would come back to haunt us in future years. John and I spent a lot of time at the Embassy—particularly John, who became the absolute star of the place. When you record an album the bass player and the drummer are usually the first to lay down their material, and they often end up with time on their hands while the other band members record their contributions. Roger had done his bit during our first couple of weeks in London, and he went back to Birmingham to be with Giovanna because he was quite anchored with her, but John stayed on in London and partied almost every night. He was starting to get a staggering amount of female attention, much more than the rest of us. The record company had deliberately pushed him into the spotlight because of his looks, and I think all the wild partying was his way of letting off steam.

The Embassy was definitely an interesting place, but, unlike John, I was never that impressed with it. I didn't mind having a bit of fun, but I didn't want to sit there all night talking rubbish with people who'd overindulged in certain substances. Hayter, who later died of AIDS, had an office at the back of the club behind a bullet-proof door. For a select few who were in the know, there would be mounds of cocaine on the table in the office after the club closed, and people would go there to party until morning. But I have never been a fan of sitting there trying to put the world to rights when you won't even be able to remember what you were talking about the following day.

The guys from Spandau Ballet were based in London, as was Steve Strange, and it was through the Embassy Club that John and I first encountered Robert Palmer. We went back to Steve Strange's house in Notting Hill one night and Robert was lying there on the bed, giggling away in a world of his own. He was behaving as if he had taken acid, just laughing his head off, until he came round a bit and we introduced ourselves. He was a proper partyer, but he *always* wore a suit and tie.

"I'll never look out-of-date like this," he used to explain.

Robert loved being around different people and going out to dinner with them. He drank wine and whiskey—the grape and the grain—and he had a great routine that involved getting up for lunch and having some wine before going to work and never dropping a beat. After that, he would go out to dinner and then go back to work again. But he never let his lifestyle interfere with his work. He was a great singer, lyricist, and all-round musician.

TRACEY and I had planned to get married in April or May 1982 in the Midlands, but after we finished recording *Rio,* the band had to shoot our videos in Sri Lanka and Antigua before playing in Japan and Australia. By the time we got back to the UK, I was exhausted and laid up with a stomach bug I'd picked up in an elephant lagoon (I'll tell you about that in the next chapter). It turned out to be a very nasty virus. At one point I was in Wolverhampton General Hospital with a temperature of 103 before Tracey and her dad persuaded me to transfer to the private hospital.

Our plans for a spring wedding had been well and truly spoiled, and now we were due to play a series of gigs in the States. Capitol Records, EMI's American division, had promised to put a lot of backing behind us if we remixed the *Rio* album for the States, which we did with the help of an American sound engineer. It gave the album a smoother, cleaner sound that went down better with US audiences, who are used to slightly more precise sound than we'd developed in the UK. We were in agreement, because we realized we needed to change our sound for the States, where the music industry spends far more time and money on mixing material. Not that we had much choice.

"Remix it and we'll support you; don't do it and we won't," said Capitol.

It was good advice, but the American tour left Tracey and me with no choice but to rethink our wedding plans again.

"Okay, if we can't get married now, let's do it in the UK in the summer after the US tour," I suggested.

It sounded like a good plan, but after we went on the road the record label announced they'd managed to book us on a second US tour with Blondie, which would immediately follow our own. We were due to play the last date of our US tour at the Greek Theatre in Los Angeles on July 27 before joining Blondie's Tracks Across America Tour in Kansas City on August 2. It meant there would be no time to go back to the UK to organize the wedding—and our families back home were beginning to wonder if we'd ever go through with it.

"Well look—in between our tour and the Blondie tour let's get married in LA," I said. "It will cut out all the headache of trying to organize things with our families, and if anyone wants to come they can get themselves an air ticket."

Tracey agreed and we booked the wedding for July 29, 1982, at the Chateau Marmont Hotel on Sunset Boulevard in Hollywood. It wasn't just the timing that made America the best location to get married, because back home Duran Duran were starting to get an enormous amount of press attention. "Hungry Like the Wolf" had been released in the UK on May 15, and we were chased by screaming girls wherever we went. Getting married in the States would create less fuss than a wedding back home. John, in particular, was still being heavily pushed by the record company as a single man who made an ideal teenage pinup. I'd never really played up to the same image, so it wasn't as if the media were going to react by saying, "The single guy in Duran Duran has gone now, girls." But even so, there were a few paranoid people at the record company who feared that the first Duran Duran wedding might damage our image as available young men.

"The fans will see the wedding and wonder who is going to be next," they said.

I had a bit more respect for our fans than that, and I argued that it was better for them to aspire to marry one of us than to just sleep with us, but in any case Tracey and I wanted to keep the day low-key, which probably suited the way the record label and our management would have preferred things if they'd had a say.

DURAN Duran were really starting to take off in the States by the time the big day of the wedding arrived. We'd made our first major appearance on US television in Philadelphia when we went on the dance show *Dancin' on Air* and "Hungry Like the Wolf" was beginning to get major airplay on US radio. Our videos were getting great exposure on MTV and we were being constantly played on TV screens in nightclubs, which helped to raise our profile all the time.

Meanwhile, we were working our butts off and played gigs across America and Canada, which included shows in New York, Boston, Montreal, Toronto, Pittsburgh, Detroit, Chicago, Milwaukee, Minneapolis, Seattle, and San Francisco. We'd travel from city to city by train, which was a strange feeling because even though we were being mobbed in public by fans in the UK, in the States we could still travel by public transport without being recognized. Our record sales were starting to earn us serious sums of money, but we still weren't at the point where we could afford to travel everywhere by private jet, so the train made sense for accounting reasons as well. But we were starting to enjoy our growing financial freedom, so we'd check into the most luxurious hotel we could find whenever we were in a major city. When you are newly in love, there's nothing nicer than checking into a palatial hotel and getting a nice room, perhaps with an open fire, and living off room service. Tracey and I did a lot of that, and it was a nice bit of sanity away from the huge amount of fuss and attention that was beginning to surround the band.

Two days before Tracey and I got married, Duran Duran sold out the Greek Theatre. Eight thousand people saw our show there. It was the first glimpse of what was about to happen across the United States—and it was fantastic. Until then we'd been opening for a couple of other bands and playing to audiences of 3,000 to 4,000, but with every show interest was growing. We'd seen what had happened in the UK, so we had a sense of where it was all going. Our attitude was "Wow—it's about to happen here, too."

For the wedding, everyone in the band had checked into their own bungalow at the Chateau Marmont. Tracey and I took one of two special apartments that stand on the top of a hill within the hotel grounds. It had its own garden, a big lounge kitchen, and three or four bedrooms, so there was plenty of room for entertaining. It was the ideal place to spend your wedding day—although the atmosphere at the hotel was slightly strange because the actor John Belushi had recently died in the bungalow next door. The *Blues Brothers* star had been found dead from a drug overdose in March, but the whole place was still covered with police tape, and all his cars were being examined by cops in the underground car park. The police were actively investigating his death, so there were lots of forensic people coming and going, but we didn't allow it to spoil things.

There was a little tree close to our bungalow and we arranged to be married there by the Dean of UCLA. The day before the wedding I went into town to organize all the wedding suits while the other band members went off to a yacht party. We all planned to wear gray top hats and tails; one of the security guards and I had to try and get everyone's sizes correct.

"Don't worry—everything is going to be perfect," I whispered to Tracey that night.

The only problem the next morning was that we nearly didn't wake up! The others were supposed to come and rouse me to ensure I didn't oversleep—but it must have been a great yacht party because they were all still out of it from the night before. Luckily I woke up just in time, and I went around all the other bungalows knocking on their doors, starting with John. He was still asleep so I had to wake him.

"You look dreadful. Fancy a livener?" I smiled.

So we downed a Jack Daniel's and Coke each, put on our suits, and off we went. But despite all the hangovers, the ceremony itself was very private and lovely. It was attended by about thirty close friends. We released a couple of nice photos of Tracey and me to the media through the record company. We also had some pictures of the five band members together in our top hats drinking champagne. Then we had a huge wedding cake and lots of pizza. Afterward, Tracey and I sipped more champagne together and relaxed in the sunshine on the beautiful grounds of the hotel.

It was a perfect rock-and-roll wedding. To cap it all, things were going great in the band and there didn't seem to be a cloud on the horizon. But although we had no way of knowing it on that day, as a band we were about to face some problems later that year.

In fact, we were about to face a whole lot of trouble.

I was in a dreamy sleep cuddled up in a hotel bed next to Tracey in October when I slowly became aware of a distant commotion that seemed to be happening somewhere far away. Slowly, as I began to wake through the fog of sleep, I could hear voices shouting outside in the corridor. For a second I thought I heard a crash and the sound of breaking glass, then things grew quiet again.

"What the hell was all that? Did you hear it?" I asked Tracey.

"Ignore it and come back to bed," she replied, sleepily.

But somewhere inside me little alarm bells were ringing. It was autumn and we were on the road in Germany, having finished touring the States with Blondie a few months earlier. I had arranged for Tracey to be picked up from the Munich airport earlier. We'd spent the evening eating pizza together in bed at the hotel, while some of the other members of Duran Duran went off to a nightclub. They'd planned to meet Bryan Ferry there; the Roxy Music guys were big in Germany and they were out there at the same time. Intrigued by all the fuss I'd heard outside my room, I got out of bed to investigate.

"It's John. Don't worry—it's all right, he's gone to bed," said one of the crew. I could see from the expression on his face that things were far from all right. "There was some trouble at the nightclub," he explained.

We were all checked into hotel rooms that had doors connecting to the same corridor, which was lined by glass light fittings that were spaced high up along its walls. I could see that one of the fittings had been smashed, and beneath it was a dark smear of blood.

I was torn between investigating further and going back to bed. Things seemed to have quieted down, so I decided to return to my room to be with Tracey. But try as I might, I couldn't sleep. A couple of hours later I got up and went to John's door, where I could hear muffled voices coming from inside.

"It's Andy. Let me in," I ordered.

The door swung open and there was John, surrounded by some of our crew members. I could see he was in a terrible state. His right hand was wrapped in a huge swath of bandages, and he looked pale and distraught.

"What the hell happened?" I demanded.

"They came at us with baseball bats in the nightclub and beat the hell out of us," explained one of the crew.

Only then did the full horror of what had taken place begin to unfold. John and Roger had been part of the group that had gone to the nightclub in Munich along with several of our entourage, including our bodyguard, Simon Cook. The group had met up with Bryan Ferry as planned and the evening was going well. No one could explain exactly what had happened next, except that they'd been sitting around a table downstairs in the club when a group of men armed with baseball bats rushed over. The vicious attack that followed had been premeditated and nasty.

"It was too coordinated to have been a spur-of-the-moment thing. They came at us very quickly and they knew where we were," the crew explained to me.

Roger had taken the worst of it. He'd been beaten close to unconsciousness after being smashed over the head. He had a nasty bump on his skull and he was probably lucky to be alive. A full-scale war had then broken out between the attackers and our own security. Simon Cook had taken a real pounding, but despite that he'd never stopped punching back while he tried to defend the band. He was a brave bloke, and he even managed to briefly drag a few of the attackers back down the stairs as they made their escape. He was a good friend to all of us, so it was upsetting to hear he'd taken such a nasty beating on behalf of Duran Duran.

It was John who had sustained the bloodiest injury. The wound to his hand would keep us off the road and force us to scrap the rest of our dates in Germany. Ironically, the wound hadn't been sustained during the fight in the club. John had actually cut his hand at the hotel by putting it through the light fitting that was now shattered and dripping with blood in the corridor. He'd suffered a deep, nasty wound, and there was no way he was going to be playing bass guitar anytime soon.

I discovered that during most of the fight, John and Bryan Ferry had been hidden away in the toilets. I suspected that by the time John got back to the hotel, he was overcome by the fact that he hadn't done anything to help the others. Band of brothers? Forget it. In my view, when he'd punched the light fitting he'd been lashing out in anger at himself. Perhaps he felt bad and wanted to punish himself for what he rightly or wrongly perceived to be his own failure to be able to join the fight? There was no need for John to feel that way. He wasn't a coward—it was just a human reaction. But I was torn between having sympathy for him over his plight and being angry with him because I knew his injury was going to cause us a lot of problems. I think you can forgive anything when someone is suffering, but in my view John had either meant to punch the light, or he'd been so out of control that he'd done it by accident—and either way he needed help.

"I mean, it's a fucking wall, there's lots of places you can punch. Why go for the most painful bit?" I said to myself.

"Right—we're going home in the morning," announced Simon the bodyguard. Despite the terrible beating he had taken he was still being the most rational of all of us. "We've got to get flights and get out of here fast. No one has got to know about this. We'll pay the hotel bill, no fuss. Dead quiet. We'll catch the earliest flights we can get."

We knew he was right, and the next morning we caught the elevator down to reception in silence. The hotel weren't very happy with us, but we were all determined to keep quiet as we checked out. Then it was quickly through the hotel door, looking straight ahead, and onto our tour bus. By now, John was out of it, half asleep with his hand wrapped in a giant ball of bandages; a doctor had dressed his wound during the night. Every one of us felt tired and ragged.

Getting married earlier in the year had been the nicest thing that had happened to me, but getting beaten up in a nightclub was the nastiest thing that had happened to the band so far. I think that some of what occurred that night got bottled up inside John and Roger, and it may have had a bearing on how things unfolded in the future. I can't believe something like that doesn't have an effect on you. Roger had been the victim of terrible violence, and John was powerless to help. We weren't a violent bunch of people, but everyone now knew what it felt like to be a target. Suddenly it was as if a whole new negative dimension had become part of the equation, and it was a turning point. Our reaction was, "Okay, we better have more bodyguards in the future." It was also a turning point for me personally, because I was on my way to becoming regarded as the king of hedonism for always being up for a party. As I've mentioned I had a reputation for having hollow legs when it came to putting away the booze, and if the mood took me, I happily stayed up all night drinking—and I was out most nights. I also continued to use cocaine from time to time. But on the evening of the nightclub incident, thankfully, I'd opted to have a quiet night in with my wife.

THE pressure had been building up on us all since the Blondie tour, which had been fantastic, but it was also a time during which early frictions began to form within Duran Duran for the first time. Before we got to Germany, things started to change over the summer with the arrival on the scene of Nick's new partner and future wife, Julie Anne Freidman.

A few days after Tracey and I got married, Tracey went back to the UK and I met with the rest of the band at the LA airport to fly off to meet with Blondie elsewhere in the States.

"Nick's got someone with him," said one of the crew in the departure lounge. "Who is she?"

It was Julie Anne, who introduced herself as a model and the heiress to the Younkers department store fortune in the States. Nick had met her at the yacht party the day before my wedding and he'd clearly been enthralled by her. The rest of us were slightly bemused, because an outsider had never been allowed to travel with us before. We were always very organized and respectful; we knew that whenever we came together to travel it wouldn't just be a free-for-all. You have a certain routine of how you do things on the road, and any disruption to that routine can cause havoc. I'd sacrificed having a honeymoon and sent my new wife home so that we could go on the road, yet here was Nick bringing his future wife with him. He had broken the unwritten

WILD BOY

band rule that said you didn't bring your girlfriend on the road. Simon Le Bon, who had become very close to Nick, seemed very surprised. He picked up on it straightaway and approached Nick by saying something along the lines of "What the fuck is going on?"

"I've met her on the boat and she's coming with me," was all that Nick said at the time.

"Yeah—you've not been laid for ages," one of us joked back.

Nick's romance with Julie Anne was the first relationship to come into the band that would start to fracture our unity, because it was the first time an outsider was allowed into our inner circle. Most of the other relationships we'd all been involved in up until then had already been in place since our days in Birmingham. Tracey and Giovanna had been part of our circle since the beginning. John could be a bit mad with the girls, but even his relationships were mostly with people whom we knew from the Rum Runner. Simon's girlfriend at the time, Claire Stansfield, was Canadian, but she was someone we knew from the UK, too. But as for Julie Anne, I remembered something that Paul Berrow had told us before we'd left for the States. "Ooh, when those bloody American birds get hold of you, you won't catch your breath," he warned. "Different set of values."

That might have been a bit harsh, but culturally, we were all very English in our tastes and our outlook. Suddenly we found a brash American heiress in our midst. As time went on, I didn't quite know whether or not to trust her. Today I joke that it was a bit like the famous scene in *This Is Spinal Tap* when the lead singer's overbearing girlfriend arrives at the airport. Julie Anne was very pushy because of her social standing, and she was used to being at the top. She wasn't a bad person, but we weren't used to having an outsider in our midst. To me, her presence in the group was like a bomb. She'd met Nick on a boat and pretty soon she was rocking the boat.

BLONDIE was huge across the States, but they were starting to come to the end of their run of success. The ticket sales on the tour weren't huge—but it was the first chance we had to play at some really big arenas. We had to pay money to get on the tour because it gave us such great publicity. Under the circumstances Blondie could have been very aloof, but they were an arty band like us and they made us very welcome. We didn't mix much with Debbie Harry, but Jimmy Destri, Chris Stein, and Nigel Harrison all knew how to party. Jimmy Destri shared a lot of substances with me; in fact, I think I still owe him on that score. My drug use wasn't at the stage where I felt it was causing me a problem, but ever since I took cocaine in the camper van I had continued to dabble with it. Blondie also introduced us to a lot of other people in the States, including some of the members of the legendary disco band Chic, who would eventually play a big part in our story.

We were on a great run, but it had been an intense year that had already seen us filming videos in Sri Lanka and Antigua and touring both Japan and Australia. After we finished in the States, we had another crushing series of gigs in Europe. The constant attention was beginning to fray our nerves. We seemed to be living in a little bubble of our own, which involved marching in and out of hotels in a line while our security guards fought through the crowds. There would be one bodyguard at the front, then a band member, then another bodyguard, and so on.

Our ordinary fans were always adorable to us, but depending on where we were playing things could often get very dangerous. The first really heavy experience in that respect had occurred about a year earlier at the famous Paradiso Club in Holland. The stage was completely overrun and mobbed, and we had to go back to our dressing room while things calmed down. Initially it was just two or three fans who came onstage, and our security had managed to grab them, then suddenly there were ten or twelve of them, and after that they just kept coming. It was flattering, but often the venues would get trashed and it was becoming more and more common for us to be billed for "Damage to first 500 seats!"

So if the truth be told, by the time we arrived in Germany in

October we were on the brink of exhaustion. The combination of everything we had done and the fact we'd been on the road for so long meant we'd just pushed things too far. Even if there had been no fight in the nightclub, there would still have been a lot of tiredness and unhappiness in Germany because we needed a rest.

In the end, it was John's gashed hand that gave us a brief respite, because we had to scrap the rest of our dates until we could find someone to stand in for him. None of us were filled with much regret over canceling the shows, and we managed to play down the scale of the incident in the media. Today it would have been a huge international incident. Can you imagine the sort of fuss that would occur if Justin Timberlake were forced to cancel a tour due to a fight in a nightclub and a gashed hand? But at the time of the Duran Duran incident only a few lines appeared in the UK newspapers. A decade later, when Oasis got into a similar scrape in Germany, it was forensically picked over by the press. In 1982, though, the media were a very different beast, and our problems slipped by almost unnoticed.

They'd have never got into that fight had I been there, I used to think to myself. I believed that I'd had the shit kicked out of me enough as a kid to know it's time to get out fast when the odds are stacked against you. But with hindsight, if I *had* been in the club, the chances are I would have been at the center of things. Tracey was like a guardian angel who had prevented me from being there, because I had been back at the hotel with her.

There was no justification for the attack. If something like that occurred today, our lawyers would track down the people responsible and make their lives hell. Looking back, I think it affected our mental state in a big way, because it was the first time we encountered that kind of violent overreaction to the band. Roger and John didn't pick the fight, they were targeted—but once that door is open it's hard to close. Despite the fact that we were victims, we should have also realized our lifestyles were partly to blame. This was the first taste of the consequences of wild hedonism. We were starting to lose control, and we should have used the incident as a warning signal. Instead, we just went into denial about it.

So, was anything ever done? Did we ever sit down and talk about it? Was there ever any consideration of whether John or anyone else needed any help coping with the intense pressure of constantly being pursued?

The answer is no. We were just glad to get off the road. Deep down inside, it was the first time that we realized how fragile we were and how big the ramifications could be if any of us went off the rails. It showed us that if one of us did something stupid, then it wasn't just the individual who would suffer. The whole crew would suffer, there would be a promoter to answer to, and thousands of fans would be let down.

We had to understand that none of us could afford to have a bad day, and from this point on there could be no more days off. *Ever.*

The Birth of the MTV Generation

ONE of the things that Duran Duran will probably always be remembered for is all the great videos that we appeared in. They were
enormous fun to make—even if it nearly killed us at times. I'm not
joking! Several of us risked being drowned, we narrowly escaped being trampled by a crazed elephant, and we were forced to flee one
shoot after being threatened by four thousand angry monks. At
various stages while filming, Simon was strapped upside down to a
water wheel and submerged in icy water, Nick risked severe dehydra-
tion during a four-hour taxi trek through the jungle wearing leather
trousers in 100-degree heat, and I spent four days in the hospital
after falling into a muddy lagoon and being struck down by a tropical stomach bug. But we also got to visit some of the most exotic and
beautiful locations in the world . . . and most of all we had a truly
fantastic time. It was as if we had nine lives and nothing could harm
us. Most of the incidents occurred while we were filming the videos
for "Save a Prayer" or "Hungry Like the Wolf" on location in Sri
Lanka or "Rio" in the Caribbean, but the studio could be just as hair
raising, as Simon found out on the set of "Wild Boys."

I remember when the record label called us in to discuss making
the video for "Rio." "We want to film everything on a yacht in the

Caribbean, and we'll be flying out some models to appear alongside you," they said.

"Sounds about right. What's the general idea?" I asked—although, to be honest, we weren't too bothered about the finer points of the video's storyboard.

"Girls, boats—yes, please!" was how Simon later described our attitude. In hindsight, letting Simon near a boat wasn't such a great idea.

Today, releasing a single and a video go together in the same sentence, but back in '81 and '82 video was a completely new medium that nobody had fully exploited. I suppose that as five young lads, we were a band that always had the potential to look good on camera, but there was a lot more to it than that. For us the music always came first, but we quickly understood how effective our sound could be when it was played to moving images. It worked alongside pictures because it was exotic and different and uplifting. It's like when you watch a movie and a piece of music comes along and the music and the image complement each other perfectly, and suddenly everything works together, although sometimes it's by accident if not by design.

We were in the right place at the right time. When we came onto the scene, video was emerging as a very cheap format that was an alternative to expensive film-based productions. The marketing people at EMI were very aware of this and had been talking to their counterparts in New York, including a guy named Ed Bernstein, whom our own management also had a lot of contact with. Ed drew their attention to the potential of using video on a new cable station called MTV, which back then was only just in the process of being formed in the States. It meant you could shoot material for broadcast for a lot less money. Also, there were a great number of talented young filmmakers who wanted to use the exotic new format to make three-minute music videos. In those days, the record labels were big moneymaking concerns that employed the best and brightest people, who soon realized what videos could do for artists. Not only could they get you an infinite amount of airplay, but people could

see you, too, without the need for you to travel everywhere. And of course, who better visually was there to show on your gleaming new MTV station than Duran Duran?

We were helped by our management, the Berrows from Birmingham, who secretly fancied themselves as movie producers. They loved everything about New York and had modeled the playlist and styling at the Rum Runner on Studio 54, so they were naturally receptive to MTV. We had successfully managed to boot Mike Berrow out of the band for his dreadful sax playing, but I think he and his brother, Paul, secretly saw video as a way for them to stay involved in the creative side of things. To be fair to Paul, he certainly understood the power of imagery, even if some of his ideas about how to make a video sexually appealing turned out to be a bit wild.

So our entrance on the video scene was due to a mixture of EMI spotting the potential of MTV and the Berrows seeing themselves as movie moguls. Having said that, even though the Berrows helped, I still believe we would have found everything without them. Everyone at the record company took one look at us and realized we were perfect for the format, particularly Simon. He had been to drama school and had even starred in TV commercials as a kid. We used to joke that you could talk him into doing anything as long as there was a camera there, and the rest of us wouldn't have done half the things he did in the videos.

Nick and John were also very visual in their whole outlook, which initially was based as much on fashion as it was on music. I think John always fancied himself as a bit of an actor, and Roger is actually very photogenic, too. I was probably the least enthusiastic about appearing on video, although at times Nick wasn't so comfortable, either. I guess it helped a lot that the record company believed we all looked good on film.

The first video we made was for "Planet Earth."

"We've got some fantastic show reels to show you by an Australian director called Russell Mulcahy," said one of the A & R men at EMI. "He's streets ahead of anybody else."

The people at the record label were right. Russell turned out to be the Steven Spielberg of video, and I have to give him credit that a lot of our best videos were driven by his genius. Russell had directed the video for the Buggles hit "Video Killed the Radio Star," which was the first music video to be shown on MTV. He also went on to become a very successful moviemaker and he directed the *Razorback* and *Highlander* films. Our first meeting with him was very frantic, and he seemed to have an attention span of only four minutes, but he had amazing ideas. We worked with other directors from time to time, but all of Russell's material for us was consistently strong—and it included the videos for "Hungry Like the Wolf," "Save a Prayer," "Rio," "The Reflex," and "Wild Boys." Russell would take our basic ideas from the songs and turn them into a whole storyboard—and it nearly always worked. There was no premeditated way of doing the music; Russell just somehow managed to marry the two mediums together.

The record label wanted to make sure that there were plenty of New Romantic overtones on "Planet Earth," so we all wore frilly shirts and we invited some camp-looking male dancers from the Rum Runner to help glam things up. If you look closely you can see that one of the dancers we used in the final cut was Martin Degville, who went on to make a name for himself in Sigue Sigue Sputnik. The video opened with a shot of Roger, who was bare-chested and floating above the earth, before cutting to all of us playing together on what looked like a platform of ice that was suspended in thin air. In fact it was all shot through Perspex and the backgrounds were superimposed. We lined up together in the same order onstage that would eventually become our signature: Simon in the center, John to the left, and me to the right (as you face the stage). We had a bit of a hiccup on the day that we filmed it: John and I didn't bring our own guitars, so we ended up playing on instruments that we weren't really comfortable with. But it came together well, apart from one shot that featured Simon, or rather a certain part of Simon's anatomy, that Nick was very unhappy about.

"What the hell is that supposed to be?" Nick scowled as we reviewed an early cut of the tape. It showed a bare-chested Simon attempting to give a smoldering look by raising an arm above his head—only to reveal a bit too much body hair.

"That's Charlie's armpit!" I explained gleefully (I called Simon Charlie because his full name is Simon John Charles Le Bon and I thought *Charlie* sounded more down-to-earth).

"Well—do you want it in the video or not?" asked Russell. Actually, we didn't want to lose the whole sequence, so it is still there to this day: a lingering shot of Simon's hairy armpit amid all the glossy New Romantic imagery. I don't think Nick was ever very happy about that one. But it didn't do us any harm, and it was largely thanks to the fact that we had a video to complement the song that we went straight to number one in Australia, hence the reason we already had a profile by the time we arrived Down Under in early 1981.

ASIDE from Russell Mulcahy, we also had the good fortune to work with Kevin Godley and Lol Creme, of 10cc, who had moved into video production. Godley and Creme directed "Girls on Film," which caused an enormous controversy and became a huge success. They later did our "View to a Kill" video. "Girls on Film" was a much bigger production than "Planet Earth," and in many ways it was a big watershed for us. It was shot over two days at Shepperton Studios and it caused a sensation when it was released, mainly because it was so sexually explicit. Even by today's standards it's still too hot to be shown uncut on most mainstream TV networks, and the DVD can be sold in the UK only to adults aged 18 and over.

One of the opening sequences showed two attractive models who were wearing see-through baby-doll lingerie as they walked hand in hand across a bridge (just like in the song lyrics). The girls then suggestively straddled a huge pole, which was strategically covered in cream, before taking part in a topless pillow fight as their breasts spilled from their outfits. You can't really get more sexual than that—

The Birth of the MTV Generation 103

and this was 1981! Later on in the video there were shots of a woman's nipple being aroused by an ice cube, and there was even a mud-wrestling bout between two gorgeous models. The video encountered no problems with audiences in America, although I suspect that might not be the case if it were rereleased today. The outcry that occurred when Janet Jackson accidently showed a bare breast on American TV a few years ago shows how much things have changed.

"Where did all that sexual imagery come from?" people would ask us.

The video was storyboarded around the idea of going behind the scenes at a fashion shoot. We were the band playing at the side of the catwalk. Godley and Creme, whom you can catch a brief glimpse of in the beginning of the video, did a remarkable job; the final cut came across as risqué and glossy rather than rude and crude. I suspect a lot of the sexual content was actually Paul Berrow's idea. He was a hilarious character when it came to dreaming up that sort of thing. Paul was the elder of the Berrow brothers and he was quite an imposing character with a high forehead and a booming voice.

I can hear him now: "Let's get a bloody pole, grease it up, and have a couple of dirty birds on it."

I remember thinking, *Oh yeah—what's going on in your mind?*

But Paul was determined to pursue his endeavors as a producer, and a lot of his ideas probably helped to make the "Girls on Film" video so memorable. We thought the whole idea was great, and we certainly weren't going to argue with spending two days at Shepperton Studios while being surrounded by beautiful models. As far as the band was concerned, it was all a right laugh, and some of the band spent most of the time trying to get the girls to give us their phone numbers. During the mud-wrestling scene we were stood next to the models, and although we were lip synching the lyrics for the cameras, John and I switched our amps on and we played for real at that point to add to the atmosphere. We knew the sexual imagery was so strong that most of it would never get shown. We just thought:

WILD BOY

Great! We'll do another cut eventually, but initially the BBC won't be able to play it and it will cause a furor.

Aside from the sexual content, it was the first video in which we wore suits designed by Anthony Price, who became one of our favorite designers because his suits were so sharp. Roxy Music, who influenced us, also wore Anthony Price suits. The video also showed us doing feminine things, like using hair spray and having makeup put on us. It was suddenly as if the styles of the sixties and the seventies had fused. We took the glam fashion of the seventies and inserted the suits, which had been the uniforms of the sixties and the Beatles.

Just as we predicted, the BBC immediately banned the "Girls on Film" video, but that only served to boost our credibility. People thought we'd done something outrageous, like you might have expected from the Stones. It was strange, because from out of what initially seemed to be nothing more than someone's sexual fantasies we'd managed to create a great marketing tool! The song itself was great, but it wasn't written as one piece of work. It was really just a concept about attractive females appearing on camera, which had originally been part-written by Andy Wickett. Then Nick and John had made their contribution to it before Simon and I came along and added our bits. Simon was the only one who could make the lyrics work—and the video exploited his words to the full. As I said before, it's the music and the pictures together that work so well. It was things like this that made it so special. No one else did it. In fact, if it hadn't been for the video, "Girls on Film" might have been regarded as just another great bubblegum pop song of the early eighties. As it turned out, the video helped to immortalize it as a classic.

PERHAPS our most memorable video is "Rio"—and Russell Mulcahy was at his very best when we came to shoot it. The concept itself was very much John's creation—he came up with the title based on the idea of it being the name of a beautiful girl. John's always been a little bit of a visionary like that. So when we did the cover sleeve for our second album we decided to create the face of Rio on the sleeve. We didn't want to appear on the cover ourselves, because we thought it might look overcommercialized. Our faces were everywhere by then, and although the label advised it would go down well if we went on the cover, we decided our photographs would appear on the inside sleeve instead. It was our way of saying, *This is also about art, not just marketing.*

The painting itself was a great piece of work that we commissioned especially by the American artist Patrick Nagel, who was an illustrator for *Playboy.* It worked brilliantly, because it's one of the most recognizable images connected with Duran Duran. Whenever we showed it on a big screen onstage, even when we were playing stadium gigs twenty-five years later, the crowd would always go wild because they knew immediately which song was coming next. The original piece of artwork was quite a big painting, and we bought it off Patrick for about £9,000. I haven't got a clue where it is at the moment, although I wish I knew because as a piece of pop art it must be worth millions—and I still own one-fifth of it!

When we came to do the video, it was natural that we would bring to life the girl in the painting. This gave everything a great continuity forward from the lyrics that Simon sang about the girl with the "cherry ice cream smile." EMI opted to shoot it all in Antigua in the Caribbean, and the model they found to star in it looked exactly like the girl in the painting. I was the last member of Duran Duran to travel to Antigua because I often tried to squeeze in an extra day at home—so I was the first to meet "Rio" as by coincidence she was traveling out of Heathrow on the same day. No one in the band had even seen her photo at this stage, but it was immediately obvious to me why they had cast her.

"Oh—you don't half look like her," I said, as we boarded the same flight.

Her real name was Reema, she was half-Lebanese, and she was on the books of the Models One agency in London. We talked a bit on the flight, and she sounded very posh and sophisticated. I was convinced Simon and John would soon be competing for her attentions but that neither would stand a chance! I think she'd been told by her agency not to get mixed up with any of us, and she was a very straight girl.

When we got to Antigua everything was a rush (as it always was), and because I'd left a day late there was no time to catch up on the jet lag. As a backdrop for the video, the island was perfect. It was completely unspoiled and still very raw in the early eighties, so a lot of the local bars were really interesting. They used to serve some wicked rum and, if you got to know the right people, some very heavy-duty ganja.

We filmed over three or four days in several different locations, including Shirley Heights, Miller's Beach, and also out to sea off the coast from English Harbour. The most spectacular scenes showed us all in our latest Anthony Price suits aboard a breathtaking yacht as it skimmed through the waves, with Simon singing his heart out on the bow. There were lots of James Bond overtones, with beautiful girls walking out of the sea, but Russell put lots of humorous touches into it to keep our feet on the ground. The idea was that we were supposed to be these guys who were trying to act dead cool, but part of the storyboard was that something stupid happens to each one of us: I got dragged up in a net, and various things happen to the other band members throughout the video.

We were quite happy to send ourselves up a bit, so I suppose it was a case of life meets art. There's even a bit where Simon is shown on the telephone trying to chat up the girl in the video! It was as if we were saying, *We know everyone thinks we can pull any birds we want—but we're not too big to have a good laugh at ourselves!*

The whole look, feel, and location of the "Rio" video made a statement about the sort of lifestyle that we aspired to, complete with the designer suits, the yachts, and the beautiful models. We were just starting to become really successful, and here we were on-screen in the first throes of the materialistic image that we would become associated with. Travel to fabulous locations and enjoying a wealthy

The Birth of the MTV Generation   107

lifestyle might seem like obvious things to aspire to today, but this was the early eighties and it wasn't necessarily an obvious route to go down at the time. Punk had consciously shunned anything materialistic, but as the rock writer Dave Rimmer said around that time, it was suddenly as if punk had never happened. A whole new fashion was emerging, and out of everyone in the band John and Nick were the most focused on it. I'd originally avoided the fashionista thing like the plague, probably due to my working-class roots in the North East, but as I started coming into a bit of money I admit it felt nice to be able to walk around a shop and afford things. In a way, the whole country was about to go through a similar transformation, because by the late eighties it was a dominant part of popular culture to aspire to be successful.

During the filming of the "Rio" video, Simon and Roger took to being on the yacht immediately. When you watch the video, you can see they're having a great time as we sailed along. John and I were more than happy to go along for the ride, too, but Nick looked distinctly uncomfortable, probably because he was seasick most of the time.

In fact, Nick later told an interviewer how much he disliked the whole thing. "God, I hated that boat, wrecking my Anthony Price suit with all those dreadful waves splashing everywhere," he said.

As far as Nick was concerned, yachts were things best left moored in the harbor so that people could drink cocktails on them. Mind you, he might have had a bit of a point, because we nearly got into some terrible scrapes. Simon hurt himself very badly when he had to pretend to fall into the crystal blue waters from the end of a pier.

"Just act as if you've lost your balance and fall backward into the sea," advised Russell.

Unfortunately, Simon misjudged things and caught himself on the jetty as he flipped over and didn't break his fall properly. If you watch the video closely you can see that instead of tumbling backward into the sea, Simon actually lands full square on his back on the platform and scrapes himself before going over the edge. It looks as if he meant to do it that way, but he ended up with a very badly bruised back. He refused to let it interrupt the rest of the shooting, but I can assure you that when Simon gets an injury it becomes a major piece of theater and he'll demand "this tablet, or that tablet" to ease the pain!

Later on we shot a hilarious sequence in which each of us individually played a saxophone while trying to keep balance on a wobbly raft as it bobbed about in the sea. Only Nick and John are shown in the final cut of the video, but you can see Nick's having a real battle to stay upright. I think we all went into the drink several times over, sometimes with alarming consequences. During the footage of when we were all on the yacht, with Simon singing at the front, you can see John and me on the left at the back of the boat. You can tell from the spray and the wind in our hair that we were really hammering along. I think we were doing about thirty knots and most of the time we were simply hanging on for dear life. We'd been given a bit of a talk about safety by the captain beforehand, which included all the usual stuff about the sea being full of dangerous currents and riptides and warning us not to mess about on deck. But it fell on deaf ears—particularly with John, whom we'd nicknamed JT by now. I can remember we were in midshoot when I tried to stand up and get my balance on deck, and I felt a shove from John and . . . "WhoaAAHH!"

Splash. Suddenly, I was in the middle of the ocean gulping saltwater and bobbing up and down as the yacht zoomed away from me at full speed. I'm not the strongest of swimmers, and for a second I felt a twinge of fear: what had the captain said about dangerous currents? A rope trailing off the back of the yacht was connected to a launch that was following about forty or fifty feet behind, so I knew there was a good chance the launch would come crashing into me if I wasn't careful. I could feel I was in a spot of bother already, so I tried to catch hold of the rope as it rushed by at great speed.

Ouch! I soon realized that a wet rope slipping through your hands hurts like hell, but I managed to hold on with all my strength. Don't forget, I was wearing an Anthony Price suit instead of a life jacket. My options then were either to do the sensible thing and get into the launch and sit out the rest of the shoot, or to try and haul myself back onto the main yacht. Of course, I chose to rejoin the fun, but it took every bit of energy to pull myself back onto the main boat. In hindsight, it was a crazy thing to do. As I hauled myself back on deck, gasping and wheezing, I could see the skipper was far from happy.

"Fucking hell, man! Do you realize what you have just done? That was ridiculous," he screamed at me, before turning his attentions to JT, who was now laughing hysterically. "You could have fucking drowned him. There are dangerous jellyfish out there and it could have been serious."

Then it was my turn to be screamed at again: "Seriously, if we'd have been forced to turn around to come and get you it would have screwed everything. That was bang out of order!"

These days, record companies build clauses into contracts which forbid artists from taking part in dangerous water sports. I suppose they might have a point—but when I fell into the sea it looked good in our video!

WE released "Rio" as a single in the UK in November 1982. Sadly, the videos that accompanied our next three singles weren't quite up to the same standard. "Is There Something I Should Know?," "Union of the Snake," and "New Moon on Monday" were all hits in their own right, but somehow the videos didn't seem to have the same continuity with the songs as our earlier work.

The video for "Is There Something I Should Know?" was shot in London before we'd started work on our third album. It went straight in at number one, which was a momentous achievement (and I'll tell you about the party we had to celebrate later on). But the video didn't seem to follow any overall concept, apart from paying tribute to the Beatles in certain places. Just like the way the song existed in isolation and wasn't part of an album, there was no theme to the video. Consequently, there were a lot of pointless sequences in it, such as all the strange men who seem to be measuring trees. It was very polished and photogenic, but a bit meaningless.

The "Union of the Snake" video, in my view, wasn't much better. It was shot in Sydney, Australia, but strangely Russell didn't do it; I assume he was tied up with something else. Simon had tried to explain to me what the lyrics of the song were all about, but I have to confess it sounded like a load of waffle to me—something about how we are all descended from lizards. Simon's very well read, but I'm not sure that even he knows where his lyrics come from sometimes, although the directors of the "Union of the Snake" video fell for the lizard stuff in a big way! The video certainly has a reptilian theme, but amid all the footage of lizards chasing people there are lots of meaningless images, too, like the juggler who suddenly appears for no apparent reason. For all I could see it might just as well have been about wandering around with a stiffy!

There was worse to come. "New Moon on Monday" was our least favorite video of all. Everybody in the band hates it, particularly the dreadful scene at the end where we all dance together. Even today, I cringe and leave the room if anyone plays the video. We shot it just outside Paris on the third of January 1984, and we were all miserable because we hadn't had a long enough Christmas holiday. Our management had convinced us to theme it on the French Revolution, and it also had historic references to the French Resistance—but, to be honest, it was just a load of gibberish. The set was dark and cold, and we spent most of the day drinking alcohol. By the time we were dancing at the end I was half cut. It is one of the few times I've seen Nick dance (watch his shoulders moving up and down if you ever get another chance to see it!). We were very uncomfortable with the whole thing. After "New Moon on Monday," we all thought, *Bollocks—let's now do something that's fundamental and solid.*

The answer was a spectacular live video in the form of "The Reflex." We also did epic shoots for "Wild Boys," during which

Simon was strapped to the water wheel, and "A View to a Kill"—but I'll tell you about those three videos later in the book.

WHEN it came to establishing a foothold in the States, there's no doubt that our videos gave us an edge over other British bands. We had a strategy for doing well in America and we believed we could make it there, but it involved a lot of commitment and hard work, and we knew we had to make more effort than any other band. It involved touring in as many American cities as possible and we were careful to always try and keep the American media on our side. Video was at the heart of our success. We couldn't have done our first American tour if it were not for the MTV following that we established. During '81 and '82 we broke into markets in the rest of the world, but initially it was very hard to get radio airplay in America. But we were consciously aware that lots of nightclubs there had TV screens in them, and as our videos took off in the clubs it created a talking point around us. "They might not be big, but they are big everywhere else and look at this video of them," was how the American media reacted. No one else had the videos so it made us larger than life. Because we were British, the US audience seemed to be willing to accept us even though we did risqué things like wear makeup and film sexually explicit videos, which might have caused a bit more shock if we'd been a band made up of all-American college boys. In particular, it was the videos that were shot by Russell Mulcahy and which accompanied our *Rio* album that first stirred things up in the States. We'd written the album mainly in London and had recorded it at George Martin's AIR Studios on Oxford Street on the sixth floor of the building where Top Shop stands today. They were called "air" studios because they were built on hydraulic stages that created an air gap between the studio and the rest of the building in order to prevent noise from leaking into the building below.

We were doing a lot of partying in London at the time and one of the girls who started to hang around with us was Paul McCartney's oldest daughter, Heather. I worshipped the Beatles, so I was delighted when she invited me and some of the other band members up to her family home in St. John's Wood one afternoon to look at some of her dad's memorabilia. It was no accident that Paul wasn't home at the time, and she showed us lots of his old clothes and things.

"Me dad would hate me hanging out with you lot. Don't ever tell him," she warned us.

A few weeks later Heather came into AIR Studios.

"Don't tell Dad that I took you up to the house and all that sort of thing, but he says he's recording in one of the other studios round at the back and would you like to meet him?"

We were all unanimous. "Absolutely, yeah."

Then all of a sudden he just walked in. Now in 1982, shortly after Lennon had gone, if a Beatle walked into your studio it felt like God himself had just arrived. We were in complete awe.

"All right, boys?" he said. "I've been listening outside over the last few weeks to what you've been doing. There's a track called "Rio" . . . That's a hit song, that."

We were openmouthed. I thought about that copy of *Sgt. Pepper* my cousin gave me in 1967. Art had met life in a spectacular way.

IN addition to the "Rio" video that we shot in Antigua, "Save a Prayer" and "Hungry Like the Wolf" also had great videos to accompany them, both of which we filmed in Sri Lanka prior to going to the Caribbean. Sri Lanka was a whole adventure in itself. It was chosen as a location because Paul Berrow had been there on holiday and had become obsessed with the place, to the point where he hatched a madcap scheme to build his own temple there! He'd been impressed by all the Buddhist monuments and wanted to plow some of his newfound millions from Duran Duran into creating something in a similar vein. I don't know whether it was purely a money-making scheme or something that he wanted to do for aesthetic reasons, but by this stage I didn't care. The management were beginning to irritate me a little bit with their daft brain waves.

"Chaps! Chaps! It's bloody fantastic out there and I'm going to build something huge," boomed Paul, before outlining his plans in detail.

"Check this out," I said to the other band members. "He's building a temple in Sri Lanka. I wouldn't let him build Lego with me, let alone a temple. And he has the cheek to say everyone in the band is mad!"

Simon had a bit more sympathy: "He's just eccentric and creative."

That's our *job,* I thought.

Judging from Paul's contribution to "Girls on Film," it would have turned out to be a Temple of Love, but whatever it was that he started to construct got destroyed in the civil war that began in Sri Lanka soon afterward. But a happy by-product of Paul's obsession with Sri Lanka was that he met a production crew out there who could make all the arrangements we needed in order to shoot there. They arranged all the film permits and were responsible for navigating us around; they even hired a herd of elephants. It was amazingly cheap—and the results were breathtaking.

Simon, John, and Roger initially traveled to Sri Lanka together, while Nick and I stayed back in London doing the final mixing for *Rio* and finishing some B sides. We went to join the others about three days later, having left the studio at 4 a.m. and grabbed just a couple of hours' sleep before getting up to catch the plane. We had a quick bit of breakfast at the airport before flying with our good old Indian airline again in the cheapest seats. In all the rush, Nick hadn't really put much thought into dressing comfortably, and he was wearing a pair of tight leather trousers. We assumed there'd be a nice air-conditioned limo to meet us at the other end, but we were in for a nasty surprise.

"Fucking hell, it's hot," said Nick as we stepped off the plane.

It was like walking into a wall of heat.

"Don't worry," I said. "We'll be in the hotel bar enjoying a nice cold beer very soon."

Wrong again. The others were all in a faraway town called Kandy, and the only way to catch up with them was by taking a four-hour taxi ride across dry scrubland on a bumpy road in 100-degree heat. The vehicle was a clunky old sedan that looked like it had been built in 1958 and it had no air-conditioning, so it acted like an oven in the baking heat. I could see Nick wilting next to me as he sweated it out in his leather pants while we were rattling and rolling along.

"Fucking hell. This place is horrible. They're bastards for bringing us here," moaned Nick.

As we watched the dusty landscape pass by, it dawned upon us that we were entering a very different world from the one we were used to.

There were beggars everywhere and many of them had limbs missing. The level of poverty was shocking. In the few shantytowns that we passed there was no sanitation, just raw sewage running down the street. We saw many sights like that during our stay in Sri Lanka, and even now I can remember vividly how shocking and humbling it was. But despite the hardships they faced, the local people were warm and friendly and greeted us with eager curiosity.

All the way along the roads, children would spill in front of the vehicle and stop us, offering us watermelons. There would be ten-year-old kids, and even five-year-olds, offering to chop off the top of the fruit with machetes so that you could drink from them. Then they'd gesture for something in return and we soon cottoned on to the fact that what they wanted from us most of all were any Biro pens or pencils that we had with us. If you gave them a Biro they would react as if to say, *Phew—fantastic,* because it meant they had something to learn to write with.

I remember thinking: *How long will that last them and where will they get another one from?*

It certainly put things into perspective: here we were as young pop stars looking forward to our glamorous forthcoming tours of

Japan and Australia, yet all it took to make these people grateful was a Biro.

When we finally reached the hotel in Kandy, Nick gingerly climbed out of the car, dripping in sweat, with his trousers virtually melted onto his skin. We'd certainly never been to a place like this before and we were anxious to get into the cool behind the mosquito nets.

"You can't eat anything but cheese sandwiches," was the first thing the crew said to us. "There's too much of a risk of food poisoning and we can't let anything jeopardize the shoot."

Nick was bright pink by now, and we must have looked a bit of a sight together. "Fucking hell, where the hell have they brought us to?" I asked myself.

But things were about to improve. I could spy a swimming pool in a courtyard at the back of the hotel. Nick and I finally got a cool beer as we watched the sun go down. The sunset was amazing; the whole sky turned a deep red color above us while we sipped our drinks.

THE poverty that we witnessed in Sri Lanka was something that moved us all, particularly when we reached the capital, Colombo, where the conditions seemed worst of all. There were crowds of children on every street corner.

"Mister, you want drink? You want smoke? You want woman?" they would shout to us. I remember following directions from one of the street kids to a shanty bar in order to buy some weed—so much for sticking to cheese sandwiches! They even had bootlegged copies of our own album for sale. But Sri Lanka was a series of contrasts, and it was also immensely beautiful. The beach scenes in the "Save a Prayer" video showed the coastline exactly as it was; we didn't attempt to change anything for the cameras. The sands were unspoiled and completely deserted, apart from the odd fisherman sitting on a pole in the sea just as you see them in the video. We didn't have to do anything to create a stunning backdrop because it was all

116   **WILD BOY**

just naturally there. Even the locals whom you see in the videos are ordinary people who just wandered by. Some of the interior scenes were shot inside the hotel foyer where Nick and I had collapsed after our four-hour taxi ride from hell.

Russell and his storyboardist, Marcello Anciano, had been out to Sri Lanka to check things out beforehand, and they had shown us some of their plans while we were still in the studio. We'd never really seen or understood anything like that, but in hindsight it's obvious that Russell understood the value of having a leading man in the videos—not just a lead singer but someone in a leading role, which was Simon. When you watch the Sri Lankan videos now, you see that what he did with Simon was really effective because most of the scenes are pure Le Bon, with the rest of us only appearing in bits and pieces, which suited me fine. Simon was Film Boy, John was Poster Boy, and I guess I was Wild Boy!

"Save a Prayer" was our attempt to do a ballad, and the Buddhist temples were a perfect setting for the song's spiritual overtones. The historic monuments that we filmed around were truly magnificent. But unfortunately, the choice of location nearly got us lynched by four thousand angry monks! We tried not to cause offense, and we always took off our shoes to show respect, but you could see that the monks were uneasy about us being there. The Berrows had persuaded us to go to Sri Lanka in the first place, but what they hadn't told us was that the whole country was on the verge of civil war at the time! Feelings were running pretty high because of the political situation, so I guess the last thing the religious leaders were in the mood for was Duran Duran turning up at their most sacred temples with a load of cameras. They had no problem with us visiting the holy sites, but it was the fact that we were filming there that upset them.

One of the temples we visited was guarded by shaven-headed monks in orange robes, who stood to attention just like the guards outside Buckingham Palace.

"Don't try to look them in the eye, because if you do, something will happen to you," one of the locals warned us.

Apparently, local folklore maintained that the guards could hypnotize you with their eyes and force you to see visions of their choice. I thought, *Oh, really?* and I remember coming face-to-face with two of them at the gates to one temple, and they were looking straight ahead and standing motionless. I tried not to look at them, but of course curiosity kept making me take the odd peek.

But the real problems started to occur when we were filming the main temple sequence in the video, the one where you can see some hills in the background. We were doing our thing when we slowly started to notice more and more monks in orange robes gathering around at the foot of the hills. What we didn't know was that a political rally connected to the growing civil unrest was about to take place. The monks were gathering because their leader was about to arrive by helicopter, so they took a dim view of Duran Duran prancing around miming a performance of "Save a Prayer" and "Hungry Like the Wolf." One of the crew came over to talk to us.

"The crowd is going to get bigger, and in about half an hour we will have to leave. When we give the order, we will all have to go straight to the buses and leave," he warned.

By now there were thousands of monks surrounding us, and most of them were glaring at us intently in silence. Suddenly we could hear a helicopter overhead. One of the religious leaders came over and spoke to us through an interpreter.

"You are causing offense. If you leave respectfully that will be fine, but you *have* to go," he said.

The message was clear. Either we got on our buses or they'd force us to leave—and with a civil war brewing it could have easily escalated into a very serious incident. I certainly wasn't going to argue with four thousand angry monks with only the likes of Simon Le Bon and Nick Rhodes to back me up. We were on the buses and gone!

ONE scene that none of us wanted to do was a sequence that Russell was keen on, in which a band member had to volunteer to writhe about while an elephant's trunk squirted water over his bare chest. It was very homoerotic.

"There's no way I'm doing that gay thing with the elephant," I said.

For once even Simon was slow to volunteer to do something in front of the camera, and Nick and Roger were having none of it, either. In the end, John agreed—after all, he was the pinup, we argued. The resulting scene appears about halfway through the "Save a Prayer" video, and we ribbed John over it for many years to come. It was shot at a lagoon where the local crew had recently helped to film a Tarzan movie. Some of the scenes we did there were also used in "Hungry Like the Wolf," which featured Simon doing his best Indiana Jones impression. The lyrics to the song were very suggestive and parodied *Little Red Riding Hood,* except that the wolf is a guy who's on the prowl for a lover. So the storyboard for the video was basically "Indiana Jones is horny and wants to get laid!"

The water at the lagoon was very dark and murky and, as I later found out, it was full of bugs—no doubt because it was used as a latrine by the local elephant herd. The shoot got pretty wild at times. There was one big bull elephant that seemed to take exception to its handler. We were halfway through the shoot when we suddenly heard a deafening roar followed by a sequence of crashes. The angry bull elephant had gone berserk, splashed through the water, then charged full speed at its handler, who only narrowly managed to get out of the way before it went raging off into the jungle. Elephants are mostly gentle animals, but we'd been warned that if they get angry they can easily kill a person. Thankfully it was going in the opposite direction to where we were standing or we would have been flattened, but it caused a bit of a kerfuffle and we were worried that the rest of the elephants might turn upon us.

By now the heat was starting to get to me, so I decided to keep cool by sipping on plenty of Jack Daniel's and Coke throughout the day. Not a great idea. Although I'd refused to do the gay scene with the elephant, I was willing to trying riding on top of one. Everything was fine until it was time to get off. As the elephant began to lie down to let me off, my right leg snagged and started going under it. I managed to whip it out just in time, and I complained vehemently to the handler, but he was a little Sri Lankan guy who didn't speak any English and so he couldn't understand me. By now a lot of moaning was going on, and I admit I was one of the worst offenders, along with Nick.

"What the fucking hell are we doing here? Which one of us is meant to be Tarzan?" I shouted. Little did I know it would soon be me falling out of a tree.

I decided I was having nothing more to do with the elephants so I climbed up into a tree and perched on a branch about ten or fifteen feet above the water. It seemed like the perfect vantage point from which to mime playing guitar, but I hadn't accounted for the effect of the Jack Daniel's on my sense of balance. I wobbled and suddenly . . .

Splash.

Falling into the sea in Antigua was one thing, but the water in the lagoon was dark and murky. It had been a long drop and suddenly I was submerged and ingesting mouthfuls of the dirty black liquid. Believe me, falling into a lake that's been used as an open toilet by elephants is not a pleasant experience. By the time I crawled out of the water I was coughing and spluttering and wondering what the effect on my health would be. I was worried about swallowing so much of the mucky water, so I thought it would be a good idea to empty my stomach by being sick. The only catering facilities on the set were these little stands that sold bags of fried red chillies, which looked a bit like potato chips. I thought if I ate enough of them it would help me to throw up, but in fact they were delicious. I ended up eating loads of them, washed down with even more Jack Daniel's.

When the shoot ended, I soon forgot all about falling in the lagoon, but it came back to haunt me with great vengeance about a week later, after we arrived in Australia to play a series of gigs. I was feeling hot and sweaty onstage in Sydney when I was suddenly doubled up by excruciating stomach cramps. I managed to play to the end of the set, but during the encore I had to quickly dash behind an amp, where I was violently ill. The next few days were agony, and I spent the whole time either throwing up or running for the bathroom. By the time we got back to England I was physically exhausted; no matter what I did I couldn't seem to shake it off. I felt completely drained and awful, and for the first time in my life I was seriously worried about my health. Things took another turn for the worse when I broke into a fever. Eventually I was rushed to the hospital and placed in an isolation ward with suspected malaria. The doctors seemed completed baffled by it until finally I was persuaded to transfer to a private hospital. As soon as the medical team realized where I'd been, I was diagnosed as suffering from a nonspecific tropical virus that I'd picked up from the dirty water in the lagoon!

IN addition to "Save a Prayer" and "Hungry Like the Wolf," we'd shot a third video in Sri Lanka, for a track called "Lonely in Your Nightmare." We did the whole lot for about £55,000, which is much cheaper compared to what they would have cost if we'd shot them using old-fashioned film techniques. "Save a Prayer" and "Hungry Like the Wolf" are like mini movies in their own right, yet they each cost less than £20,000, which illustrates how video allowed us to do things that we otherwise could not have done. It helped us to connect with our audience a bit like the way the Internet helps new bands to do the same today. I guess the flip side is that a lot of people still think we spend all our time messing about on yachts. When it came to video, Russell surpassed everybody else. Loads of bands use video to bling things up today, but he did it back then . . . and on a tight budget.

And as for the virus that I picked up in the lagoon: the private doctors managed to get rid of it almost immediately, but I spent four days in the hospital before I was fit enough to leave. I suppose there's a lesson there somewhere, along the lines of: "If you smoke dope and drink Jack Daniel's in the tropical heat, don't fall into a lagoon full of elephant's urine and wash it all down with more booze and a bucket of chillies."

But I guess some people never learn.

CHAPTER SIX

Princess Diana's Favorite Band

IT was almost impossible to describe how beautiful Princess Diana was when you met her in the flesh. She possessed a rare aura and a timeless grace that you perhaps come across only once or twice in a generation—and we were lucky enough to be her favorite band. Diana never made it to the throne, but as far as the world was concerned she was already the queen of fashion and glamour and all things that glittered, so it was inevitable that the royal seal of approval would give Duran Duran an enormous boost. Unfortunately, it also made us a target for terrorists. Simon, John, Roger, Nick, and I didn't know how close we would come to paying with our lives for our royal association.

The IRA secretly intended to assassinate Prince Charles and his attractive young wife on the night of July 20, 1983. A huge bomb was planned to go off while the royal entourage watched us perform live onstage. The device was designed to cause maximum carnage. Killing the heir to the British throne and wiping out the UK's most popular band in a single attack would have caused pandemonium and handed the Irish Republican Army its biggest-ever coup.

I obviously would not still be around to tell the tale if the IRA plot had been successful, but it was only thanks to a remarkable piece of counterintelligence work by Scotland Yard and their colleagues in the Garda that the attack was foiled. It would be several years before we learned the truth about what was planned for that evening, but we now know that a man named Sean O'Callaghan was secretly sent to London with orders to kill. His mission set off an incredible chain of events that we knew nothing about, but which could so easily have ended in tragedy.

Terrorism, however, was the last thing on our minds when we were invited to meet royalty for the first time. We were midway through recording our third album in Montserrat in the Caribbean when a telephone call came in from London to inform us that the Prince's Trust had invited us to play before a royal audience.

"They want you to be the headline act at a gala charity show in the summer at the Dominion Theatre in London," explained our agent, Rob Hallett. "You'll all be personally introduced to Charles and Di in person before the gig, so everyone will need to be on their best behavior."

Bloody hell—it must all be true about Diana being a fan of ours, I thought to myself.

We'd read in the newspapers about Diana's supposed fondness for our music, but up until now we'd taken it all with a pinch of salt. It was certainly good PR, but we wondered if it was just something that our record company had spun up for the publicity.

Normally we would never interrupt our recording schedule for anything, let alone a stage performance, which would mean having to rehearse thoroughly and get fully stage-ready. This was an enormous task that would involve organizing clothes and crew and everything else associated with a major show, not least of which was cutting down on our alcohol intake in order to look our best! But this was in an age when there was still an insatiable fascination for royalty, and a command performance was something you wouldn't even dream of turning down. So it was easy for us to say yes, despite the fact it would cause us an enormous logistical headache.

"How are we gonna rehearse properly while we're stuck in the studio out here?" I asked, aware that planning such an important event would normally involve weeks of working with our stage crew back in the UK.

"No problem," said Rob. He explained that the record company were planning to fly all our backing singers and a saxophone player out to the Caribbean in order that we could rehearse there and so cause minimum disruption to our schedule.

The prospect of meeting Princess Diana caused huge excitement for all our families. In 1983, the public still had enormous respect for the Royal Family in a way that was different from the disinterested manner in which some people often regard them today. Back then, the Royal Family seemed to be more fundamentally part of our lives, and they were held with a regard that still bordered on reverence. It sounds silly today, but they somehow seemed less *mortal,* yet at the same time we felt as if we'd grown up knowing them, albeit from afar. When the Queen celebrated her Silver Jubilee in 1977 to mark twenty-five years on the throne, the whole nation came out to celebrate with her, and there were kids' street parties everywhere. But despite our respect for them, the Royals somehow existed only in a formal world that was cold and beyond our direct reach.

When Diana came along she gave the Royal Family a whole new dimension. Young people like us at the time could relate to her because we saw a beautiful English rose who was the same age as us and who shared similar tastes and beliefs to our own. It was a great thing for the nation to have someone who was so touchable, and she was never afraid to show she cared for ordinary people. She hugged and kissed children with AIDS without fear and she brought love back into the Royal Family at a time when protocol tried to dictate that you couldn't show feelings. Not surprisingly, she became the most iconic lady in modern British history, and young women, in particular, shared a strong empathy with her. So all things being considered, I was much more excited about meeting Diana than I was about meeting Prince Charles.

There was a huge feeling of anticipation within the band, but for me the day held an extra significance because it was also the first time I was due to see my mother since the awkward meetings I had shared with her in my teens. Our latest attempt at a reunion had been planned at Tracey's instigation.

"Why don't you let me get in touch with her?" Tracey had insisted. "It would do you a lot of good to talk to her, and it might give you some answers about some of the things that happened in your childhood."

I wasn't so sure that there was much to be gained by opening up old wounds, but I had conceded that if I was going to try and form any sort of meaningful relationship with my mother in the future, then the royal concert seemed like an ideal opportunity to turn over a new leaf.

"Okay, let's get in touch with her," I said.

So we invited my mother along, although I chose not to tell my dad because I wanted to spare his feelings. He was very proud about the royal concert, but I knew he'd be content to read about it at home.

MEANWHILE, the IRA were busy making plans of their own. Sean O'Callaghan, the man ordered to assassinate Charles and Diana, had slipped into the UK unnoticed. Traveling with a woman in her late twenties and two small children in order not to attract any attention, O'Callaghan had quietly caught a ferry to Fishguard before making his way to Liverpool, where he checked into the Central Hotel, close to Lime Street railway station. He lay low there for a few days while he waited for a message.

Of course, we in the band still knew nothing about this at the time, but like everyone else in the UK we were aware that the conflict in Northern Ireland was at its height. Terrorism was a very different threat from the one we face today from Al Qaeda but it could be just as deadly. During the thirty or so years of conflict in Ireland the number of people who were killed in "the troubles" was similar to the number of people who lost their lives in the 9/11 attacks.

After three days O'Callaghan received word that the "equipment" he needed would be delivered to another hotel in London. As he moved down to the capital, he must have looked like any other traveler. In reality, he was a high-ranking member of the IRA's GHQ staff, and he had already killed twice during active service. He booked into the Russell Court Road Hotel and made his way to the Dominion Theatre in Tottenham Court Road. Incredibly, he then simply walked in through an open door, climbed the stairs, and entered the royal box. He discovered it to be a wooden balcony at the side of the stage with a men's lavatory located about fifteen feet away. He estimated that if he planted a bomb in the toilets that contained twenty-five pounds of an explosive called Frangex, it would kill or seriously injure everybody within a sixty-foot radius . . .

WE flew into the UK a couple of days ahead of the concert on first-class flights that were sponsored by PanAm. (Our days of traveling economy with our trusty Indian airline were finally over.) We'd been sheltered from the press in the Caribbean, but when we arrived in London we were given VIP treatment, and it caused a massive amount of fuss and media attention. From the airport we were whisked to the Grosvenor House Hotel in Park Lane, where we planned to spend the day before the concert with our families.

The next morning outside our hotel, there was still a huge media presence that caused mayhem, with photographers spilling out into Park Lane and blocking all the traffic. Motorists were honking their horns like crazy, and there were police everywhere trying to sort things out. We looked tanned and healthy from being in the Caribbean sunshine, and we were more than happy to play up for the cameras.

Inside the hotel, I met my mother over breakfast and she brought along my younger half brother. Our conversations were polite and friendly, but just like the meeting we had in Kent when I was fifteen there was no real warmth between us. I can't even remember much of what we spoke about, but it was mostly just meaningless pleasantries.

WILD BOY

There were so many significant things going on that day that even something as important as meeting my estranged mother didn't make much of an impression on me. Perhaps there's still part of me that wants to block out the memory, because I can't recall much about our meeting at all.

Bizarrely, one thing I do have a vivid memory of from that day is the complete chaos that was caused within the sumptuous confines of the Grovesnor House Hotel by my pet Jack Russell dog, Charlie. Simon used to joke that because the dog was a Jack Russell I should have called him Jack Daniel's, which would have been appropriate given the amount of the stuff I'd drunk in Sri Lanka. Charlie was a mischievous little pet who scampered around like lightning in excitement, but he had an embarrassing habit of occasionally relieving himself in awkward places. When our entourage descended on the hotel, we completely overran the place and we caused lots of disruption in the restaurant, where all the well-heeled guests were exchanging polite pleasantries over a quiet lunch. Suddenly, they were surrounded by five thirsty rock stars and our families, our various senior crew members, and all our security, while the world's press camped on the pavement outside.

Meanwhile, I was delighted to discover that the hotel was so posh that it had its own dog food menu, which they served up in silver doggie bowls.

"That's just what Charlie needs," I said eagerly.

Looking back, I suppose taking your Jack Russell to lunch at the Grosvenor House Hotel might seem like an odd thing to do, but when you're in a band you get used to doing eccentric things like that. In any case, we were spending so much money at the hotel that they probably wouldn't have minded if I'd insisted on getting down on all fours myself and eating out of a dog bowl. Sometimes we'd find the fawning attitude of hotel staff hilarious, and Simon in particular became a master of winding them up. Years later, when hotels started to show adult movies as part of their in-house entertainment, Simon used to complain about the quality of the films at the front desk for a joke.

"About your porn," he'd say with a completely straight face as we checked out. "It's crap and it didn't even get me moist. I want it all off my bill!"

"Oh, yes, sir," they'd reply, and then cancel the charges. I don't know if it was a gag that Simon had copied from a movie scene, but it used to crack me up every time.

We were in a similar sort of mood in the Grosvenor, and soon Charlie was running around under the tables and yapping all over the place. Then, to my horror, I noticed he'd stopped running around and had decided to empty his bowels instead under the table of a particularly posh group of diners nearby. I had visions of one of them calling over the staff and complaining in a plummy voice, "Waiter, I'm afraid a rock star's dog has taken a dump on my shoes." Well, it certainly beats having a fly in your soup!

In fact, the hotel staff were very good about it and didn't kick up too much of a fuss, although it was probably no coincidence that we never went back there. I used to refer to it afterward as the Famous Dog Dumping Incident, and it proves anything can happen to you when you are in a band.

THE security on that night was incredible. Police with sniffer dogs were everywhere, and the whole place was thronging with men from MI5 in plainclothes. Our own minders were all ex-military and they knew exactly what sort of security operation was taking place.

"Make sure you are not carrying anything," they warned us. "If you've got any spliffs get rid of them, don't even think about taking a beer in there. This is the tightest possible security and you will never see anything like this again in your lifetime."

I don't know whether or not our management or our label were aware of a possible threat from the IRA, but in the band we still had not been told anything. Once we were inside we were asked to all line up alongside Dire Straits, who were also on the bill, while the protocol for meeting Charles and Diana was explained to us. The officials weren't too bothered about us bowing, but we were asked to call the royal couple "Sir" or "Ma'am." I was pleased that we were not expected to bow, because my father's harsh treatment by the church meant I still had a healthy disregard for authority. Even though I respected the Royals, bowing wasn't something I wanted to do.

And then they arrived.

We saw them coming and there was actually a certain glow that surrounded them. The car was so shiny, everything glittered and their arrival was coordinated to perfection. Diana, of course, looked immaculate. She wore a billowing designer dress with a nautical-style lapel. As I watched her work her way down the line, she seemed to be greeting everybody quick, quick, quick so that she could get to us. Then it was our turn.

"Ma'am . . . this is Duran Duran," explained an aide.

She smiled. "I don't need any introductions to these boys. I know *exactly* who they are."

And she went straight over to John! Diana then stood chatting to us for what seemed like ages, while John stood in the middle with Simon and me on either side of him. A photographer then took a shot of the four of us together like that, and that made all the front pages the following morning. You can see from the photo that she looks just as pleased to meet us as we were to meet her, and the chemistry between her and John is obvious. In fact, Simon even looks a tiny bit jealous as he stares at John from the side! We felt as if Diana was telling the world, *This is my band!* as she shook hands with John. She knew our names, what we were about, everything.

"I'm so looking forward to the show," she told us, smiling and tilting her head backward in that special manner she had.

"Wow, this is great—nice to meet you, Ma'am," I said, thinking how excited my nan back in Newcastle would be to hear all about this.

Then Prince Charles came walking up, and he seemed a bit crusty in comparison. She wore designer gear, but he seemed to always wear hand-me-downs, he was so outshone by his wife. Diana had walked ahead of him, but I got the impression she wasn't supposed to and that he was a bit pissed off about it. I was a bit puzzled by it, but if we'd known then what we do now about the fact that Charles had a bit of a problem with her celebrity, it would have made sense.

"I hear there were lots of ladies waiting on the tarmac at Heathrow when you arrived yesterday," Charles said to Simon.

Nick then spoke to Charles and Diana both for some time, and they asked lots of questions about Montserrat. They certainly seemed well briefed.

Sadly, when we finally got to play onstage it was a bit of a disaster. We were plagued by technical problems and our timing was all over the place. John had trouble with his bass, which sounded out of tune, and we were generally underrehearsed despite our makeshift efforts to get up to scratch in Montserrat. It takes a lot of time and effort to get stage-ready, as we'd just discovered. The *Daily Mirror* was so unimpressed by our performance that it changed its early edition headline from DIANA'S DELIGHT to DIANA'S LET-DOWN in later editions. But it didn't take any of the gloss off the event. It was a fantastic experience, and the reaction from the general public and the buzz it gave us was great.

And as for the IRA? Incredibly, the plot was foiled because the very man they had selected to plant the bomb was a double agent. Sean O'Callaghan had secretly tipped off the security services about his mission, and he had simply been going through the motions when he traveled to London so as not to arouse the suspicions of fellow terrorists. Scotland Yard leaked the fact he was believed to be in the UK to the media, who wrongly reported that his intended target was Margaret Thatcher. This gave O'Callaghan an excuse to flee to Paris, complaining to his IRA bosses that his mission had been compromised by a leak and therefore could not go ahead. It explained why the security had been so overwhelming on the night of the concert. So much for them being worried about drugs.

The first I learned about it was years later when I picked up a newspaper and read an account in which O'Callaghan confessed everything. He described the plot as "potentially the most dangerous scheme ever devised by the Provisional IRA."

"Duran Duran don't know how lucky they are," he later said on television.

I was angry that nobody had told us about the threat. What did the authorities think I was going to do, go and start a fight with an Irishman? But in a perverse way O'Callaghan was right, we were lucky. We might have been only a secondary target to the Royals, but if it wasn't for O'Callaghan's actions, the bomb would have killed Charles and Diana and everyone in the band.

If we had nine lives, then one of them had just been used up.

REHEARSING for the royal gala in the Caribbean had sounded like a good idea, but it was never really going to be an ideal way to do things. Recording for our third album, *Seven and the Ragged Tiger*, was already proving to be very difficult, and we were secretly worried about being able to deliver it on time. We'd flown to Montserrat so that we could concentrate on work there, at studios that were owned by the former Beatles producer George Martin. We'd already started on the album earlier in the south of France, but we'd done a lot of partying there and precious little real work.

In truth, we were probably missing the UK deep down inside, but we'd taken an important financial decision to become tax exiles in March. This meant we couldn't have gone home for more than a few days even if we had wanted to. It was a controversial thing to do at the time because some people read sinister overtones into it, but we'd already paid a huge amount in tax and we were aware that whatever we were earning now might have to last us a very long time. Our records had all gone screaming up the charts, but our financial and legal advisors told us to consider that rock and roll can be a very fickle industry and we shouldn't bank on always being so fortunate.

"You might have one or two more successful albums ahead of you, and then it could all be over," they warned us.

We were doing very well financially by now, but I can remember very clearly that the first check we sent to the taxman was for £600,000, which was the amount of tax we paid on the first £1 million that the band had earned between us as a partnership and we all had to sign off permission for the check to be sent. The top rate of tax in the UK had previously been 83 percent, but even the rate of 60 percent at which we had to pay would mean that a colossal amount of our earnings would continue to be handed over to the Exchequer. Today the top rate is capped at 40 percent—but back then, once the Berrow brothers had also taken their cut, and other expenses and costs were deducted, it left each member of the band with a share of around £80,000. This was still a handsome amount of money in the early eighties—and none of us was complaining at the time—but it hardly compared to the riches that could be bought with £1 million!

So it was against that background that we followed the advice to locate overseas for tax reasons. It all made perfect sense on paper, but in reality it was a tricky game to play because it meant we were on a strict "sixty-day rule," which stated we could spend no more than that exact number of days in the UK. At the time, leaving the UK didn't seem like such a big deal because we'd gotten used to living on the road while touring overseas. But we didn't realize how precious each and every one of those sixty days would become. Our nasty experiences in Germany should have sent us a warning signal about the dangers of being away from home for too long, and in that sense leaving the UK permanently was probably the worst thing we could have done for the sake of our long-term sanity. Sometimes you'd end up just sitting in a hotel with nothing to do but keep out of the country. But we also felt it was the only thing we could do if we wanted to secure our financial future. We were starting to do well in America, and although we'd earned good money up until now, we hadn't earned *American* money, so we were keen to invest as much of it as wisely as possible.

The decision we took (to be tax exiles) made us much more aware financially and Nick and I began to question how much money the Berrows seemed to be making from us. Instead of charging us a straightforward management percentage, we had a complex deal with them under which they technically owned some of the rights to our music. It meant that we had to pay them a far greater proportion of our earnings than might otherwise have been the case. The Berrows did a great job in helping to launch us and they negotiated a very good deal with EMI so they definitely played a part in our success. But I was beginning to question why it was they should own rights to our music when we were the ones who wrote it. There was nothing illegal about it, but I think Nick and I were both a bit uneasy about it and we were in favor of tackling them about it head-on. But Simon meanwhile was becoming increasingly close to the brothers. Roger avoided confrontation and John was probably the least financially astute of all of us. I used to say that John would bury his head in the sand with a checkbook hanging out his backside if he could and I was only half joking.

Our decision to move abroad had definitely contributed to the fact that by the time we arrived in London for the Prince's Trust, we were unsettled and underrehearsed for a show of such magnitude—as discovered on the night itself. Further problems followed when we played another charity gig soon afterward at Aston Villa's football stadium in Birmingham in aid of a charity called MENCAP. The charity had been promised a substantial amount of money in profits, but the problem was that the ticket sales were far lower than expected. Meanwhile costs had been allowed to escalate. We were employing enough accountants at the time to ensure this sort of thing couldn't happen, but it all went horribly wrong and the charity ended up being sent a check for just £5,000, which its director, Brian Rix, refused to cash and instead hung on the wall in his office. Even though we felt it wasn't our fault, each band member felt so bad about it that eventually we put £50,000 into the kitty between us to try and raise a reasonable profit, but the fallout continued to cause negative headlines for several months.

DESPITE the problems that lay ahead, the year had started with a huge high, thanks to "Is There Something I Should Know?" going straight into the charts at number one, which was a big achievement in those days. It was our fastest-selling record, and it was probably also the quickest song to write. Simon and I did most of it together over Christmas in an apartment we shared on Green Street in London while we were recording there. We needed a single between albums. We came up with the main riff while we were messing around, and it was followed very quickly by the rest of the chords and the main melody. It felt as if it only took about ten minutes to come up with but it was probably a bit longer. We then ran it by the rest of the band and Nick came up with "deh dah dah" bit on top of Simon's "Please, please tell me now" lyric. It was a neatly timed little idea that was influenced by the Beatles track "Please Please Me."

EMI loved it, and "Is There Something I Should Know?" was released on March 26, 1983. We knew immediately from the sales figures that it was doing well, but we weren't able to get the chart position until it was officially announced by the BBC at 10 a.m. on a weekday morning. In those days it was rare for a single to go straight in at number one in the UK and it had only been done ten times in the previous twenty years (Slade and the Jam did it in the UK three times, no one else more than once). Today sales of 50,000 will do it, but back then you had to sell bucketloads, close to half a million singles in a week, in order to pull it off. We were confident we'd done it, but we still needed to hear it officially confirmed.

I was with Tracey in Wolverhampton with the champagne on ice when we received the good news by telephone. I spoke to a girl named Lynn from our fan club office, and Tracey could tell by my voice getting higher and higher as I said, "Yeah, yeah . . . *Yeah*!"

Pop, pop, pop. Plonk.

WILD BOY

Straightaway we were drinking Buck's Fizz at ten o'clock in the morning. For me, it was one of our most significant achievements, because we'd galvanized close to half a million people in one country over a five-day period. It was a great pop song that I had a lot to do with, and I remember how happy it made me feel. It came along at the height of the time when we needed to deliver something, between albums and amid all the turmoil created by our decision to become tax exiles.

The only slight downer was that when we mimed our lip-synched version for *Top of the Pops* we had to do it in advance, before we had any idea how well the single had done. When the nation saw us on TV a lot of people thought we looked a bit miserable. I have to confess we didn't look like a band that had just gone straight to number one!

IN April we finally split the country. We rented a big old château at a place called Valbonne, on the Côte d'Azur near Cannes in the south of France. It had a great big communal room where we all used to hang out. There was a rehearsal room, a mobile studio outside, and loads of bedrooms upstairs. We'd planned to get cracking on *Seven and the Ragged Tiger*, but unfortunately we hadn't banked on how strong the lure of the bright lights of Cannes with its film festival would be. Looking back, it was the start of the megadamage because my cocaine use began to accelerate and John had developed similar habits of his own. We were living the high life to the full and soon we were partying every night.

I think John was driving his gold Aston Martin by now, but Mike Berrow went one better and turned up in a beautiful, brand-new browny-red Ferrari. Nick and I wondered how much of our earnings had gone toward purchasing the car, and I admit we had a quiet snigger when Mike came out of a nightclub to discover someone had smashed all its windows. He probably thought we'd done it, although that wasn't our style.

Meanwhile, we discovered that Elton John was in town filming his new video for "I'm Still Standing" with Russell Mulcahy. This was before Elton became teetotal, so he was still a steaming party animal. We went up to see him at his hotel and spent the afternoon getting blasted on martinis. We decided it would be a laugh to get him drunk and we were literally slinging the drinks down him.

"Ooh, you are lovely boys," he screeched, loving every minute of it.

We got him so drunk that eventually he went upstairs and threw a huge wobbler and trashed his suite, which was decorated with expensive antique furniture. The hotel weren't very happy and Russell was shocked because it caused all sorts of chaos—but it was a great party.

Daytimes were spent mainly lounging around the pool as a constant stream of visitors attended our château. We were interviewed and photographed there by *TV Times*. The British TV personality Paula Yates came down to film a special episode of *The Tube* with us for Channel Four. One unexpected guest who arrived around about the same time was the model who'd been crowned Miss UK at the time. Needless to say she was gorgeous, and it was hilarious to see the effect she had on Simon and John. Suddenly they were both running around like lapdogs after her.

"Can I get you a drink? Would you like to go for a swim?" they would ask.

I can remember sitting inside the château with Tracey, watching them together in the pool as they swam up and down trying to impress her. Occasionally Simon and John would exchange a dark look with each other as if to say *Go away, she's mine.* At one point they temporarily abandoned the hunt and came back inside the house. Then John came out and sat back by the pool with her.

"The bastard!" said Simon as he spied him out of the window, before running back down to the pool. This went on like a real life sitcom all afternoon. The irony was that neither of them had a hope in hell as Miss UK wasn't in the least bit interested in them!

But despite all the fun and games, it was also a time when cracks began to appear between us. In particular, a rift between Nick and me started to grow. It first came to a head in an explosive way due to a row between us that I felt was caused by his partner, Julie Anne, who gave Tracey the impression that I'd been flirting with a model during an air flight. I'd been over in the States for some promo work and was flying back on the same flight as Julie Anne. I think we'd all been ribbing Nick a bit because he'd had to stump up for her ticket cost, whereas everyone in the band was traveling for free courtesy of the record company. During the flight I'd innocently sat next to a woman on the plane who turned out to be a model, and we'd chatted politely for part of the journey.

In truth I didn't even know the model's name and I certainly didn't try to pull her, but when I saw Tracey her face was like thunder.

"What's wrong?" I asked.

"Nothing," replied Tracey.

"Come on, what have I done?"

"Who were you sitting next to on the plane?"

"I don't know, some model," I said, protesting my innocence.

Tracey wasn't normally a jealous type of person. I'd had a few glasses of champagne, and assumed rightly or wrongly that Julie Anne had been gossiping to someone about the model on the plane. In my mind, I could imagine Julie Anne telling everyone "Well, the girls were all over Andy on the airplane. Oh my God, you should have seen it! There was this beautiful model sitting next to him."

I knew something like this was going to happen the moment I saw her, I thought to myself as I rushed off to find Nick.

"Nick, for fuck's sake! What was that all about?" I demanded. My face was red with anger, but he was dismissive.

"Yeah, well. She doesn't know the rules," he replied flatly. Everywhere we went we were surrounded by female attention and the rule was we had to accept this without anybody making an issue of it.

"You will not survive if we live like this," I raged. "Don't fucking do that again. You can both keep your mouth shut in the future, okay? Otherwise the next time you even *appear* to be at fault I will tell her.

Imagine if everyone started blabbing their mouths off about things that aren't even fucking true."

If I'm honest, it wasn't very constructive of me to shout at Nick like that, but I was simply furious, and I remained wary of Julie Anne for a long time afterward. Nick and Julie Anne's bedroom was directly below the room Tracey and I were in at the château, and there was a secret back staircase that led down to them. I was so suspicious of her that it nearly crossed my mind to sneak down and listen in on them in case they were talking about us. It might have seemed like an overreaction, but there were a string of little incidents that started to wind up some of the others, too.

Things started to appear in the press, including the location of where we were staying, which caused us huge problems with the paparazzi. Roger was photographed by the *Sun* holding an air gun inside the château grounds, which he'd borrowed from security. We were really angry about that because of the negative image it sent out. We even phoned up the *Sun* to warn them that we'd set the dogs on their reporters if they returned. Privately, the finger of suspicion pointed at Julie Anne, which may have been completely unfair, but as the only outsider among us she became the one whom I trusted the least. I found it interesting that when it was time to go to Montserrat somebody stole her passport.

"Passports," said the woman at the check-in desk.

One guy always carried all our passports, usually the tour manager, who was accompanied by a bodyguard. "Julie Anne, have you got your passport?" he said.

"Ain't you got mine?" she asked.

"No. We haven't got your passport. Come on. Chop chop. Check in."

Now it was Nick's turn to explode. "You can find her fucking passport or I am not going," he snarled.

Eventually, things calmed down and the missing passport miraculously appeared, although I'm sure that later on the plane, one of us discreetly suggested to Nick that there might have been a reason the passport had disappeared. Ironically, Tracey and I were due to share a villa with Nick and Julie Anne in Montserrat, and I feared there would be more trouble, but in fact things calmed down a bit after that.

Montserrat was beautiful. I found some great bars, and I was soon sampling the delights of Caribbean rum punches again. We would all whiz around the island together on these little Mini Moke vehicles that the locals used. We had a big Jamaican chef at the studio, and if we dared to leave any of his food he'd soon be out of the kitchen, knife in hand, to ask us why.

"What's da matter with you, man? I used to work at the Hilton in Kingston, Jamaica—you don't like ma cookin'?"

"No, no—your pumpkin soup is great," we'd reassure him. He was a real character who became a friend to us all, and years later, while sorting through a cupboard, Tracey and I found a load of photos of him, which brought back fond memories.

BUT even life in a paradise like Montserrat wasn't without serious incident—and this time it was Nick's health that would suffer. Tracey and I were in bed one evening when there was a knock on the bedroom door. It was Julie Anne.

"It's Nick. You've got to come and see this," she pleaded. I could see from the worry on her face that something serious had happened, and all memories of the previous friction between us were forgotten.

When I got to Nick's room he was in a terrible state, sitting up in a chair clutching at his chest and gasping. He was pale and sweating, and he seemed to have trouble breathing.

"My chest hurts," he gasped.

He looked like he was about to have a heart attack, which is clearly what he feared was happening. I was terrified for him.

"Don't worry, we'll call the air ambulance. Everything will be fine," I tried to reassure him as he rocked back and forth.

The doctors were so worried that Nick was eventually airlifted to Florida, where he was taken to a hospital in Miami. After a few days he was fine, and I suspected he had basically just had a bit of a panic attack, which can cause trouble breathing. It was later reported that Nick had been suffering from paroxysmal tachycardia (or abnormally fast heartbeat) and that the problem may have been hereditary, but the stress of being in Duran Duran can't have helped. Nick was no angel when it came to excess, but after that he stuck to a modest intake of red wine. In my opinion it was another example of how our manic lifestyle took its physical toll on us in different ways: I'd been struck down by the virus in Sri Lanka, John had badly gashed his hand in Germany, and now Nick was the one who needed medical treatment. I admired Nick for being straight with himself about it, and whatever he might or might not have got up to in the past, he stuck to red wine from then onward. It was a sensible move.

After Montserrat and our brief interlude in the UK for the Prince's Trust gig, we flew down to Australia to finally finish the album. We rented a nice villa for Tracey and Giovanna on the outskirts of town. Recording at EMI studios in Sydney turned out to be hell. We were mobbed there, and security had to fight a way through for us every time we went in or out. It was flattering, but after a while, day in day out, it began to wear us down. I would wake up and dread having to go there. The third album was hard work because everyone expected so much from it, but we managed to record a version of "The Reflex," which would later become one of our biggest hits after it was remixed in America.

As usual, John and Roger were the first to complete their contribution on bass and drums, and John was once again partying as if there was no tomorrow. His destructive demons were beginning to surface once more, and he crashed his car on Sydney Bridge while Nick, Simon, and I continued to work on the top of the songs. John would often go off and party on his own. We'd had a lot of fun together as a band when we were on the road, and going out drinking together in clubs was great fun, but problems would occur when we were in the studio. These were mainly creative tensions or problems caused by John wanting to go off and party to the extreme after he'd finished laying down his bass. It seemed to me that in his mind, his work was finished. At one point John was required to come back to the studios to do a bit more bass, and for some reason it seemed to send him over the edge.

"I'm not fucking doing that!" he raged.

Later, we discovered he'd hurt his hand again, this time accidently cutting it on a shower door. It was less serious than last time, but it was another disturbing omen for what the future held. As the year drew to a close, we planned to release "Union of the Snake" in the UK at the end of October. We were convinced we would repeat the same success as we'd had with "Is There Something I Should Know?" So the whole band got together and filled up a giant bath full of iced water in a hotel suite and stocked it with every type of champagne and fine wine we could possibly want. All we were waiting for was the news from London to give us the signal to drink it all.

But when the call came it was a huge disappointment. The best the single could do was to eventually make it to number three. What went wrong? I wondered. Was it a bad song? Was it because we weren't in the UK to promote it? With hindsight, the song was up against "Karma Chameleon" by Culture Club and "Uptown Girl" by Billy Joel in the charts so it didn't do so badly, but I still felt deflated at the time. Still, at least we'd finally finished the new album, and we were looking forward to getting back to Britain in time for Christmas and using up some of our allotted sixty days there.

We were glad to go back, and we played a series of great gigs while in London during December. We were shown on *Top of the Pops* on Christmas Day doing our lip-synched version of "Is There Something I Should Know?" as part of a seasonal round-up of the year's number ones.

Christmas 1983 held a special significance for me due to the wonderful present Tracey was about to share with me.

"I've got something to tell you," she confided, when we were alone together in our cottage in Wolverhampton. "I think I am pregnant . . ."

Princess Diana's Favorite Band   141

CHAPTER SEVEN

"The Reflex" . . . and Cracking America

A HELL of a lot of blood, sweat, and tears were spilled during our tour of America in 1984. It was the year that we finally conquered the United States and we were duly anointed on the cover of *Rolling Stone* magazine, which billed us as the Fab Five in comparison to the Beatles. We were honored with two Grammy Awards, and we fulfilled our lifelong dreams of performing in front of a sellout audience at Madison Square Garden. It was fantastic. For a while everything that we touched seemed to turn to gold. But adulation comes with a price; and over the next few months we were about to experience a series of deeply disturbing incidents. The US leg of what fans referred to as our Sing Blue Silver tour that year was the last time that all five of us went on a major tour together during the 1980s. John, in particular, would end up in a very dark place, and I would finish the year secretly questioning whether or not I wanted to remain in the band. But for the time being, things seemed to be going perfectly.

I was overjoyed that Tracey was pregnant, and we were looking forward to becoming parents. I'd met and married the woman I loved, so starting a family was naturally something that we wanted to do. The timing was going to be difficult, with me having to be on the road for so long, but Tracey was very close to her mother and brothers, and I knew they would look after her while I was away. Before we went to the States at the end of January, we were due to play a series of gigs in Japan to warm up. Tracey and I decided the traveling would be too much for her to come along to Japan, although we arranged for her to join me later in the States.

The tour was preceded by an enormous high—and on this occasion that high was the first time we heard the finished version of the remix for our new single, "The Reflex." We'd originally recorded the song as a track for our third album, *Seven and the Ragged Tiger*, which had a very difficult birth and was finished way behind schedule. The track on the album isn't the greatest version of "The Reflex," and it was very different from the remix that we eventually released commercially as a single. We'd learned about the value of remixing for the American market from our experience with *Rio,* so we asked Nile Rodgers of Chic to produce versions in both 7-inch and 12-inch formats. Before CDs or digital downloads, 12-inch vinyl discs were often the only way you could achieve a truly rich depth of sound, so it was an ideal medium for Nile. As well as being hugely successful as a guitarist and founder member of Chic, Nile was just about as hot as it got at the time, having worked with INXS. He'd produced "Let's Dance" for David Bowie and later did "Like a Virgin" with Madonna. Nile agreed to work on "The Reflex" with an Italian sound engineer, Jason Corsaro, and together they came up with something very special.

We were on the road when we got a phone call from our management, who were the first to be sent a copy of Nile's version of "The Reflex."

"Chaps, I have got the remix and I think you ought to come and listen to it in person," boomed Paul Berrow in his deep voice.

He didn't say anything else, so I didn't really know what to expect when we all arrived at his hotel suite in the Midwest to hear it. I can remember that as we walked into the room everything smelled strongly of mint, and we were greeted by the sight of Paul, who'd just finished having a massage with mint oil by his new girlfriend, Miranda, whom he later married.

"I hope a massage is all you've been having, you dirty bugger," I joked, rather unkindly, under my breath.

"I've only just got this from Nile, chaps," Paul explained. "Miranda, can you just pop this on play over there."

Suddenly the room filled with the magical sound of the opening bars of the new remix: *Ta nah, nah, nah. Ta nah, nah, nah.*

"Fuck me! That's good," said Simon, on behalf of all of us. "That's *exactly* how we want it to sound, exactly."

Within a second, you could hear that the vocals were brilliantly engineered, the bass was fantastic, and everything about it screamed *hit, hit, hit!* If you do this for a job, after a while your instinct always tells you very strongly if something is good—and all of us, to a man, just went: "Wow!"

Paul seemed less convinced.

"Well, no . . . hold on," he stammered, but we wouldn't hear any of it.

"Go back to your massage," I said.

Nile's mix sounded different to anything we'd done up until then, yet somehow it still retained all the qualities of a great Duran Duran song. One of the things that was so groundbreaking about it was that it was the first time a black producer had really exploited sampling to its full potential on a commercial single by a leading white band. Nile had taken Simon's vocals and reworked them using new forms of programming to give the single a brash, funky, and futuristic sound that instantly stuck in your head. Twenty years later everybody would be doing it, but Nile was way ahead of the times.

"Fle, fle, flex," echoed Simon's voice, hauntingly.

Unfortunately, it turned out to be too far ahead of the times for the likes of Capitol Records. Incredible as it may seem today, we initially faced a battle to persuade them to release it. The first thing we did after hearing it was arrange to sit down with our management the next day to talk about a strategy for marketing "The Reflex" with an accompanying video. We were determined to film something that represented the core of what we were about as a way of bouncing back from the "New Moon on Monday" video, which contained those embarrassing dance sequences. Our tour was sold out and people were clamoring to see us live, so the time seemed right to do a live video. At the time, we were the only British band that could pull off those huge arena shows (Spandau were dust by now!), so we put together a grand plan. It included shooting the video, filming a *Sing Blue Silver* documentary, and recording a live *Arena* album. The only drawback was that when it came to "The Reflex," the record label had other ideas.

"We have a problem. Capitol Records don't want to release it. They think it is too black," explained the Berrows.

"Too black? What do they mean, too black?" we asked.

"They think it's the wrong sort of association. It sounds too much like something a black artist might do."

I was incredulous. "Well maybe that's because it's been fucking mixed by the world's leading black producer," I spat back in anger.

I'd never encountered this attitude before, not on this scale. Where I grew up in northeastern England there were no black people. As far as I and every other member of the band was concerned, Nile Rodgers, Tony Thompson, and Bernard Edwards of Chic were successful artists who we respected and admired. Everyone rated Bernard as one of the greatest bass players in the world; our appreciation of him had been one of the things that John and I had discussed together on the very first day that we met at the Rum Runner. I could hear Bernard's influence in John's playing at that first jam session. Chic were people who were great inspirations to us because of their music and their style . . . and then suddenly we were told we couldn't work with them. No way!

But you have to remember that this was 1984, and even the likes of MTV, which was very progressive, in the main aired only videos by white bands. In those days, shameful as it may seem today, it was very hard for black musicians to get airplay, and the people in charge of the record industry were very open about it.

"No, it's too black. He's black. Don't release it."

It's shocking to think that just a generation ago things were so screwed up, but all five of us in Duran Duran were indignant and we were determined to fight our corner. Michael Jackson's video for "Billie Jean," from his *Thriller* album, had already been a huge success on MTV in 1983, so thankfully things were starting to change for the better, but it was a slow process.

Ironically, John and I had already had some initial discussions with Tony Thompson in Sydney the previous year about the possibility of working together at some point in the future. We'd also become good friends with Bernard. There was still an awful racist streak in America, but the Chic guys were so cool about it, and Bernard had actually explained to us what it had been like for black people to grow up in the South in the fifties and sixties. I think their characters were a lot tougher because of all the things they'd had to deal with in the past. It was a hard struggle for them, but the one thing that can bridge most divides is music—and in this case we were determined not to back down.

"Well, actually, you haven't got a choice about whether or not to release it," we told the suits at Capitol. "Go and call EMI in London because you will find that you can't do that. Our contract says you don't have the power to prevent us."

Capitol were an American subsidiary of EMI and they were ultimately controlled from the UK, so we knew that whatever deal we had in Britain would have to be honored in the States. Thanks to the clause in the contract that we had signed as fledgling artists four years earlier, we had retained creative control over our music—and we had learned from the flop of our second single, "Careless Memories," not to let the record label dictate to us about release decisions. But it was a risky strategy. We could force Capitol to release "The Reflex," but we couldn't make them spend money promoting it unless they genuinely believed it could be a hit. And without proper promotion even the best singles can struggle. We didn't often meet with the record company at this point. We would normally just sit down with them for ten minutes and let them know what we were doing—and this was going to take more than a quick meeting to resolve. When the five of us were united about something we were a powerful force to be reckoned with, so the Berrows were dispatched to London to sort things out. Meanwhile I phoned our old ally Dave Ambrose at EMI.

"Dave—do you know what's been going on?" I asked.

"Yeah Andy—I've been thinking about it as well. It's one of your best pieces of work, you've got to release it."

Fortunately, everyone else in London backed us to the hilt, and eventually they managed to get their American counterparts excited about it. "The Reflex" became our eleventh single and it was our most successful. It gave us a hit just when we needed it most, after we'd struggled to complete our third album, and in that respect it saved our careers from going off the boil. It got a fantastic review in the *New Musical Express* (the first track of ours to be praised in print by their journalists), and it reached number one in both the UK and the USA. It also got to number four in Australia, and it won an Ivor Novello award for International Hit of the Year—but most important of all, it bridged the divide.

Some things are worth fighting for.

AT first, America seemed like a great big playground, and we were flattered by the constant comparisons that the US media made between us and the Beatles. John, Paul, George, and Ringo were our heroes, so it was a huge accolade to be mentioned in the same breath as them, and it became a regular talking point. In early February, we held a press conference at the Magic Castle pub in Hollywood, which was attended by a crowd of 150 journalists, who treated us as if we were the original Fab Four. We'd worked out a few lines together beforehand, and it became a very humorous affair as the reporters moved their way down the line and each of us introduced ourselves.

"Hello, I'm Simon and I'm the singer."

"Hello, I'm Roger and I'm the drummer."

When it got to my turn I joked: "Hello, I'm Ringo and I get pissed a lot!"

We had this thing about trying to make the American media laugh with us and it worked. They saw us as quirky English eccentrics and they loved us. It was a relief for such an important big press conference to go so well, and we later showed some brief sound bites from it in our *Sing Blue Silver* documentary. Duran Duran were finally accepted into American culture, and we were probably the last British band to achieve that. The tour itself was sponsored by Coca-Cola, and they couldn't have asked for better publicity—even though at one point John pissed them off by admitting he preferred Pepsi!

They were happy times. It was as if we'd suddenly moved up another notch. It was the first time that we used a private plane on a tour—a big 727, which Simon jokily nicknamed the Excess-a-jet! The entourage that we traveled with was very large by this point—there were around 150 of us, including the road team and our camera crew.

The scale of each gig was enormous, and it was like a military maneuver each time we needed to assemble or disassemble our stage set. If we were due on the road the next day, a small army would descend the moment a show finished, and they would work quietly through the night in order to transport all our gear to the next venue. When a major band goes on the road it's like undertaking a civil engineering project every day. There's a whole science that has grown up around getting everything in the right place at the right time.

We had a convoy of eight or nine big trucks that would start loading as soon as we came offstage at around 11 or 11:15 p.m. The crew could get incredibly ratty if anyone was hanging about in their way—and with good reason. They'd be on a tight schedule, which meant they had to get the first truck out and onto the road by 12:30, after which the vehicles would come out one by one as they became ready. The order of the truck flow is very important, and it has to be planned with precision—otherwise, everything arrives in the wrong order at the other end, which can delay building the new set. Depending on the nature of the itinerary, the crew have to start building the new stage while bits of it are still on the road. It's tough, physical work and it takes a lot of discipline to get it right. Everything is overseen by a stage manager, whose job it is to mastermind the ins and outs of the setup and breakdown. The head trucker then has to organize things to run smoothly and makes sure that none of the trucks go missing along the way.

The crew themselves travel on buses on which they eat and sleep throughout the night until they arrive at the new venue the next morning. Next, it's a quick shower at the venue before they get called to assemble their gear from around 6 or 7 a.m. In addition to the stage, there's all the equipment and a massive sound system; a complex lighting rig with hundreds of spotlights and projection gear; plus all of the backstage equipment needed for the dressing rooms, wardrobe, makeup, TV room, band room, hospitality, and greenroom. In all, there are many hundreds of thousands of pounds' worth of specialized equipment, all of which seems to weigh a ton! Then there's all the catering and merchandising stands that have to go up—and that alone can involve twenty or thirty stalls. I remember explaining it all to my dad one time and he was fascinated. It's like UPS or FedEx on a busy day. The loading and unloading can go on around the clock for twenty-four hours, from the first truck leaving to the last truck arriving. It's a phenomenal deal, every day.

Every show has to be perfect—or as close to perfect as you can get it. For the band it might be show number 27 on a 100-date tour, but for a fan who has paid his or her hard-earned money for a ticket it still has to be every bit as good as the first night. Without a really excellent crew something is going to suffer, and it will usually be the show. Fortunately, in Duran Duran we were generally surrounded by a really good crew made up of intelligent guys who were always smart and on the button. We paid them well and we always made sure they had plenty of food and drink on their buses, which they basically lived on for the duration of the tour. The guys who made the most money were the riggers, who would assemble all the lighting. It was breathtaking to watch them at work 150 feet in the air, suspended above the stage. We had a very high-tech show and a lot of the moving lights that we used were new and varied. For safety reasons the riggers' work always had to be spot-on—you don't want a two-ton lighting rig crashing down on Simon Le Bon in the middle of a performance.

As well as our regular entourage, don't forget that during the Sing Blue Silver tour we also had a full-sized film crew accompanying us everywhere in order to shoot our documentary! It was a big old show. No British band had done a set quite on this scale before, certainly nothing that involved big video screens and such intricate lighting. It was a nice feeling for everyone in the band to be the bosses of something so big. I can remember taking a step back and watching it all happen with Simon one day.

"We've created a whole little industry here just from wearing makeup and all hanging out together in a Birmingham nightclub!" we mused.

We performed in front of more than 500,000 people during the American leg of that tour, and there was always something happening on the road to keep us talking. There were plenty of interesting characters in our crew: most of them were English and we knew them well. We'd persuaded a couple of the Stones' fixers, Jim and Paddy Callaghan, to work for us, and there wasn't a trick in the book that they didn't know. They were tough old Cockneys of Irish extract and they'd seen it all. Meanwhile, I even had my own spliff roller in order to save time on rolling joints (which gives you an idea why our plane was called the Excess-a-jet).

Every day the crew would be buzzing with banter about who'd done what the night before. Contrary to popular perception, unlike the free and easy days of the Rum Runner, no member of the band slept with fans while we were on the road. It was just something that we never did because we simply didn't allow outsiders into our inner circle, plus we all had partners by now. In addition to Tracey, Giovanna, and Julie Anne, John was dating Janine Andrews (my ex) and Simon was close to a model called Claire Stansfield. It was as if we were in our own little bubble with its own community that was separated from the fuss and chaos of the outside world.

Of course, some of the younger crew members were more than happy to reap the rewards of being besieged by gorgeous women, and I daresay that quite a few rock chicks were invited onto their buses. During shows, our fans would throw their knickers onto the stage with phone numbers attached, and as a consequence our road crew were constantly sweeping the stage! It was unbelievable—we'd get backstage after the gig and there'd be 2,000 teddy bears, 150 pairs of knickers, 300 bras, 50 joints, and God knows how many hotel room keys.

Of course, the theatrical streak in Simon thrived on all the attention, and he loved to go crowd surfing. He'd puff out his chest and dive into the audience so that they could catch him in a forest of open arms. I used to joke afterward that there must have been a few sharp intakes of breath when they caught him because he's a big bloke! On one memorable occasion, the audience were treated to an eyeful of Simon's crown jewels when his bulging leather trousers tore open. He was energetically bouncing around in full flow onstage when he dropped down on his knees with his legs apart in order to belt out some vocals.

Rip!

Unfortunately, Simon wasn't wearing any underwear, and his entire undercarriage went on show to a packed auditorium. It made Janet Jackson and Justin Timberlake's Super Bowl faux pas look like kid stuff. Fortunately for everyone in Duran Duran it wasn't televised, and the incident made only a few lines in the press. We were always ribbing Simon for being a bit podgy, so the fact his trousers had torn open simply added to all the hilarity.

"Don't worry," I reassured him afterward. "It was only a very small thing so I don't think anybody noticed!"

Despite our good-natured gags about Simon's weight, we were all very physically fit, including him. Life on the road can be very grueling, and if you're playing energetic shows for two and a half hours a night for three or four nights a week you soon start to build up levels of fitness similar to those of a young footballer. I used to love to let rip onstage and I'd climb onto amps and jump off in order to entertain the crowd. It played hell with my ankles, so I used to wear specially strengthened boots so that I wouldn't end up breaking a leg. Our energy onstage was very important to Duran Duran and at heart we always wanted to be a great live band.

We hoped this would come across in the video for "The Reflex," which was put together using footage shot at several different shows. The main one was a performance we gave at the National Exhibition Center in Birmingham, but major portions were also shot during a gig we did during the Sing Blue Silver tour at the Maple Leaf Gardens in Toronto. Russell Mulcahy once again did a fantastic job as director, and in my opinion "The Reflex" is one of the best live videos ever made. We wanted the atmosphere to feel as if we were performing in an amphitheater, which is why there are Roman columns at the side of the stage. The set was based on something extravagant that Nick had sketched out while we were in Montserrat together the previous summer. The video is the best representation of the energy of the band. You can see the fun we were having onstage during that tour etched across our faces.

The camaraderie you experience on the road can be one of the best things about being in a band, and we'd often play practical jokes on each other. On my twenty-third birthday we were staying in New Orleans for a gig when Jim Callaghan (whom we called JC) laid on a surprise as we left the hotel. We were all going together to a bar called O'Brien's with loads of the crew to celebrate my birthday by getting bladdered on cocktails with big straws. Tracey was with me as we walked down the road, and as we got to the corner there was a street musician standing there playing.

"Yo! Andy—Happy Birthday to you!" he sang out of the blue, just as I walked past.

Suddenly crowds of street musicians seemed to appear from everywhere, and they all surrounded Tracey and me, singing "Happy

Birthday!" It seemed like JC had secretly tracked down every street musician in New Orleans and arranged for them to give us our own special serenade as we walked to the bar. It was a lovely gesture and it really made our day.

I think all of us were enjoying things at this point. It seemed as if we were at the peak of our indestructible youth. But sadly, even though we were enjoying things for now, there was plenty of trouble just around the corner. As I said earlier in this book, life in the rock-and-roll industry is like being on a roller-coaster ride with its highs and lows. Well, if the early part of our American tour was a peak, we were about to go into a dip. The danger signs had been there a few months earlier while we were in Australia recording our third album. Going to the studio to fight our way through crowds every morning in Sydney had been a morale-sapping process that had eaten away at our resolve to make great music.

As Tracey described it, "Every day all the band seemed to do was get up, go to the studio, and work. Then you'd come home and go to bed. Day after day after day."

Worse still, the experience had chipped away at the band's unity. After John and Roger had made their contributions and were therefore no longer required in the studio, it had seemed as if Nick had constantly wanted to change things, and some days I felt as if I was fighting to protect our input. Nick seemed to want a more arty electronic sound than John, Roger, and I, and Simon often seemed happy to go along with it. John, meanwhile, seemed to struggle to fill all the extra time on his hands and resorted to his familiar trick of wild partying. By now his relationship with Janine Andrews was becoming increasingly fiery. When the producer of our third album, Alex Sadkin, had asked John to rerecord some of his bass work, John's reaction said it all: he lashed out in anger and hurt his arm in a fury. Roger, meanwhile, was likable and quiet, as usual, but we later found out that he was becoming dangerously exhausted. It seemed as if every time we were away from home for long periods of time the pressure would eventually begin to take its toll on all five of us—and America was no different.

Another negative factor was that the friction between certain band members and the Berrow brothers continued to fester. Nick and I were increasingly hostile toward them because we were unhappy with the financial deal we'd signed with them back in 1980. We had no objection to them making a living from Duran Duran—after all, they'd helped to make everything happen so quickly in the first place—but we felt their share of our profits was simply too great. Worse, in our minds, was the fact that they had some of the ownership rights to the music that we had created. It was ironic that Nick and I, who rarely saw eye to eye on most things, were united over our concerns about the financial arrangements.

At the end of February 1984, my relationship with the Berrows reached an all-time low and exploded in a violent row—and it was over something that should have been one of our finest moments. Unbeknownst to anyone in the band, we had secretly won two Grammy Awards—and our esteemed management didn't tell us.

To receive *one* Grammy, let alone *two,* is a once-in-a-lifetime achievement that most rock acts can only dream about. It still makes me furious to this day that I didn't find out until it was too late for us to collect them in person because I didn't know that we'd won until the actual day. I don't know exactly when the Berrows knew, but I was furious with them because I felt it was their job to keep us informed about things as important as this. We were performing a string of gigs at destinations that included Kansas City and Pittsburgh, and at the time I assumed that someone thought the disruption would be too much to handle on short notice.

Instead, we were told we'd won at the last minute, and we had to make do with accepting the award trophies on the road via a live video link. Our first Grammy, and we fail to attend the biggest television rock-and-roll event in America. I was furious. If there was even the slightest chance we could have won, all we would have needed to do was postpone one gig—the fans would have understood, and we could have rescheduled the gig. For the record, we won Best Short Video (for our "Girls on Film"/"Hungry Like the Wolf" video 45) and Best Video Album (for our *Duran Duran* video album), but the row totally soured the achievement. It was a horrible thing to miss out on and it stole our thunder. I was incandescent with rage and I was soon shouting at Paul Berrow.

"We win a Grammy and you don't tell us?"

Paul tried to argue there hadn't been time to arrange things.

"Are you fucking kidding me?" I screamed. "There was time to bring the Grammy trophies here to us but we're not allowed to go to LA to accept them?" By now I had completely lost it. "You might be a tall streak of piss compared to me, but one day I'm going to run up you and fucking head-butt you," I raged.

As usual, the Berrows were full of excuses, but I wondered if the reason they didn't tell us was because they were afraid of losing a little bit more of their control over us in LA? I was twenty-three years old and married with a pregnant wife, but maybe they thought I was too naive to handle it. Simon was twenty-five, yet I felt they were treating us as if we were still teenagers.

"Right, you motherfuckers. That's it," I threatened. As far as I was concerned, I'd had enough of the Berrows.

The sooner we ditched them the better.

CHAPTER EIGHT

America . . . and Cracking Up

WHEN you burn the candle at both ends, pretty soon something has to give—and in America it happened during April 1984 at the Four Seasons Hotel in San Francisco. I can't remember who it was who first called me in the middle of the night to tell me that John Taylor's hotel room was drenched in blood. What I can vividly recall is the horrific scene that greeted me when I arrived there in the early hours of the morning.

Everywhere, blood.

It was all over the bed. I can remember it on the covers and on the sheets, I can remember it on the wall up by the window, and I can remember it on the floor and all over an antique chair. In fact, one whole side of the room was covered in blood and there was a broken bottle of Stolichnaya vodka on the floor. It had smears of red gloop congealing on its broken edges. John sat on a chair in the corner, whimpering.

I couldn't get any sense out of him, and it took a second or two for my brain to try and make sense of the scene. I'd been drinking heavily that night and I'd also taken cocaine; so had John. I assumed John had been involved in some sort of argument with a girlfriend. The room was in a state as if there had been an argument. Things had been turned over, but the room wasn't completely trashed or smashed up. John continued to rock back and forth, crying in pain and clutching at himself.

Then I saw where all the blood was coming from.

The soft underside of his foot was covered in a mass of cuts that seemed to have shards of glass sticking out of them. I assumed that he must have stepped on the broken vodka bottle with the force of his full weight, but I couldn't tell if all the mess had been caused by his foot spurting or whether or not in his semiconscious state he'd walked around the room with bits of glass embedded in him.

I grabbed the telephone. "Emergency. We need a doctor . . . ," I said, as the adrenaline in my veins began to sober me up.

I could now see that John was very emotional. He was crying and screaming out in pain, but his eyes looked out of it. I didn't think he was necessarily aware of what was happening to him. He was breathing deeply, as if that was the only thing keeping him sane. I put my arm around him to try and comfort him, but I could feel panic beginning to rise within myself.

"It's going to be okay. It's going to be okay. It's going to be okay," I repeated over and over.

I don't know if I was trying to reassure John or convince myself. I kept thinking, *Fuck me, please don't let him bleed to death.*

I could see that he'd suffered a horrible wound. By now his foot was a really nasty piece of work, all purple and swollen, with lumps of flesh hanging from it. I don't know how long it took for the medics to arrive, but pretty soon it seemed as if the whole world had descended upon John's room. The first thing the medics wanted to establish was whether or not there was any tendon damage. I could see from their demeanor that they regarded it as a serious wound, but they reassured John that they would do their best to patch him up.

"Calm down, John. Breathe deeply, everything is going to be all right," they said to him.

The incident would be downplayed in the media. It was later reported that John needed twenty stitches, but I think it was more like forty-two or forty-three stitches. Believe me, this was not a minor incident. Slowly, I started to feel relief that John was receiving proper medical attention, but I still had an awful, sick feeling in the pit of my stomach. I was scared for John and what this would mean for him, but I was also scared of the implications it could have for everyone else in the band.

"My God, how is this going to look?" I asked myself, when I eventually got back to my room.

I was in a state of numb shock and I started calling various members of our crew. "Right. Meet me here now. We've got a serious problem," I told them.

It dawned upon me that the timing couldn't have been worse. We were due to shoot some major sequences of a show for our *Arena* film at Oakland Coliseum in California the next day—and the preparations for that were due to start in a matter of hours. I'd seen enough of John's foot to know he would be lucky to walk anytime soon, let alone be in a fit state to run up and down onstage with a bass guitar.

"Andy, it's going to cost several hundred thousand dollars to scrap the shoot," I was warned. "Plus, there are the insurance implications to think about."

I was more concerned about John at this point, but the question of the film shoot was something that we'd be forced to deal with as soon as the sun came up. I feared our insurance company would not cover the losses if they could argue, rightly or wrongly, that the injury had been caused by reckless behavior or if it could in any way be construed as being self-inflicted. I obviously wasn't in the room when John got hurt, so I don't know how it happened—all I saw was the mess and a man who I cared for who was in trouble. But getting drunk and dancing on vodka bottles was hardly the sort of thing that our insurers would be in a rush to pay out on. John would later deny (both to the band and later to the media) that he did anything on purpose or in a rage that night, and at the time we were more worried about dealing with the fallout than apportioning blame.

A group of us sat down in my room and tried to work out what to do next. If John was unable to play, then there would be no show . . . and no show meant no film shoot, which in turn would jeopardize our whole marketing plan for the next few months. All in all, we estimated we could have kissed good-bye to a cool $750,000, which would be worth several million dollars today.

"How are we going to get through this, then?" I asked.

"Well, we are near to the end of the tour. Maybe we can call in the Rock Doc and John can just hobble through it," said someone in reply.

The Rock Doc is the name we gave to a friendly medic whom we could call upon if things got heavy and we wanted something dealt with quietly. Most major rock bands have them and in an emergency they can often medicate you with whatever it takes to get you onstage, even if it involves some slightly unorthodox medical practices. So that's what we did. John was patched up during the night and the next morning we called the Rock Doc, but I knew this wasn't going to be easy. It was no coincidence that I was the first band member who'd received the phone call about John's injury. Ever since Australia he had been increasingly erratic, and I was regarded as the only member of Duran Duran who could really talk to him because we were close—and kindred spirits when it came to cocaine. It shows how disjointed we'd become as a group. One thing that was certain was that John was going to need a serious amount of morphine to kill the pain. Of course, apart from easing pain the other thing that morphine does is turn you into a zombie, so John also needed something else to keep him awake.

When the Rock Doc arrived the next morning I was the only guy in the room with John.

"Come on, we'll get through this," I said to him.

In the end, John had to be fired up at both ends. The doctor gave him huge amounts of morphine in the foot. Then John took pharmaceutical cocaine through the nose to keep him awake. It was the only solution; otherwise, the morphine would have knocked him out. The doctor was there and he was actually letting John snort it. That's how crazy things had gotten: a doctor was actually allowing us to take Class-A drugs.

"Here, Doc, while you're at it," I said, pointing at the cocaine. He looked at me sadly.

"Fuck it—do you know what we have been through in the last twenty-four hours?" I said, helping myself to a line of the drug.

And that was how we got through it all day. The doctor injected John in between the toes and wrapped up his foot. Then it was sniff, sniff, and onstage. Forty minutes later John was back in his room.

"Arrggh!" he screamed, as the bandages came off while he leaned back in his chair.

Sniff, sniff. Wrap. Then it was back onstage for another forty minutes. I want to stress for legal reasons that the doctor involved wasn't a member of our regular circle. Let's just say that when you work in the rock-and-roll industry, there are always ways and means of contacting people like that. We went through the process of John coming offstage to take more drugs three or four times until we finally got the filming done.

Unbelievable.

Looking back, it was all so surreal. When I replay it in my mind it's like watching the sort of mayhem you'd expect to find in a Quentin Tarantino movie. John would later be quoted as saying that he felt as if his body had left him and his soul was pinned to the ceiling—and that's exactly how he looked: as if his soul had left him. Anybody looking down on us from the ceiling of that hotel room the night before would have witnessed a morbid sight, with the stark red of all the blood against the white sheets and me panicking as I cradled him.

We got through the video shoot, but I think maybe we both lost a bit of our souls that night.

NO lessons were learned from what happened to John and no one talked to him about it. In Duran Duran we liked to identify something if it was causing us an external problem, like when Capitol refused to release "The Reflex." But when it came to sorting out our own problems we didn't connect. I wish I knew why that was but I don't have an answer, we just came from different directions when it came to communicating, so it was often easier just to leave things unsaid. After the filming took place, we didn't know what we had in the can or whether or not it would be of any use, but nobody kicked up a fuss.

My feelings toward John were very mixed over the next few days. On the one hand I felt enormous sympathy for him: he'd been through a horrific ordeal and he, more than anyone, had suffered the most from the pressures of twenty-four-hour attention. Being at the center of the circus was something that was starting to eat away at all of us, and it would eventually affect every one of us in a different way. For now, John was the one who was suffering the most. But besides feeling sympathy, though, I was angry with him, too, and there were moments when I didn't feel sorry for him at all. It was the second or third time that something like this had happened to him, and I was beginning to lose patience. There were plenty of times when I had felt like punching our management but I'd held back, so I reasoned that John should have done more to avoid getting into bad scrapes.

"You don't fucking do things like that at our age," I cursed to myself.

Officially, the injury to John's foot was due to an accident. All he said afterward was that he was drunk and dancing around his room when he accidently stepped on the vodka bottle. In my view drugs had been an aggravating factor—and it says a lot that the thing we turned to to get us out of the mayhem had been more cocaine. Sadly, the incident wasn't the only time blood was spilled. There was more to come at our end-of-tour party. A lot more.

We had two or three more shows to do, and I was counting the days before I could go back to the UK to spend some time with Tracey. Our baby was due in August, and I was beginning to long for the peace and tranquillity of Shropshire. The madness of being on the road seemed never-ending, and despite the fact that the tour had started with such a high due to all the adulation we received, our moods started to dip. A rock-and-roll lifestyle has no structure. When you are young you don't look back, but later on you realize it's a series of highs and lows. You can get high on creativity as well as drugs, but what goes up must come down and it can drain your energy. "The Reflex" was about to go to number one, but in addition to the incident with John, there was more trouble ahead—and it would further take the shine off things.

As the tour had progressed, our schedule had become increasingly intense. We might have been physically fit, but the sheer number of shows we played left us feeling increasingly exhausted. When you are spending seven days a week in hotels and traveling constantly, it can start to wear you down. Apart from brief trips back to the UK, we'd been away from home almost full-time for ten months since the previous June. Every time we went in or out of a hotel we had to hustle through crowds. You start to believe that every minute of your life someone is trying to find you. It seems as if it is happening daily, monthly, yearly . . . and there's a very real danger that it can make you agoraphobic and irrational. It's easy to fall into a routine whereby after a show you get into a blacked-out limo, which whisks you straight to a private airport so that you can go back to your satellite hotel and sleep all day until 6 p.m. Then it's up and off to the next gig, and often you don't return to the hotel until two the next morning, where you stay up all night eating pizza and getting indigestion before the whole cycle starts over again at 6 p.m. You become divorced from reality, and tiny little niggles become magnified in your mind.

The friction between Nick and me continued to rumble and Julie Anne, who'd been with us throughout the US tour, continued to grate on my nerves. Tracey says that in a lot of ways Nick and I are total opposites, and even though I obviously respected him as a fellow member of Duran Duran, I guess she's right. Certainly Nick and I had very different ideas musically, which had become increasingly apparent during the recording of the third album. I felt Nick always insisted on doing things Nick's way, and he was increasingly dismissive of the contributions from John, Roger, and me.

"This is how it is fucking going to be," he would insist when trying to argue a point.

Not even Simon was immune from his criticism; I used to joke that Nick was the head of the Lyric Police. I was also fed up with how pompous and dismissive he could be of people from outside the band.

I felt as if Nick's attitude was always along the lines of: "I don't like that. What the fuck is this?"

I wasn't alone in noticing this, but, to be fair to Nick, we could all be a bit frayed at times, myself included. I could be just as single-minded when it came to music, so it was sometimes like the proverbial irresistible force meeting the immovable object. Nick and I had never really cleared the air since our big row over Julie Anne, and things were about to get worse over a practical joke that we'd decided to play on him on the last night of our tour. Our final gig was in San Diego, and all the people from Capitol Records and everyone connected with the tour were due to be there, including a big group from the sponsor, Coca-Cola, who were throwing a corporate party for us later that evening. There was a growing feeling among several of us in our entourage that Nick needed taking down a peg or two, so we decided to spice things up by secretly sending a stripper onstage to drape herself around him during the show's finale. We knew he would squirm with embarrassment, and it was bound to cause fireworks with Julie Anne, so I asked a member of our entourage to make the arrangements.

"What I want you to do is to find the dirtiest, ugliest stripper you can get, right?" I said. "Then when we do the encore for 'Girls on Film,' send her out while Nick is playing his long solo."

"Great, he's going to hate it," he replied. "We'll have to talk to everyone else to warn them so that it's not a surprise for them, otherwise it'll go wrong."

Everyone was in agreement, and we had a bit of a debate about whose credit card we should charge the girl's services to. I can't remember who picked up the tab in the end, but at one point we were thinking of sending the bill to Coca-Cola!

When the time to perform the encore came, I could see Julie Anne standing at the side of the stage as the stripper was ushered toward us. Julie Anne copped to what was going on immediately. I don't know how she knew but, fair play to her, she raised absolute hell to try and stop it! I could see her from the corner of my eye, just out of view of the audience, as she grabbed the stripper's arm in a fury. A member of the stage crew had grabbed the girl's other arm, and there was a violent tug-of-war going on to the side of me onstage. It was a bizarre sight, with the seminaked girl being pulled back and forth by a burly roadie and an angry American heiress.

Eventually the stripper managed to burst free and she darted onto the stage and went straight to Nick. At first he was totally bemused by it all and he tried to carry on with the show amid all the confusion. I was pissing myself with laughter, and by now the rest of the band was doubled up, too. Julie Anne, meanwhile, was fuming at the side of the stage, and I could see that she was now being held back from coming on to join us. I dread to think what would have happened if she'd succeeded in breaking free—she would probably have brained the stripper there and then onstage! Nick's confusion soon turned to fury, and by the time we came offstage he was too angry to speak—unlike Julie Anne, who let rip with a tirade of abuse that would have made a Geordie coal miner blush with embarrassment.

"You bastards!" she screeched.

I felt a bit sorry for Nick afterward, but as far as a lot of us were concerned he'd brought it on himself with his high-minded ways and his withering put-downs of other people. Anyway, I had other things on my mind that night. Coca-Cola were throwing a big celebration in Los Angeles at the Chateau Marmont, and I had a limo booked to take me there. Our support band for that final gig on April 17 had been a group called Chequered Past, in which Michael Des Barres was the singer alongside Steve Jones, one of my guitar heroes from the Sex Pistols. I was keen to get to know Steve better, so I offered him a lift back from San Diego to Los Angeles. He was swigging from a bottle of Jack Daniel's all the way . . . and so was I.

"We are having a little end-of-tour party that Coca-Cola have paid for. Why don't you come along to that?" I said to him.

Jonesy (as he's known to his pals) readily agreed, and as the journey progressed he guzzled more and more Jack Daniel's until he was completely out of it. I remember thinking, *Blimey! I know he's a Sex Pistol, but he's really pushing it, even by my standards!* When we got to the Chateau Marmont, Steve literally fell out of the vehicle and lay in the gutter with one leg still under the limo, bottle of Jack in hand. It was exactly what you'd expect from a Sex Pistol, and we laughed our heads off. When we got inside, Steve was all over the place while we had a drink with some of the guests from Coca-Cola in one of the suites where they were hosting the party. It was all behind closed doors, so it didn't matter too much that Steve was staggering around, but eventually I sent him home safely with a driver because he was so smashed.

I was hanging around with the guys from Coca-Cola when we heard a commotion kicking off in the room next door. That was when things started to get very bloody again.

We rushed next door, where a violent struggle was taking place. I saw the flash of a knife and a group of people who were desperately trying to pull a man to the ground as he lunged forward with the weapon, screaming in fury. I soon worked out that someone had been stabbed, and our corporate party now looked like a scene from a Los Angeles gang fight. I recognized the man with the knife as one of our backing musicians, whom I'll call Rick (not his real name). He was a brilliant musician, but he was also a proper little hard guy from the streets.

"Fucking hell, what's happening, man?" I shouted at him.

It turned out that Rick had fallen asleep at the party while leaning back in one of the big comfy chairs at the Chateau Marmont. Somebody had apparently then gone up to him, and they must have done something to suddenly wake him. In his fuddled state, Rick assumed he was being robbed and that his assailant had gone into his pocket looking for money or drugs. Rick was a knife-carrying individual, and his instinct was to go for his weapon. He cut the person in front of him, and the whole thing had then kicked off.

Looking back, I think he would have killed someone if they hadn't held him back. There were a lot of people in the party, and he just went at them and tried to stab them a few times. He managed to cut his main target, but fortunately it wasn't a life-threatening wound, and the other guests managed to stop him before he could do any serious damage. Nonetheless, I was horrified—how could our end-of-tour private party end in a stabbing incident? I knew it was time to shut the party down—and quickly. This was LA and things were already seriously out of hand. We couldn't afford for it to get any worse or we'd finish our tour by being locked up—and this was supposed to be the Land of the Free.

"Everyone's got to go—the party's over," I said.

The very next day everyone decided not to stay in LA any longer but to go straight home. Tracey had gone back to the UK a few days earlier. I'd seen enough blood in America; there was no reason to hang around. Tired and dehydrated, I went to the airport and caught the first plane I could back to the UK. During the flight I wondered where it had all gone wrong. We'd conquered America, made the cover of *Rolling Stone,* and we'd been honored with two Grammy awards. Yet here I was, tired, stressed, and sweating on a plane while my ears whined with exhaustion and vivid images of John's disfigured foot and Rick's bloody knife flashed through my mind. Still, I consoled myself that I would soon be home with Tracey, back in the sanity of the real world. Little did I realize that there was still one last nasty surprise awaiting me when I got to England.

Simon was with me on the plane. Despite his normal cheery optimism, I think he was just as shocked and disturbed as I was over all the events during the last few days of our tour. We were too tired to discuss things in any detail, but I think we both realized we were increasingly finding ourselves in situations we didn't want to be in, and which were also completely out of control. I mean, staff pulling knives! Why the hell was anyone near us carrying a knife in the first place, let alone using it in a fight? Until now, my feelings about this sort of thing had been along the lines of, *Ah well, this sort of shit happens when you are on the road.* But I was beginning to think, *This sort of shit* shouldn't *happen. It's unacceptable and I don't want to be around it.*

After we finally touched down at Heathrow, Simon and I trudged wearily through Customs. Look on the bright side, I thought, at least Tracey would now be waiting for me outside the airport in a car.

"Excuse me, gentlemen. This way, please," growled a uniformed Customs officer with a gruff voice.

There were two Customs and Excise guards based at Heathrow who were well known for taking a great delight in searching incoming rock stars. Aside from the IRA, there wasn't much by way of international terrorism in those days, so I guess they had nothing better to do. Simon and I didn't know it, but we were in for a very tough time. In the States we'd each been presented with an electric guitar as a gift by the Novation guitar company, and in the rush to leave the country we had failed to declare them to Customs. We were coming home after months on the road, and we had about a gazillion pieces of luggage, and the guitars had slipped our minds. It was a simple oversight, and we'd have been more than happy to pay the import duties, but the officers weren't going to miss an opportunity like this to humiliate us.

"Oh dear, what else have we failed to declare, gentlemen? I am afraid we are going to require a strip search," said one of them, whom I'll call Mr. Gruff Voice.

"My wife is five months pregnant and waiting outside in a car," I protested. But they insisted in frog-marching Simon and me into separate rooms. I don't know why; maybe they thought one of us had an amplifier stuck up his backside that he'd also failed to declare.

It was a horrible experience. I was made to strip naked and bend over, although thankfully they spared us a full internal search. We were then interrogated for four hours. Where had we been? Did we have any drugs? What else had we failed to declare? We might have been famous pop stars from Duran Duran, but as far as Mr. Gruff Voice was concerned we were going to get the full treatment. All the time I was with him I had a sick feeling in my stomach about Tracey waiting outside. Did she know where I was? Would she be panicking?

My fears were correct because while I was in that dingy holding room, Tracey was actually going through a far worse ordeal. She'd been waiting outside with a driver to pick me up from arrivals when the car had become completely surrounded by a baying crowd. Word had leaked out that Duran Duran were flying in, and thousands of screaming fans were now trying to ransack the vehicle. Until you've seen mass hysteria sweep through a crowd it's difficult to understand how dangerous it can be, but believe me, it is *very* dangerous and *very* frightening. If you're stuck inside a vehicle at the center of it all, then it's absolutely terrifying. The noise is deafening and you are surrounded by an endless sea of faces squeezed up against every piece of glass until the light gets blocked out. All the time there are people banging—and I mean really *hammering*—on the car roof. The fans at the front start to panic because of the crush, and the mood soon turns very nasty. People start to faint, and before you know it lives are at risk. It had started to happen to us a lot, and I was shocked at how aggressive the crowds could be. It was as if a mob mentality took over and they were in pursuit of a strange emotion called hysteria. I guess they are just trying to get your attention, slamming on the glass to say, *Look at me.*

For a pregnant woman to be caught up in it all must have been completely terrifying. When I was finally freed by Customs, Tracey was shaking like a leaf and white with shock. She'd been trapped in the vehicle during what amounted to a small riot, helpless for at least fifteen minutes before the police had finally managed to control the crowd. These days they would have thrown a protective cordon around the car to begin with, but the ferocity of the crowd had taken even the police by surprise. I felt powerless and guilty for keeping

WILD BOY

Tracey waiting in such dangerous circumstances. I was also furious with Mr. Gruff Voice and his sidekick. If the same thing had happened today I would have sued them. But all I cared about at this moment was Tracey. It was bad enough when things like that happened to members of the band, but it's worse when it starts to affect your family. Thankfully we employed an aging Cockney driver, Old George, who had been with Tracey in the car and he'd done what he could to try and keep her calm.

"It's okay, it's safe now. We're going home," I reassured her when we eventually reunited.

As the car pulled away from London, it finally felt as if we were leaving all the chaos behind. As we drove around a newly opened section of the half-built M25, I held Tracey tight and she began to calm down. By the time the car reached the M1 and turned north toward Shropshire, I could feel the pressure beginning to lift from my shoulders. The blood-drenched hotel rooms, the fights and arguments in the band, and the booze and drugs—all seemed to be left behind as the car sped through the darkness toward the comfort of home. All I could think about was how much I loved Tracey and how glad I was to be briefly away from the madness of life on the road.

Fuck it. I am leaving it all behind. Thank God.

CHAPTER NINE

"I Saw Duran Duran Go Crazy on Cocaine"

I'M at the Plaza Athénée hotel in Paris, and I'm about to discover how it feels to wake up and find yourself suddenly splashed across the front pages of the tabloids for cocaine abuse. The date is May 8, 1984, and John and I have hooked up in France to try and do some demo tracks together in the studio. The hotel we are staying at is just a stone's throw from the bustle of the Avenue des Champs-Elysées. In my opinion it's the best in Paris, better even than the Ritz. The walls are beautifully decorated and padded with silk, and John and I each have our own suite at the very top of the hotel, which is famous for its distinctive slanted windows and its fabulous architecture. We've come a long way since our days at the Rum Runner, but our wild partying during our time in Birmingham is about to come back to haunt us.

I was curled up asleep in my suite with the Do Not Disturb sign on the handle when a knock on the door awoke me before breakfast.

"Guv, Guv . . . Wake up. I need to talk to you."

It was one of the personal assistants who had stayed on with us in order to deal with our accounts and various other things after we had come off the road in April. When you get an unexpected knock on the door early in the morning, and there's no telephone call beforehand, you know it's not going to be good news. This time it turned out to be real trouble, something that would affect all our families and change the public's perception of Duran Duran. I grabbed a bathrobe and opened the door.

"There's been a story published in London, Andy. You need to read it straightaway."

He passed me a copy of the *Sun* newspaper, and I felt a sick twinge in my stomach as I read the headline: COKE CRAZY DURAN DURAN. There were photographs of Simon, John, Nick, and me on the front page, and the paper didn't mince its words. "Simon Le Bon put his head into a packet of white powder . . . and sniffed. Andy Taylor laid out huge lines of coke on the kitchen sink unit." I continued to read with disbelief: "They are hooked on the stuff, says ex-minder. They need it to perform, they need it to have a good time, they need it to cope with the pressures of stardom." Inside, across the center pages next to a big photograph of the five of us, was la pièce de résistance, a lurid account of our drug use which was headlined, I SAW DURAN DURAN GO CRAZY ON COKE!

It was by Al Beard, the former head doorman from the Rum Runner, who had been entrusted to look after our welfare by the Berrow brothers. I cast my mind back to that cold Christmas Eve four years ago, when I'd first snorted cocaine in the camper van outside the club in Birmingham. Al's bouncers had watched me go in and out to buy drugs that night. Al knew everything, and I mean *everything*. His story contained wild accusations from start to finish—but it was the first real act of public betrayal that we'd encountered as a band. A lot of his claims were inaccurate, and some of the details would have been comical were it not for the repercussions that they had.

"Soon after Duran Duran made it big, John Taylor announced he had found a new use for his gold American Express card," claimed Al Beard. "He pulled out a little packet, emptied a load of white powder onto the table and chopped it finely with his credit card. Then he sniffed it up his nose.

"One gram of cocaine? That'll do nicely, sir."

I was singled out as the worst offender, but Beard made allegations about all of us, with the exception of Roger, whom the paper was careful to point out did not take drugs.

"Andy Taylor is top of the coke league," claimed Al's article. "Andy is wild . . . the effects of coke do show from time to time. Andy Taylor has been known to collapse on tour." The newspaper was also promising its readers more revelations for the following day: TOMORROW: HOW I FIXED GIRLS GALORE FOR THE LADS.

I was staggered. Al Beard hadn't been around us for nearly four years and yet here he was, claiming to know our most intimate secrets. A lot of what he said about Simon and Nick was exaggerated. Certainly at the time the article was published Nick, far from being hooked on drugs, actually disliked being around cocaine. But the central allegation, that Al Beard had witnessed some of us taking cocaine at the Rum Runner, *was* true—and it had the potential to be hugely damaging to us. John and I had not tried to hide our drug use from our inner circle at the club, but until now it had remained a secret from the wider world.

This was going to be a tough one for the band to get through, but what really scared me was that I knew the story would also give the press carte blanche to approach our families. Until now we'd been marketed as a band who wouldn't even take an aspirin, yet here we were being exposed for drug abuse. Our record label had promoted us as the squeaky clean darlings of teenage pop magazines like *Smash Hits*, so it was about to become open season on us in the media. By now all the other newspapers would be desperate to follow up the story and there would be teams of reporters on the doorstep of everybody who knew us back in the UK. Our staff had woken me up because they realized my dad would have seen the story before I did, and they knew it would be initially more of a problem for our families than it was for us.

"This is a fucking nightmare. We've been stitched up," I groaned.

When I get nervous I often want to eat—so the first thing I did

WILD BOY

was order some food to get something inside me to try to calm myself down. They served the most amazing scrambled eggs at the Plaza Athénée, really creamy and perfect, so I called room service. I tried to reread the article while I waited for the food to arrive. My mind was racing. Was this going to open the floodgates and cause lots of other people to come out of the woodwork? Who had we sacked recently? Did they have a confidentiality clause in their contract? *Right, I need to get on to everybody . . . get the lawyers on the phone, give out a warning. This could go on and on forever*, I thought to myself.

I left most of the eggs, but I managed to pull myself together enough to call my dad in Cullercoats. It was a difficult telephone conversation.

"Hello, Dad, it's Andy. How are you?"

Silence.

"I am a bit upset," he finally answered. "When I went to the paper shop this morning, I got a few funny looks."

"I'm sorry, Dad," was all I could say. I knew that he always walked to the paper shop every day, and he often said that he encountered different attitudes, depending on what was happening to me in the news.

"Well, you know, son, I know I once found hash in your pocket when you were a little kid," he said quietly, in his hushed Geordie accent. "I know you take drugs, just as long as you are all reet, yah know?"

This was heartbreaking.

"Dad, it's not as bad as they are making out and—"

"Well, it sounds like you've been having loads of shagging and fun," he said, trying to lighten the mood. "It's not bad, son. You are a human being and I know you are all right."

There he goes, I thought, *he's doing the same old thing he always did when I was a kid, pretending everything is all right when he must be hurting like hell inside.* He wouldn't tell me how he really felt, but I found out later that he was petrified. He didn't understand why we took cocaine, and he was terrified of what we were doing to ourselves.

The reporters' door knocking started almost immediately. My dad absolutely hated it and slammed the door on them, disgusted and fearful of what the neighbors might think.

John's family were Roman Catholics and he was their only son, so they were mortified, too. They'd had to put up with more crap than any of us, including the occasion when they had to pick up the papers and see photos of their son naked in bed with a girl. John's mother, Jean, is a sweet, churchgoing woman, and this would have been soul-destroying for her. Simon's mother, Anne, is also a really warm person. Normally she was very strong and could take anything in her stride, but how would she react to this? Nick's dad, Roger, was next on the reporting pack's list. Nick's dad adored our band, and he had a room full of all our memorabilia. He was too polite to tell them where to go and let one of them in for a cup of tea in the hope that it might calm the storm, but it didn't really work. From this point onward the association with cocaine never left us. But when all was said and done, deep down inside I also knew that the real blame lay with me for dabbling with drugs in the first place. It had left a stain on the doorstep that our families had no control over—and none of them had ever said anything or done anything to deserve it. I was ashamed.

Al Beard had more "ammunition" against us for Day Two of the exposé, although this time we were labeled as womanizers. HERE ARE THE GIRLS YOU ORDERED, SAID POSH PORTER, screamed the headline. According to the story, Al Beard arranged for girls to be delivered to us in hotels via room service. In fact, most of the details in the story related to half truths about events at the Rum Runner four years earlier, and once again he accused me of being the chief culprit.

"The band used [the Rum Runner] a lot, especially Andy Taylor. He was very good at chatting up the girls . . . I remember driving around Birmingham with him once when we spotted a beautiful blonde on the pavement," claimed Al.

"We stopped and picked her up. She was a model . . . Within

minutes of climbing into the back of my car with Andy she had all her clothes off," he wrote.

I certainly couldn't recall that, but now it was Tracey's turn to be inquisitive.

"It doesn't really say anything nasty, but who is that model?" she asked me.

"The story is four years old. Read it," I reassured her. "Look at what it says. It was when I worked in the Rum Runner, everything was before I knew you."

Meanwhile, I had plans for Mr. Beard. We had sixty full-time staff working for us, including five full-time bodyguards who were all ex-military. One of our senior people arranged a discussion about how to react, and the first thing I wanted to do was find Al Beard.

"Right, where is the fucker?" I asked.

"Oh, we know where he is. He's gone to Marbella."

"Marbella! That's a stupid place to go. Don't people disappear there?" I said. I felt I had every right to be furious, but in hindsight I was letting off steam and acting as if I was a Ray Winstone character in a movie. If I'd seen Al Beard while I was out in a car, on the spur of the moment I would have gladly run him over. I was all in favor of sending private detectives over to Spain to track him down. Al had buggered off there because he probably feared that if he was in the UK we would send people round to confront him. What I actually wanted was for someone to sit him down for a chat. I presumed he'd been paid about forty or fifty grand for the story, and I wanted him to hand it over. I wanted to say, *You know, Al. Give us the money back and you can get on with your life. We'll forget about it, I'll make a deal with you, but you are not having the fucking money.* Sending the boys round would probably have been the worst thing we could have done under the circumstances. It would have just led to more squealing in the papers, not to mention landing us in serious trouble with the law. Thankfully, I was the only member of the band who was in favor and the idea was dropped. Simon and the others were levelheaded enough to know it would have just caused more trouble.

"Fuck it, let's leave it. He can't go back to Birmingham anyway," was the general view.

Al Beard was finished in Birmingham. No one would trust him on the door anymore, and the Berrows, the Cook brothers, and everyone else who we knew there would be just as angry with him as we were. The reason I was so furious wasn't so much because my cocaine secret was out, it was the act of betrayal. Today I know that drugs are dangerous, and I can understand why the newspapers exposed us. But at the time I felt that Al Beard had failed to explain why, if he was such a moral person, he had kept quiet for so long while drug dealers operated at the club. He even admitted in the story that when pushers arrived at the Rum Runner he would go through to the back of the club and tell us they were there. I never got to ask him. As far as I know no one has ever seen him since, and I never had any contact with him.

ONE thing Al Beard had been correct about was that there was a relationship between copious amounts of cocaine and the Rum Runner. There were two big stainless-steel sinks in the kitchen, which is where lines of the drug would be chopped up. We might have seemed too clean to take an aspirin, but if you'd have crushed one up I'd have certainly known what to do with it.

Drugs were beginning to permeate society on a scale that had been previously unseen. The early eighties were a period of immense and sudden change. Thatcherism, corporate branding, and the birth of the Yuppie culture all came along in one big wave. There was still plenty of poverty, as the riots of 1981 in the UK had had demonstrated, but for the first time many young people were starting to attain huge disposable incomes compared with a generation ago. Cocaine arrived on the scene along with that wave of wealth, and by 1985 the streets were virtually covered with the stuff. There was a naive acceptance in certain circles that it was okay to indulge because it was a young drug and people didn't think it could cause any damage. Nothing could be further from the truth.

I'm not going to be a hypocrite and start moralizing against drug use when I've taken them in the past myself, but people need to understand that if they use drugs it can have dangerous consequences. You might wake up one day and find that when you weigh everything up, you might have been better off never taking drugs in the first place. There's no doubt that as a society we are still paying the price today for the cocaine explosion of the eighties. But we are never going to solve the problem until we acknowledge one brutal fact: people take drugs because it makes them feel good. It's a form of self-medication. By 1984, John Taylor and I were certainly self-medicating in a major way. We'd even used cocaine to get us through the incident with his blood-soaked foot.

When you first start taking them, the drugs work. There's a time when it feels as if cocaine fills you with confidence, overcomes tiredness, and gives you the energy to get through the day. It doesn't last forever, and after a while it goes into reverse and the drugs start having the opposite effect—as we were about to discover. Drink and drugs may feel as if they help you to communicate and break the ice, but really, you're still hiding from whatever it is that stopped you from communicating in the first place. You might get away with taking drugs heavily for two or three years, but eventually there's a price to pay. That's when you start to wonder whether it was all worth it.

From around 1981 to 1985 I wrongly thought the drugs were working for me. Not every day to begin with, but I'd have the odd line in the recording studio during the late afternoon and early evening—and let's face it, being in a studio is not like operating a chainsaw, so you can get away with it. I'd even taken speed on the day we'd shot the "Girls on Film" video, and my drug use slowly became more regular. For the first six months that I was taking cocaine in 1981 I don't even think half the band knew, but when we recorded the *Rio* album and spent more time in London my drug use accelerated. We'd seen that drugs were rife in New York when we went to Studio 54 and a lot of people there were doing them openly, so it was inevitable that sooner or later the same thing would happen in the UK.

For a time I thought drugs even helped me to cope with the workload. Our record company would often expect us to get up early in the morning after a heavy night to do some promotional work, which you can easily manage to do for a few years even though you are living to excess. But eventually the drugs go into reverse. You become too weary to promote yourself for the fourth year running, and you start turning up at radio stations grumpy and tired. Suddenly the drugs are now making you ill and irrational. Your temper starts to fray and you become unpredictable. I remember on one occasion we were threatened with being banned from appearing on the BBC's *Saturday Superstore* because I swore at a caller. I felt he was being rude to me, so I told him to fuck off on the air—I wasn't in the mood to be diplomatic.

In John's case I'm not sure the drugs ever worked even in a superficial way, because his destructive behavior began at a very early stage, around the time he cut his hand in Germany in 1982. It's no coincidence that it was just a few months earlier that John and I had started to take cocaine together while we were in London and hanging out at the Embassy Club. After Al Beard's story appeared, Pete Townsend wrote an open letter to us in the press begging us to stay away from booze and drugs.

Despite the headlines, we were never a band that took drugs collectively. Drinking was something that we all did together, and I always liked to smoke dope or have a drink as a creative way of relaxing. Drinking as a band, after a show in the dressing room, or in the hotel bar, or even going out to a club and laughing together, was something we enjoyed doing. When Nick gets a bit wobbly-legged after a drink he can be very friendly and amenable; we all could. If we went to a restaurant we would order a bottle of Dom Perignon and lobster. "If you can afford it, spend it" was how we saw it. In contrast, any drug use that occurred tended to be furtive. But by the time we were in Australia putting the finishing touches to *Seven and the Ragged Tiger* in late 1983, John's cocaine use was secretly out of control and I was a heavy user, too. John and I even did coke together in the recording studio. On one embarrassing occasion someone found me staggering about next to a Coca-Cola machine. I was so wired that I actually thought I could get a line of coke from a vending machine.

John later confessed how bad things got for him. "It got to the stage where cocaine was literally given to me on a plate every day," he said in an interview published years later in the *Sunday Mirror.* "I was drinking every day and taking cocaine every day. I didn't eat that much. I took drugs—that was my diet. I convinced myself it was cool."

Not everyone in the band had the same attitude about drugs as John and I. Roger was never really inclined that way, and I hadn't seen Nick indulge in anything stronger than red wine since his health scare in Montserrat. Simon, however, did admit on record a few years later that he dabbled with some types of drugs, and I am not going to add to that—although clearly he never did anything on the same scale as John or I.

"I got involved in drugs more than most people I know. I loved some drugs," Simon said in an interview with the *Daily Mirror* in the nineties. "I enjoyed a very hedonistic life and had some great experiences, but drugs are dangerous and I am certainly not advocating people using them."

Dangerous is the right word, but it would not be until at least another year after the Al Beard story hit the newsstands that John and I would discover just how destructive drugs could be.

THE cocaine scandal had an immediate effect. The police pulled in our road crew and started to question all our top boys. They didn't touch any of us in the band because we were mainly out of the country, but from then on every time we returned to the UK we would be turned over by Customs. The indignity and hassle that Simon and

I had suffered at Heathrow a few weeks earlier started to become a regular occurrence. The Rum Runner was already experiencing problems with its license at the time the story appeared, but from this point on it was obvious that the police's main objective was to close the club down for good. On August 1, the Rum Runner's management found themselves before Birmingham's city magistrates and were fined after admitting to selling drinks without a license. DURAN DURAN WERE DEEPLY INTO DRUGS, said the headline in the *Daily Mail*'s report of the court case the following day.

"Pop group Duran Duran were alleged yesterday to be regular users of cocaine and cannabis in the nightclub which launched them to stardom," reported the paper.

"There is no question that members of the group were regular users of cocaine and cannabis as is common in that world, not only in their private lives but in the club also," solicitor Stephen Lineham told the court, according to the *Daily Mail*.

"The claims about Duran Duran will come as a shock," added the *Daily Mail*. "For it was the appeal of their clean cut image which three years ago set them off to international stardom . . . In July last year, Princess Diana said they were her favourite rock group."

The police activity at the Rum Runner continued. During another raid they eventually found what they were looking for, and seized some cocaine which had been discovered hidden behind a brick in the wall. They arrested an associate of the band. He'd been on the road with us at one stage to organize some of our merchandising. It was terrible, because in many ways he was just the fall guy. Meanwhile, the Rum Runner had a compulsory purchase order served on it. It was bulldozed to the ground and a Hyatt hotel was built on the site. The party was over.

A strange and unexpected postscript to the cocaine scandal was that it actually made us more acceptable to certain sections of the public. "The Reflex" sold better than ever, and we were suddenly seen in a new light by the *New Musical Express*. Nobody necessarily admired us for taking drugs, but the story humanized us because it made people realize we were fallible. It showed that we weren't perfect and that we had our flaws just like everybody else, and it gave us a gritty realism in some people's minds.

Drug use is very common in the music industry, so the people immediately around us were not actually that shocked. It's true that we had a young teenage audience, which sat very uneasily with the drug revelations. But we were all teenagers ourselves when we started out, and we didn't consider our audience to be younger than ourselves—and we certainly didn't ask to be role models. Drugs grew out of the circumstances that we found ourselves in, when really all we needed to do was to take a bit of time off to relax. But like I said earlier, there were no days off. It would eventually drive me to the brink of a breakdown and force John to go into rehab, but at this point all that was still in the future.

I always used to maintain that I never needed to go to rehab; I just needed to go home. At least back at home I always had Tracey, who remained the one constant in my life. She was unaffected by all the madness.

Or so I thought . . .

CHAPTER TEN

Wild Boys . . . and Darker Still

I need to slightly rewind the clock to the moment I arrived back in England following the stabbing incident at the Coca-Cola party in Los Angeles in April. As our car sped up the motorway through the darkness of the night to Shropshire, it felt as if the pressure of life in Duran Duran diminished with every mile that we traveled up the M1. Tracey was expecting our baby in August and our home life, for the time being, seemed settled and stable compared with the chaos that surrounded the band.

We had decided to stay at our cottage in Tracey's old neck of the woods so that she could be near her family when the baby arrived. I used the next few days to take stock of where my life was—and where it might be going. For the first time I began to wonder if things might actually be better outside of the band. We'd had a fantastic time and enjoyed enormous success, but was it starting to take an unacceptable toll on all of us?

The first person I confided in was my brother-in-law, Sean. We'd been out together at some of the fantastic old country pubs in the area, and it turned into a late-night drinking session that ended with us watching the sun come up. We were lying down in a cornfield looking up at the sky. I can see us today in my mind's eye, as if I'm looking down from above, with the vivid greens and yellow of the corn all around us. I'd been bottling up my feelings until now. They say that's what cocaine does. It cuts you off from your own emotions. It makes you bury things. It was the first time I admitted that I was starting to get very weary of life in the band.

"Would it surprise you, Sean, if I told you that I don't necessarily want to do this anymore? I don't know if I should stay in Duran Duran," I said.

I think Sean was shocked, as we had it all: money, success, fame.

"It's probably just something you are feeling because you are tired. You've been on the road for a long time," he said. "With Tracey being pregnant you'll need a break at some point. You probably just need a rest."

It felt good to talk to somebody, and I knew Sean had a good head on his shoulders. I decided to make a go of things. Now that the tour was out of the way, we mainly had just postproduction work to do on the *Arena* album, so it felt as if we had some breathing space. Roger and Nick both planned to use the spare time to get married over the summer. All of us were still tax exiles, which was part of the reason I was in France later when the Al Beard story broke, but I was hoping to spend as much time in England with Tracey as possible.

WITH all the births, marriages, and escapes from death that occurred over that summer, you might think there wouldn't be time for much else, but the other thing we managed to cram in was the video shoot for "Wild Boys," which took place prior to the weddings. The opulence and expense we went to on that video outstripped everything we had done until that point. Once again Russell Mulcahy was the chief architect. It was filmed during a ten-day shoot at Shepperton Studios, on the huge soundstage that had been built by George Lucas for *Star Wars,* and the cost was staggering.

The title of the song came from a William S. Burroughs novel that Russell had acquired the song rights to, so it was an unusual project because the idea for the video came along before the track itself. The book tells of how a gang of teenage marauders from North Africa terrorize a population, but when all the cocaine revelations started to emerge it seemed like a great song title for us. The first line starts with "The wild boys are calling . . . ," and people assumed it had been written about us. Underneath, I suppose it was, but on the surface it is based on the book. We were putting together the *Arena* album with footage from Toronto, the NEC in Birmingham, and San Francisco, and we needed an extra track.

"Let's go in the studio with Nile Rodgers and see if we can come up with something with Russell's Wild Boys idea," somebody said.

When we first started doing the track we set up a really interesting drum sound with Roger, and I had a little riff that I thought I could weave into it. The problem was that by this time I was mostly staggering into the studio drunk or flying high as a kite on cocaine, or both. By 10:30 at night I can remember standing up and trying to play guitar, but I'd had so much Jack Daniel's that I gave up.

"I'm going," I said. So we went down to the Cafe de Paris, where a group of us sat in one of the cubicles they have there.

When the time came to leave I tried to stand up and fell over. It was the first time I had gone out and gotten so plastered that I had to be assisted out of the place. It was also the first time that I didn't care what people thought anymore; I had enough bodyguards to carry me out. In those days there were very few paparazzi around, so I escaped being plastered all over the front pages. Fortunately, during the sober parts of the day we managed to come up with a good track with the help of Nile, who gave it a dance edge—but it took a few weeks to do.

When we came to shoot the video, the scale of the event was enormous—and Russell had bizarre plans for Simon.

"Simon I want you to be stripped and strapped to a revolving waterwheel, and you will then be fully submerged upside down as it rotates through the water," said Russell.

"You want me to do what?" said Simon.

It was a dangerous stunt, but we could all see that he secretly loved the idea of all the attention it would create. Fair play to Simon, he was always willing to do something if it would help the band, especially if it appealed to the natural showman in him. This was something we would all want to see.

AS well as the William Burroughs references, the subplot of the video was that we would have Milo O'Shea's original Durand-Durand character under the stage, snatching people into his dark underworld. There were a lot of men running about in loincloths, and it was all a bit too camp for me, but it was at a time when there was a lot of hedonism, drugs, money, and ambition to outdo anything that even Michael Jackson had done in a video. Russell had decided to really push the boat out. I was sitting in one of the dressing rooms at Shepperton when one of our accountants came in.

"I've just had to take ninety thousand pounds out of the account of each band member towards the cost of the shoot," he said.

"Ninety thousand pounds!" I winced. "Why does it have to be a ten-day shoot? What's the matter with five?"

With £90,000 from each of us the band's contribution added up to a cool £450,000, and with EMI's contribution at least matching it, the total bill for the video came to around £1 million. Don't forget this is at 1984 prices, so the idea of a band making something so extravagant today would be an impossibility; the economics simply would not work. I grumbled a bit about the cost at the time, but in hindsight we probably got our money's worth over the course of our lives, because it was such a memorable project.

As well as Simon being tied to a waterwheel, I was due to be strapped into a Superman-style harness so that I could swing back and forth through the sky, while Roger would be fired up and down on a jet pack. John was due to be tied up in a derelict car, and Nick, meanwhile, would stick to playing his keyboards in a cage. The set was enormous, with lots of big scaffolds, and there was a giant statue of a gargoyle-like character with a high forehead (which we joked looked a bit like Paul Berrow). At the end of the ten days, Russell planned to blow up the entire set in a giant fireball. Give the man some credit—he liked to go out with a bang.

One interesting departure from all our other videos up until now was that there were no girls in this one and there was a lot of comment at the time about how homoerotic it looked. One touch that I added was the ripped-jeans look—as far as I know we were the first to do it, so maybe that's my one contribution to fashion!

Simon's waterwheel stunt was the obvious highlight of the shoot. There had been a few injuries so far, with people falling from scaffolds and so on, but thankfully Simon came through it unscathed. There were two divers on hand the whole time in case anything went wrong, but it still must have been very scary and claustrophobic for him. A lot was made in the press about the fact the wheel stopped turning at one point while Simon was underwater and the papers assumed he'd been trapped and had to be rescued. I think it was more of a case that the wheel was always supposed to pause and arrangements had been made for Simon to breathe through an air pipe. It was actually a very complex stunt worthy of a Bond movie, and our very own "Simon Le Bond" performed brilliantly. The final video was breathtaking (quite literally in Simon's case), and the waterwheel scenes were very hypnotic to watch. It was released to critical acclaim, and it won a Brit Award for Best Music Video.

TRACEY and I were at home at our cottage when her water broke, and our son, Andrew, arrived right on time on August 20. It was a long delivery, but we were both elated. I was present at the birth, and the first thing I did after cutting the umbilical cord was to count every finger and toe! The midwives wrapped him up in this little white towel and handed him to me, the medical procedures were over, and we had a little baby to care for.

CHEEKY SMILE: An early photo from the Taylor family album of me as a baby in 1962.

SHARPSHOOTER: Here I am dressed as a little cowboy at the age of three in 1964.

All photos from the Andy Taylor Collection, except as noted.

ARMS ALOFT: A happy shot of me (above), taken while touring in 1982.

PHONE HOME: Simon Le Bon (below) pictured on the telephone at the flat we shared in Moseley in 1981.

LIVE GIG: Simon Le Bon (left), John Taylor (center), and me, onstage with Duran Duran during the eighties.
Photo by Brian Rasic/Rex Features

NEW ROMANTICS: An early shot of the band taken in London in August 1981, soon after the release of "Girls on Film." From left to right: Nick Rhodes, me (with blond hair, foreground), John Taylor, Simon Le Bon, and Roger Taylor.

Photo by Andre Csillag/Rex Features

ON SET: Me attending a photo shoot for the inside sleeve of *Rio*.

STARRY-EYED: Tom Sheenan, former *Melody Maker* photojournalist, with our *Rio* album cover.

FORTY WINKS: Nick Rhodes tries to grab a nap while on the road during an early Duran tour.

AUTOGRAPHS: Me (center) signing autographs for fans with Grant Hilton (left).

LAUGHTER: Me (left) with Russell Thomas (a colleague from EMI) and John Taylor (right).

THUMBS UP: Members of the band with bodyguard Simon Cook (center). From left to right: Simon Le Bon, Nick Rhodes, Simon Cook, and Roger Taylor.

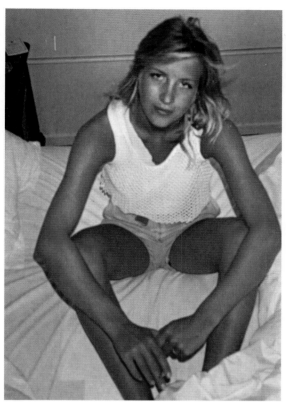

SOUL MATE: Tracey in San Francisco in 1982.

ON THE LINE: Me on the telephone while on the road in 1983.

BOW TIE: Me at some pre-dinner drinks in Australia in 1983.

THREE'S A CROWD: Mike Berrow (left) with me (center) and
Roger Taylor during the eighties.

"He's gorgeous," I told Tracey.

Nothing prepares you for the delicacy of holding a newborn baby. He was like a piece of fine bone china, and the first thing I thought as I sat down in a chair was *Christ—don't drop him!*

We had two bodyguards with us, and we kept the location of the hospital really quiet. I wasn't going to chance any repeat of the horrible incident Tracey had suffered at Heathrow. The local newspaper found out where we were, but they weren't intrusive and we went home safely with a midwife to our cottage. I found changing a nappy difficult at first, but you soon learn how to pick up the little legs and get on with it. As well as the midwife, we had a lot of help from Tracey's mum, who taught me how to sit a baby on my knee and burp him while you gently hold his neck with your other hand. It requires you to be completely gentle in your approach, and I found the whole thing mind-blowing.

Lots of Tracey's old friends lived nearby, and there was an extended network of people from the Midlands who were all there and all very happy for us. Sometimes it would get to eight in the evening and everything would be dead quiet, so I'd slip out to a great cider pub around the corner and wet the baby's head with a few close friends and family. I'd found a completely new form of happiness that was so different from anything I was used to in Duran Duran. I was still going back and forth to London, making plans for the release of *Arena* and "Wild Boys," but it was a big relief to know I had a beautiful family and my own tranquil little world away from the band.

LIFE then took a very dark and completely unexpected twist—and it made me realize that all the success and adulation can suddenly count for nothing when a loved one's life is in danger. Sadly, it is often only tragedy or the threat of it that reminds you that you are still human.

Tracey had been a bit tired in the weeks that followed the birth, but we both thought that everything was fine. In fact, she was about to become very sick and it would rock us both to the core. The only way I can describe what happened is that I came home one night and there was a different person in the house. At first I thought Tracey was just giving me a hard time about something or other, but she was swearing at me and behaving very belligerently, which was completely out of character.

"What are you talking about? Calm down," I said.

She seemed to be confused about who she was. She started to make up things that she claimed had happened to her in the past, including a horrific account of how she'd been attacked by a man. None of it was true, but I later found out that she was going through some experiences in her mind that were demonic and seemed very real to her at the time.

"Are you okay?" I asked, putting my hand on her arm.

"Get off," she growled, as she lashed her arm back. I could feel the strength in her as she pulled herself away from me and it scared me.

I thought maybe I'd done something to upset her, but then I noticed that her eyes had changed and I realized that something else was going on. To this day, I've kept two photographs of Tracey that were taken a few days apart. In one her eyes are beautiful and bright, sparkling with life soon after she gave birth to our son. In the second photograph, which was taken after she became ill, her eyes are dull and dead. Every time I tried to physically calm her by putting an arm around her, she became aggressive and her strength was frightening. I later found out that increased strength can be a side effect of psychosis. When I touched her hand it was so tense that she felt like rock.

"I'll make you a cup of tea and run you a warm bath," I said, hoping it would relax her.

Eventually I managed to get her in the bath and I went downstairs for about twenty minutes, wondering what to do. Our cottage was old, so I could hear everything upstairs. I heard the floorboards creak as she got out of the bath and went into the bedroom where our baby was asleep. A tiny little alarm bell started ringing inside me. I went upstairs and I found her standing at the open window with little Andrew in her arms. I spoke to her softly, but there was no reaction from her—she didn't seem to know what she was doing. Then the penny dropped and I knew there was something very, very badly wrong. She was completely unrecognizable, and for one fleeting moment I thought maybe she was possessed. I don't know what her intention was, but I was terrified she was going to jump.

"Give me the baby, Tracey, and come away from the window."

I tried to take Andrew from her but she wouldn't let me. I managed to move her away from the window and I closed it. As soon as I'd made things safe, I called Tracey's mother and I rang a doctor.

The medics knew what was wrong pretty quickly. The psychologist explained Tracey had suffered a nervous breakdown brought on by a full-blown postnatal psychosis. Many women experience postnatal depression, but only one in a million suffer something as severe as this. There was a danger it could become life-threatening.

"How long will it last?" I asked.

"The level of seriousness depends on the patient because it's a hormonal thing, but it could be up to eighteen months," explained the doctor.

Eighteen months! I felt that Tracey would be better off at home rather than in the local hospital, so we organized twenty-four-hour medical care. Our doctors made a decision to sedate her by putting her into an enforced coma for six days. It was for her own safety because she was so ill that her brain needed complete rest—and the only way to do it was to medicate her.

It felt as if everything in my life had just evaporated into ether. I looked at our little baby and I prayed Tracey would be okay. I couldn't think about anything else. Everything that happened to me up until now was insignificant compared to this. I was terrified that even if Tracey pulled through it would be too late for her to bond with our child. I'd seen enough to understand that a baby smells and feels its way through the first few weeks of its life with its mother, and any disruption could only be a bad thing. The lowest moment was when the doctors suggested that one of the treatments that could be suitable for her was electroshock therapy. It sounded like something from Victorian times.

"No thank you," I said. "There's no one else here who you can ask about that so don't mention it again."

For six long days and nights I helped the medics and my mother-in-law care for Tracey. The nurses worked in shifts. They told me it was important to get a routine going so that everything stayed as familiar as possible for Tracey when she briefly awoke from time to time. I ate breakfast and watched TV each morning, and during the breaks in her medication I would help to bathe Tracey whenever she roused a little. At one point the doctors had to put her on a drip to get some nourishment inside her and to keep her hydrated, so there was a lot of equipment up in the bedroom. We'd recently decorated the room for the arrival of the new baby, and now it looked like an emergency ward. Tracey's medication was increased during the evenings so that she could sleep for ten to twelve hours without being disturbed. I tried to cuddle her at night but she was all floppy. The nurses explained that she couldn't react to me emotionally because she was so heavily sedated. The only thing we could do was to look after her hygiene while her brain relaxed and the medication did its job. The whole point was to prevent her from reacting to anything and let her calm down.

Thankfully, it worked.

Slowly, the doctors reduced the medication and she started to come around. I held her hand and it felt gentle again. The anger was gone, and the woman I loved was back. She managed to hold a glass by herself for the first time in a week, and I knew she was going to recover. Food was still not easy, but slowly she began to improve and the dark rings around her eyes began to vanish. Once Tracey had calmed down, the doctors were able to balance her hormones by giving her drugs, and her condition began to stabilize. Inducing the coma had been necessary so the doctors could control her mental psychosis before they could start balancing her body. A lot more is known about how to treat the condition today than was known in 1984, but she pulled through.

It was a great relief when things started to return to the way they had been. I needn't have worried about her bonding with the baby; I only needed to watch her splashing with him in the bath to realize everything was fine. But the doctors warned us there was a danger the psychosis could return in the future.

"We don't advise you to have any more children or you could find yourself suffering again," the doctors told us.

I would sit and wonder what had brought on the illness. Was it anything to do with my lifestyle in Duran Duran? Being trapped in a car at Heathrow Airport while it was ransacked and she was pregnant couldn't have helped. Had the time Tracey spent with us in the States taken a heavier toll on her than I'd imagined? Was the furor over our cocaine use a factor?

The honest answer is that I don't know. It's a rare illness, but it can strike any woman after childbirth. Tracey never smoked while she was pregnant, and she has never been much of a drinker, so physically she didn't put any stresses on herself during pregnancy. In fact, she was a strong, energetic woman who went riding almost every day and kept herself very fit—and all those things helped her pull through.

One thing that the whole episode taught me was that your priority in life should always be your family and the health of your family. If ever that collides with work commitments you should always choose family first. Sometimes it can be hard to juggle both. There were times during this period when people would call me with updates and assessments of how our release plans for *Arena* were going and I'd think, *You know what? It's not that interesting to me at the moment. I've got more important things to care about.*

Tracey later told me that she had some very deep spiritual experiences while she was unconscious. She went through the sort of thing that you hear about people going through when they are very near to death. You can't really describe it unless you have been through it yourself so I won't try, but afterward Tracey became very religious. She hadn't been in danger of losing her life, but she had experienced what it was like to lose her mind. As a result her Catholic faith became very important to her, and she became close friends with a sister at our local convent. There was still a very nasty relapse ahead (which I will tell you about later), but Tracey eventually made a full recovery. She is now much more conscious of how important it is just to have a normal life—for her, being normal each day is a gift. We've been married now for over twenty-five years. Despite the warnings from the doctors, we have three more beautiful children, in addition to Andrew. Tracey is a healthy and well-balanced person.

She is also a very brave woman.

I explained about what had happened to Tracey to the rest of the band, but I don't think any of them really understood. To be fair, nobody from London had really been around us at the time, and I was glad to keep things separate from my life in Duran Duran. Tracey and I were more interested in slowly learning to stand on our own two feet again and learning all the things you need to know in order to bring up a baby—which is hard work even when you have plenty of help. I think I told John about it in a bit more detail than the others, who were mostly busy getting on with their own lives.

Everyone was managing their own affairs. I didn't know it, but at the same time I was questioning whether or not I wanted to remain in the band, Roger wasn't feeling too grand about it, either. He'd gotten married to Giovanna in Naples in late July, and the newlyweds managed to escape from the crowds by going on holiday to Egypt.

Nick's wedding, meanwhile, was a much more public affair. It had taken place at the Savoy Hotel in London two days before Tracey had given birth to our son. Everybody wore pink, including all the guests, and when we arrived at the hotel there were pens filled with pink flamingos. Nick's "best man" on the day was his ex-girlfriend Elaine Griffiths, and you had to hand it to him and Julie Anne—they knew how to cause a stir. I went to the wedding with Simon and his girlfriend Claire Stansfield, and the papers were full of speculation that they too would soon be wed. What they didn't know was that Simon would soon have his eye on an attractive young model named Yasmin . . .

So after the chaos of our US tour, everybody was really getting on with their own lives for a while. We all needed the breathing space.

We had less contact with each other than normal during the second half of 1984, although we still got together for the odd promotional event or TV appearance. One memorable occasion was when we recorded a Christmas edition of the BBC's *Pop Quiz,* with Mike Reid. The publicity about the rivalry between us and Spandau Ballet had gotten so great that the BBC begged us to go head to head with them on the show.

Neither band would ever live it down if they lost, so I had a quiet word with Jimmy Devlin, a legendary A & R man at EMI who knew everything about how to pull strings and plug bands.

"We can't get beaten by that bunch of tossers from London; we'll never hear the last of it," I told him. "We'll probably know how to handle the easy questions, but we need you to get the answers to the hard ones."

"Donnea worry," said Jimmy, who was a burly Glaswegian.

It was my idea, but he was happy to oblige. This was going to be a real-life case of "Jim'll Fix It"! A while later he came back to me with some great news: he'd secretly got hold of the answers for the final round. I sensed a major coup. On the day itself things had been ramped up so much that there were sets of fans of both bands queuing outside the BBC. John was our captain, but all five of us took part against all the members of Spandau Ballet. Nick answered our first question correctly to give us an early lead, but by the time we went into the third round both bands were dead even on fourteen points each. The finale ended on a cliffhanger with Mike Reid asking us a really obscure question.

Bing!

I thumped the bell and gave the correct answer—we'd won! You could see immediately from the faces of Tony Hadley and Gary Kemp that they knew they'd been stitched up. When Jimmy confessed everything to Tony Hadley a few years later, Gary Kemp came up to me afterward and laughed: "I always fucking knew you fixed it."

For us it had been a bit of a prank, but everyone took it totally seriously. Even today clips from the show still regularly pop up on YouTube—and our fans still argue with theirs about who deserved to win. Of course, Spandau never went on to crack America like we did, so all I will say is that Duran Duran might have been from Birmingham (which Spandau's manager Steve Dagger liked to claim would put us at a disadvantage), but at least we did our homework!

CHAPTER ELEVEN

The Power Station . . .
and Power Struggles

I was looking for a bridge to take me in a new direction, and I found it in the Power Station, the band that John Taylor and I formed with Tony Thompson and Robert Palmer during a gap in Duran Duran's schedule in late 1984. It was a very satisfying experience, so much so that John and I ran up a hotel bill of $450,000 while we were recording the Power Station's first album in New York (and that was without the tip!). Not surprisingly, the project itself didn't make us very much cash and neither did it stop us from being self-destructive, but it did give us a renewed focus, and for that I was grateful. The music that John and I made together in the Power Station was born partly out of frustration at not being able to play the way we wanted in Duran Duran. The memory of how painstaking it had been to record *Seven and the Ragged Tiger* was still fresh in our minds, so when the opportunity came along to do something different we seized it with both hands.

The first conversation I had with Tony Thompson about us doing some work together had occurred at the end of 1983, when John and I went to see him playing drums with David Bowie while we were in Sydney. Bowie had just released *Let's Dance*, which was a very influential album, and the drumming on it sounded phenomenal. We had the same agent as Bowie, so John and I were invited back to his hotel for a private party after the show, and it was all very friendly. Tony was one of those rare drummers, like John Bonham, who could create an individual sound of his own. John and I bumped into him in the loos, and we spent the rest of the evening chatting about music. He confirmed my suspicions that he was a big fan of John Bonham, and John Taylor and I both felt we'd made a good connection with Tony. He was famous as the black funky disco drummer from Chic, but he was really a rock drummer at heart. A member of Bowie's entourage came over and interrupted us while we were talking.

"David would like to talk to you downstairs," we were told, rather grandly.

I hope this doesn't spoil my fun, I thought. I'd learned pretty early on in life that meeting your heroes doesn't always live up to expectation. But we went downstairs and were introduced to Bowie. He was very opinionated and quite odd to talk to, but then I thought, *Well, he's supposed to be odd—he's David Bowie.* (No offense, David—most people who meet me say I am much shorter than they imagined!)

I didn't hang around too long. I went back upstairs with John and we carried on talking to Tony, whom I remember was drinking Seagram's 7 whiskey with 7UP soda, which he called a seven and seven. We obviously came from very different backgrounds, but we had all enjoyed a tremendous amount of success, and I think he was as fascinated by us as we were by him. He knew that Nile Rodgers, one of his former band members in Chic, had already agreed to mix a track for us. He was intrigued to know more. I would later discover that Tony was one of the funniest people I'd ever met; the man had a sense of humor, and when you worked with him you always knew he performed best when he was laughing. He was a very happy sort of guy. Nothing in the industry had really taken its toll on him like it had on John and me. He was just a big, powerful, superfit drummer with a great spirit. *I can work with this guy,* I thought.

"We are going to have to talk again," I said, when it was time to go our separate ways.

WILD BOY

When we eventually got together it was Tony Thompson who anchored the Power Station, not John or I. Tony was the true inspiration for the sound because he played the drums with alarming power; it was his loudness and his reflexes that originally inspired the whole thing. I heard from him again during the early part of 1984, while we were in New York.

"I want you to come and meet my good friend Bernard Edwards," he said.

We were staying at Le Parker Meridien and we had a meeting in the Black Suite there. It has walls that are painted completely black, so when you pull down the blinds you don't know what time of day or night it is. We explained to Bernard that even though John and I were already in a band, we were thinking of moving sideways with some of our music. I wanted to retain certain values of Duran Duran, but I felt it was time to change the rhythm of our sound and be a bit more creative, with a harder guitar edge. I had always wanted a slightly more rock-based sound than we'd had on the third Duran Duran album. Bernard was widely acknowledged as one of the world's top producers and everyone's favorite bass player, and he understood us in a way that only a good producer can.

"Okay, it's a deal. I'll come over to England and we will do some sessions together," he said.

So in late '84 Bernard, Tony, and I met up in the UK and went into the studio together. John wasn't around (I think he was busy out crashing cars), but I broke the ice by suggesting we start by doing a cover version of "Get It On" by T-Rex. I chose it because it was a song we all recognized, and it was something we could just play straight off. Together we came up with a new groove for it, and we were pleased with the way it started to shape up. Prior to forming the Power Station, John and I had already written and recorded an early demo of a piece of music in Paris, which John titled "Some Like It Hot." I played it to Bernard and Tony. We cut a new version of it together, without John's bass, and Tony's drumming brought the track to life in an impressive way. (Some of John's bass was added later on.) It was during this period that Bernard and I really hit it off. The drum intro at the beginning of the track was sensational, and we had to position thirty-seven microphones around the studio to get that echo sound that it became famous for.

When John surfaced he loved the results, and he enthusiastically sent a copy of "Some Like It Hot" to Robert Palmer, whom we knew from our Embassy Club days. John included a note saying we needed some lyrics for it. Robert listened to it on the beach at his home in the Bahamas, and he came up with a very clever vocal harmony for it on the spot.

"Listen to this, it's fantastic," John told us when he heard the results.

Everything was now set, and we arranged to start recording at the Power Station studios on Fifty-fourth Street in New York. It was an impressive building that had an elevator into which you could drive a limo and be taken up to the relevant floor. It was where Michael Jackson and all the rock greats like Bruce Springsteen went to lay down their material, and we decided to name our band after the studio. We were in Power Station Studio Three at the top of the building, and Mick Jagger was recording a solo album on a floor below us at the same time. Robert Palmer was in a booth with headphones on when Jagger walked in with Jeff Beck, who had been playing guitar with Mick. Robert didn't spot them and proceeded to perform a very complex set of lyrics for "Some Like It Hot." Jagger started hopping about in excitement, and we could see that Jeff was impressed, too. Soon more and more people started to trickle into the studio to listen to Robert sing, including the famous producer Arthur Baker and Nile Rodgers, and they were all hugged by Mick Jagger when they arrived.

"Come on. Come and listen to Robert Palmer sing," was the word that went around the building.

When Robert finished, he came out of his cubicle to discover a small crowd of his fellow musicians had gathered.

"Fookin' hell—a full house!" he said, displaying his dour Yorkshire humor.

Would he hug you like Jagger? Not Robert. It was interesting to observe the contrast between him and Mick, who was bouncing around just like he does onstage. Robert was calm and understated in his formal suit and tie.

"Oh yeah, man—that was great," clucked Mick enthusiastically.

Jagger's ears had also been pricked by Tony's drumming, so he asked Tony if he would be willing to do some drums with him, too, and Tony agreed. Tony would find humor in everything, and he would come back to us after a session and give us a progress report on Mick's antics.

"He's mad. He was doing all that stuff in front of me that he does when he's onstage," laughed Tony. He described how Mick would strut up and down like a giant cockerel. Apparently, Mick sang every number with great theatrics, even though there was only a bemused Tony and Jeff to appreciate his preening. Tony would be thinking, *Calm down, Mick!* That's the lovable thing about Mick Jagger: he's one musical hero who is *exactly* the same in the flesh as you imagine him to be.

We had a lot of fun of our own while we were recording. John's art-school credentials came out in him while he planned the album cover; in Duran Duran he'd been stifled by Nick, Simon, and EMI. I gave him free reign and didn't interfere. I, too, was allowed to really pursue guitar, so Tony and I were the noise in the band. John and I moved into the Carlyle, New York's most luxurious hotel, on East Seventy-sixth Street. Virtually every major politician or senior dignitary stayed there, including the Reagans. John and I enthusiastically set about working our way through the room-service menu, which contained just about every fine thing you could ever think of. Our suites were enormous, and whenever we decided to change them from time to time we would leave a little surprise for the next guest.

"Look at this, John," I said. I uncurled one of the suite's posh toilet rolls and drew a giant pair of breasts on it and scrawled a rude message, aware that the next guest to read it would probably be a head of state. It was childish, but fun!

The Power Station . . . and Power Struggles   199

The other thing we would do was to dismantle the toilet system itself so that it no longer flushed. We used to laugh hysterically at the idea of a world leader taking a dump, then having to call up maintenance and ask them to come and remove a turd. It was like we were reliving our Hyatt House antics from 1981 all over again. On one occasion the manager came and knocked on my door.

"Would you mind putting a towel under the door, sir? I am afraid it is rather noisy, and there is a bit of an aroma that's disturbing the other guests," he would say distastefully, referring to the pungent smell of marijuana that would often seep out from our suite. We were still indulging in bad habits at this point, and we had a man who would come to visit with a toolbox filled with every pill or substance you could imagine.

We would call room service any time of day or night demanding our laundry be done or to order some exotic food. Our rooms alone cost $750 a night, and with all the fine dining and extravagance it's no wonder that we ran up such a huge bill. We hammered the room-service menu so heavily that it almost became boring. I can remember sitting there with John one evening and looking down the endless list of fantastic dishes.

"Lobster?"

"Had that."

"Foie gras?"

"Had that."

"Truffles?"

"I'm sick of them."

Eventually we decided to order a Chinese carryout from the local fast-food joint instead, and we arranged for it to be delivered to the Carlyle!

OUR recording sessions at the Power Station would mainly start at 10 p.m. or midnight and go on until six or eight the next morning. But we were still recognized and photographed every time we went in or out, so we'd always dress in our full rock-star regalia. We caused a lot of attention. At one point a camera crew turned up with a woman and a baby, and they claimed the child was John's kid. Her story was soon proved to be false. A similar thing happened to me not long afterward, when I received a phone call from Jim Callaghan telling me that an underage girl had made a false allegation that I'd taken her back to my suite. Fortunately the hotel logs and my travel records proved she was lying.

Despite all the attention and high jinks away from the studio, Bernard Edwards always ensured that we stayed focused.

"What's the point of being here unless you record a song? Let's make an album quickly and then get the fuck out of here," he would bark. "Life's too short. It's only music and if you learn to play well you won't have to be here all day."

It was a good attitude and a good mixture of hedonism and focus, very different from the laborious plod of recording *Seven and the Ragged Tiger* with Duran Duran. When John and I had announced our plans to Simon and Nick, they'd been a bit prickly.

"Well, I'm going to be away sailing for a while, anyway," said Simon dismissively.

As far as I can remember there was never actually a row over it within the band, but Nick and Simon knew it had the potential to disrupt Duran Duran. They responded by announcing that they would be doing an album together called *So Red the Rose*, so two camps had now emerged. There were John and I on one side in the Power Station, and Nick and Simon in Arcadia on the other, with Roger (who was becoming increasingly weary of life at the center of the storm) floating in between. Both camps chose a hotel to set up their new headquarters, with us at the Carlyle, and Nick and Simon staying at the Plaza Athénée in Paris, where from all accounts Nick's lifestyle was just as extravagant as ours. From then on it became a bit of a challenge between us as to who could make the best album—and the power struggles with our record company began soon afterward.

"You can't do this," EMI bluntly told John and me. The person we were speaking to was someone I didn't even know, and yet here he was trying to order us around.

"Either call someone who gives a fuck or get somebody on the phone who knows what they are talking about," I said in reply.

But EMI stuck to their guns and said they would refuse to release our Power Station album. It reminded me of the struggle we'd had with Capitol over "The Reflex" because they considered it to be too black.

"This will really freak people out. Two white boys from a pop band and two black dudes from Chic. They won't be able to get their fucking heads around it," laughed Tony Thompson.

But on this occasion it wasn't about race, it was more about control.

"Right, well, if you won't release it we will take it to another label," I told EMI. John and I then did exactly that and approached an independent record company in New York. As soon as we did that, EMI caved in and we agreed to work with them. "Some Like It Hot" was released as a single and charted in March '85, around the same time as the album. We announced plans for a Power Station tour during the summer, and both the album and the single sold well. More important for me, I'd proved to myself that I could cut it outside of Duran Duran by doing what I loved best, playing guitar music. The Power Station made me very happy for a long time. Sadly, I don't think it did the same for John because he had too many personal demons to deal with and he didn't have the same creative relationship with Bernard that I had.

As for the $450,000 bill that we ran up during the six months or so that we lived on and off at the Carlyle . . . it was worth every penny.

THERE was, however, one nasty incident that occurred in early 1985 that served as a stark reminder of the problems we'd been through the previous year—and once again it concerned Tracey's health. While I was recording with the Power Station she had spent some time staying with friends down at Robert Palmer's place in Nassau, but in February Tracey went back to the UK.

"Why don't you catch the next Concorde over with a friend and spend some time here with me," I said.

Tracey agreed, but when she arrived and came to the studio, I noticed she seemed a bit withdrawn and didn't connect with any of the people there that we both knew. I assumed it was just jet lag, and I agreed when she said she'd go back to the hotel for an early night. I came in late and crashed out after a long recording session.

When I awoke the next morning I slowly became aware that there was no one else in the room and those little alarm bells started ringing inside me again: *There's no one here.* I sat up and realized Tracey was gone, which was completely out of character. I called the restaurant downstairs in case she had gone down to breakfast, but she wasn't there, so I rang the friend's room, but she told me Tracey wasn't there, either.

Fuck.

The illness was back. I called the cops and then gathered as many of our group at the hotel as I could find. Simon Cook, the trusted bodyguard who'd taken such a beating for us in Germany, was there, along with several other staff from London. Everyone went out to look for Tracey, and I told them to scout the whole of Manhattan. The police checked the security cameras, and they established that Tracey had left the hotel. Because we had already been through so much as a couple I didn't panic, but a voice inside was telling me to fear the worst.

Someone is going to do something fucking horrible to her, I thought.

It was midmorning. I knew that if we didn't find her soon we'd have to put it on the news in order to appeal for help, "The wife of the guitarist in Duran Duran is missing in New York City."

Fortunately one of our staff found Tracey wandering, dazed,

near Macy's department store. We discovered that someone had taken a bundle of dollars that had been in her pocket and replaced it with bundles of ripped-up newspaper. I thought, *If she has been attacked then whatever has happened we will get through it again.* But fortunately she was unharmed; she had just been mugged in a very passive way. She had suffered a relapse and was telling the same false story as before about being attacked by a man. This time the doctors were able to control her condition far more easily, and within about ten days Tracey was back to normal. But it had been a frightening scare.

NOT long afterward, John got to talking at a party to Albert "Cubby" Broccoli, the James Bond mogul.

"When are you going to get someone decent to do a Bond theme tune?" asked John.

It was a brash question (John was probably coked up to his eyeballs at the time), but they kept talking, and the next day John announced to the rest of us that Duran Duran would be doing the title track for the next Bond movie. John would often come back from a party and say something was going to happen, and nine times out of ten it would come to nothing. But on this occasion there seemed to be something to it, so we pursued it.

When we learned that the new James Bond movie, starring Roger Moore and Grace Jones, was to be called *A View to a Kill*, we thought, *Bloody hell—that's a great title for a Duran Duran song.* After all, the band itself was named after a character from a movie (which we exploited in the "Wild Boys" video) so this seemed to be another good film connection. I was slightly apprehensive about going back into the studio with Nick after all the freedom we'd enjoyed on *The Power Station,* but recording a Bond theme tune was too good an opportunity to miss.

"Let's do it with John Barry, he does all of the Bond theme tunes. He'll put the Bond into the band," suggested someone.

"Yeah, we'll do that," replied John.

John Barry turned out to be a hilarious character. He was a very posh old composer who played the piano with a tumbler of whiskey by his side. John Taylor and I were both heavily into booze ourselves at the time, and we set about heavily leading him astray with more drink. There was a great little pub just down the mews street from where John Barry was based, and we would all disappear there for long afternoons. Pretty soon after our first meeting, John came up with a wisp of a tune for the opening part of the song.

"I think we have got a start here," said Simon hopefully.

Simon worked on it a bit more with John Barry, and they came up with the first line, "Meeting you, with a view to a kill." Roger and I then developed a hybrid drum/electro sound that sounded great and Simon added the chorus. Originally he sang it as one flowing line, "Dance into the fire."

"No," I said. "It's not quite right. Try putting a pause into the line for a drumbeat. It's 'Dance. *(boom)* Into the fire.'"

Simon sang it again, leaving a pause, and it sounded right. We knew we had another Duran Duran hit on our hands.

Working with Nick, however, was not so easy. He absolutely hated cocaine, so he wasn't appreciative of JT's and my behavior. He seemed to regard us in much the same way as he had during the *Seven and the Ragged Tiger* sessions.

"It doesn't matter if you have got a great song—you've done it in a way that I don't like." That seemed to be his general attitude toward us.

Nick seemed to be resentful of the whole project because it was organized by John Taylor. At times it was impossible for all of us to be in the studio together without having a row, and it was Nick who seemed to be swimming against the tide. John Barry challenged him a few times about things he'd done musically, which seemed to annoy Nick.

"I'm fucking not doing that," Nick would say flatly.

"You can say all you want, but I know what I am talking about and at this time, you don't," said Barry in his posh voice. "I've worked with people like Shirley Bassey and Roger Moore, and this is *my* gig, young man."

Simon, the eternal optimist as ever, did his best to make peace between the warring camps. But this was a power struggle that deep down we should all have known could only end in tears for Duran Duran.

THE record label didn't have to think very hard about "A View to a Kill." They just put their stamp on it and watched it fly out of the shops until it became the best-selling Bond theme tune of all time. John had been right to be so brash to Cubby Broccoli.

For the video, we approached our old friends Godley and Creme, who'd directed our "Girls on Film" video in 1981. The plan was to hire the Eiffel Tower for the morning and shoot a series of gravity-defying special sequences. I was to play a character called Agent Spiff, who was pretending to be blind with a white stick (that was Godley and Creme's Northern humor). In truth, I wanted to get it over and done with after all the friction in the recording studio, but there was a big nasty incident at the Plaza Athénée before I got a chance to flee Paris.

A couple of days prior to the Eiffel Tower shoot I was talking to Ronnie Wood, who was recording with the Stones at EMI's famous Pathé studios in Paris. He invited me down, and I accepted. I'd always wanted to go and see the Rolling Stones recording, because their studio setup was legendary. My intention was to go alone, but on the night a little posse of us went, including John. When we got there we found a small crowd of people already hanging out. I was in the guitar room admiring all the Stones' instruments with Ronnie, when Keith Richards arrived in a foul mood.

"Oh yeah—down here on a fucking coke deal are you? Well, get it out then," he snarled.

I'm going to have to give him a line and I'll make it a right big one, I thought.

"You lot are just down here for a line of fucking coke and a mooch about," he repeated aggressively.

"No, no. Keith, it's all right," said Ronnie.

I chopped out a line of cocaine for Keith and it seemed to pacify him. I'd known what to expect from him, because he'd been obnoxious to Simon when we'd all met previously, and Keith felt so bad about it afterward that he wrote Simon an apology. Despite the hostile reaction from Keith, it was amazing to see the Stones' studio. Everything was perfect, from the bar stocked with ice to the instrument cages that contained all their beautiful old guitars. Bill Wyman wasn't there, but it didn't seem to bother any of them. They just swapped instruments around and all got on with each other. *God, I wish our band was like that,* I thought.

I just wanted to sit in the corner and enjoy the rawness of it all. They were a real band's band. But as the night wore on I could see that John was all over the place, and he started making a real spectacle of himself. At first he was just swaying all over the place and going "woo whoooo," but after a while he started to get very emotional about something. I don't know whether or not one of the Stones said something to upset him, but he ended up crying his eyes out on Jo Wood's shoulder. Jo was used to dealing with mad rock stars, but I thought, *Shit, I wish I had come on my own.* Keith Richards might have behaved obnoxiously, but he was right—most of the people present were just there for "a mooch," and they didn't have any real interest in what was going on.

"Come on, John, let's go," I said.

I went off to a club in Paris with Nick and his wife one night around this time, but the things between us went from bad to worse. Julie Anne got up on the dance floor on her own, and it seemed to make Nick a bit moody.

When we got back to the Plaza Athénée all hell broke loose.

From what I could gather, Julie Anne locked Nick out of their suite and she barricaded herself inside. She was screaming at the top of her voice out on the balcony, and it caused a big commotion, because some people feared she might fall off.

The whole thing then descended into a farce when the fire brigade were called. I was feeling the worse for wear by now, and I watched Nick charging up and down the corridor, not knowing what to do next. Despite our differences I felt sorry for him, as his marriage was clearly not going to be a happy one. They'd had a blazing row and the following day his new mother-in-law and father-in-law flew over from the States.

When I woke up early the next morning, the day before the Eiffel Tower shoot, a wave of depression hit me as I recalled all the events of the last few days. I felt embarrassed at the memory of John staggering around at the Stones session, and I felt exhausted by the nastiness of the commotion at the hotel. Suddenly, I was uncontrollably upset and I kept crying.

This can't go on, I thought.

That's when I made up my mind that I'd do the Bond video and get the hell out of there. I called one of our accounting staff whom I was friendly with and confided to him how badly I was feeling. The booze and the drugs and the carnage that surrounded Duran Duran were all just too much. I knew I was fast heading for a nervous breakdown if I didn't change my lifestyle.

The next morning I got up at five, put on my dark sunglasses, and went to the video shoot. I left the Plaza Athénée soon afterward and I've never been back since, didn't even want to walk in there again.

Looking back, when John and I formed the Power Station prior to "A View to a Kill," Duran Duran had already split up.

We just didn't know it.

CHAPTER TWELVE

Live Aid: The Final Curtain

I wasn't looking forward to Live Aid. Sure, the scale and the grandeur of the event was something that I wanted to experience. But by the time we gathered in Philadelphia I was apprehensive about seeing Simon and Nick again. I think we were all starting to feel very frayed one way or another, particularly Roger. He was always very much the quiet man of the band, but somebody whom I respected immensely. I think the pressure of the constant attention, the touring, the traveling, and the whole circus just became too much for him and he started to become agoraphobic. He was naturally quite a shy person, and he began to dislike being involved in promotional appearances for our *Arena* album. Years later, I asked Roger how he'd been feeling at this point.

"I was hanging on by my fingernails," he said.

Roger was right. The whole band seemed to be hanging on by our fingernails.

We were recording with John Barry in his mews house in Kensington when the call came in from Bob Geldof asking us to take part in Live Aid. We'd already sung on the Band Aid single, which had raised funds for starving people in Africa, and we'd also appeared in the video the previous Christmas, so we were top of Bob's list for his grand plans that summer.

"I'm going to organize a great big fookin' gig like you have never seen, and I need you boys to come on board first," he said. "You're the only UK band with any sales in America, so if you come on board it means America will come on board."

I wasn't much of a fan of Bob at the time. I thought he was a bit of a gobby Irish singer whose band hadn't achieved much, but you had to admire his determination. We'd had a bit of a laugh shooting the Band Aid video, because we'd been in Germany the night before with Billy Idol. We had been playing out there at the same time. We'd all gone back to the same hotel, only to be told the restaurant was closed and room service was finished for the night. Rather than go to bed hungry, we waited for the hotel staff to bed down for the night, then some of us crept downstairs and raided the kitchens. We spent the night helping ourselves to everything in the pantry, all washed down with copious amounts of booze. The next morning I was so hungover that we nearly missed the plane taking us to London for the Band Aid shoot. If you watch the video closely you'll see I'm wearing a hat because I wanted to hide how scruffy and hung-over I looked! I wasn't the only one a bit worse for wear; the guys from Status Quo kept everyone amused at the shoot with some boozy antics of their own. The episode had been a brief interlude of fun away from the usual hassle, so initially I hoped Live Aid might be the same. I was wrong.

After doing "A View to a Kill," John and I were busy with our Power Station tour. We took a bit of a blow when Robert Palmer pulled out, saying he couldn't spare the time. We were determined to go ahead, though, and we asked Michael Des Barres if he would take Robert's place. The Power Station was still going to be my bridge out of the madness, with or without Robert. One thing I was determined to do was to make a clean break from the Berrows, who I remained unhappy with over the large slice of our earnings that they were entitled to under the terms of our contract with them. To my mind they were one of the causes of a lot of the madness, always driving us on to do more shows, public appearances, interviews, and dire projects like the embarrassing video for "New Moon on Monday." And all the time they were earning more and more money for us to pay for their gleaming new Ferraris and expensive escapades abroad. So it was around about this time that I checked through all the paperwork and realized there was a legal way I could sever my ties with them.

Under our deal with the Berrows, they owned some of the rights to our music, which was something I couldn't change, but there was a time clause that allowed me to employ my own management after five years. It meant that even though the Berrows still owned some of our publishing rights, I no longer had to work for them directly. It had the potential to get messy, but I eventually phoned them up and told them of my intentions. John was in agreement with me and I phoned the Berrows up from his house.

"You don't represent me anymore. Your five years are up—you're fired," I said.

Of course, the Berrows still looked after the others (until 1986, which I'll come to later).

I knew some of the other band members were beginning to feel the same way as John and I, but the sticking point was going to be Simon, who was much closer to the Berrows than the rest of us. Simon had two big passions in his life at this point: his future wife, Yasmin, and sailing—which was something he had in common with the Berrows, who shared his nautical ambitions to sail around the world. Together, they'd purchased an expensive yacht called *The Drum*, and they intended to enter the Fastnet yachting race on some of the most dangerous seas in the world. To me it was just another of the Berrows' daft plans, like the time one of them had tried to build a lasting temple in Sri Lanka. Coming from a fishing family, I knew the sea was something to treat with respect. Simon's plans to sail around the world would also mean him taking off the best part of a year, and I knew the chances of us resolving our differences with the Berrows while he was away with them were very remote.

When I raised it with Simon, it exploded into a spectacular row.

"I think we need to reconsider our contract with the Berrows. Things are not working the way they should be," I said.

"No, it's all right. Everything is okay, it will be fine," insisted Simon.

His optimism would never dampen, but on occasions like this it would infuriate me. Simon is a kind, decent person, but at times he gets lost in Le Bon Land. *Which Simon have we got here today?* I wondered. *The one from the real world or the one from Le Bon Land?*

"Take the blinkers off, Simon. Everything is not okay. It's not okay to feel like this," I argued.

"Oh mate, come on. You just need to calm down a bit," Simon replied calmly.

Don't give me that big brotherly "I am the oldest" load of shit, I thought. *Take the blinkers off, Simon. Don't address me and my problems until you've addressed your own.* As far as I was concerned, he shouldn't have been taking a year off and going on a boat with the Berrows. It just opened the door up to make everyone else feel contemptuous of both him and them for leaving the rest of us behind.

"Well I want to do it," said Simon flatly, his expression hardening.

"So we've got to wait for you to take a year off? I want to get rid of them and you are protecting them," I shouted.

"Well, I am doing it," said Simon sternly.

I lost it completely: I used some very blunt language along the lines of accusing Simon of wanting to "wank off around the world with them on a fucking boat."

"Well . . . I am doing it!" he roared.

YOU can understand why there were a few awkward silences when we got together for the Live Aid rehearsal in Philadelphia. We were at number one in America with "A View to a Kill," and we were about to perform at the biggest show on Earth, but you wouldn't have known it from our demeanors. Physically, John and I were lean and concert-ready from being on the road with the Power Station, but Simon seemed bloated and distracted. Roger was suffering in his own private hell and Nick was . . . well, Nick was just Nick. The five of us hadn't been on the road together since San Diego the previous year (the night of the stabbing at the Coca-Cola party), and when we started playing together it showed. There seemed to be scores of people whom we didn't know milling around at the rehearsal.

"Excuse me," I shouted into a microphone. "Can everyone who is not actually working please fuck off out of the room." It was something I'd learned from the Keith Richards School of Charm.

The next morning—the day of the show—I awoke in my hotel room and had breakfast in bed while watching the TV. Live Aid had steamrolled into being an enormous phenomenon. There were events all around the world to raise money for the starving in Africa. The principal gigs were at Wembley Arena in London and at JFK Stadium in Philadelphia, and virtually every major artist in the rock world was taking part. It was a culturally defining moment, like Woodstock had been a generation earlier. The day raised millions and it saved lives—but whether or not the awareness and the goodwill that it generated had any lasting good is another matter, because twenty years later Africa is still in poverty. Like I said at the beginning of this book, half the world watched the show while the other half starved.

Because of the time difference between London and Philadelphia, I was able to watch the opening act at Wembley from my hotel room before we left for JFK Stadium. Status Quo were first onstage in London, and their rousing performance reminded me of their antics at Band Aid. When it was time to leave my hotel I went down and got into our limo. As well as with Duran Duran, John and I were performing with Tony Thompson in the Power Station that day—and in turn Tony was due to play drums with Phil Collins and Led Zeppelin. So in our entourage we had elements from three groups: Duran Duran, the Power Station, and Led Zeppelin. We were joined by Danny Goldberg, a very shrewd LA showbiz agent who'd agreed to look after my affairs now that the Berrows were soon going to be off the scene.

It was a sunny day, and there were crowds thronging about on the streets everywhere. Inside our limo the five members of Duran Duran sat in silence, as if we were going to a funeral. I suppose that in a way we were, because Live Aid was our final curtain. Only Danny and Tony Thompson spoke occasionally to break the ice. Tony was trying to crack the odd joke, but I think even he could sense the tension.

The bustle behind the scenes at the gig bordered on mayhem, with trucks and trailers parked up as far as the eye could see behind the stadium. Ronnie Wood and Keith Richards gave us a good laugh when they turned up drunk and fell out of their limo. I spent most of the time backstage gulping white wine and eating Domino's Pizza; there was no fancy catering. Bill Graham, a powerful American music promoter who'd famously played a rock promoter in *Apocalypse Now*, was calling the shots. When the time came for John, Tony, and I to go on stage with Michael Des Barres in the Power Station I pulled in my guitar and . . . boom. Both amps were dead.

Shit.

I am about to appear at the biggest show in history and I can't play a note. I turned to Keith, my technical assistant.

"What are we going to do?"

"Give me ten minutes," he said.

"I haven't got ten minutes."

I could hear the roar of the crowd. The two noisiest audiences in America are usually Seattle and Philadelphia, and today Philly was really up for it. Then, above all the cacophony of noise I heard Bill Graham shouting.

"What the fuck is happening? We've got to get this show on the way!" he bellowed.

I looked at Keith. Suddenly he went charging off and grabbed one of Jimmy Page's amps from the Led Zeppelin crew.

"Can I borrow this?" he said, and grabbed it before waiting for an answer.

Keith and the crew carried out the amp and I plugged in my guitar. Every second counted to prevent the audience from becoming impatient. I spoke to one of the other technical staff in the live broadcast truck to explain to them they'd have to make some adjustments.

"We are off the rig, just crank it up," I shouted.

We managed to get everything working after four minutes and we performed "Get It On," "Some Like It Hot," and "Murderess," but we had to drop one number to make up for lost time. When I came offstage Bill Graham was still ranting.

"Why don't you shut up?" I shouted at him.

"Steady on, Andy," Jim Callaghan said to me. He was aware of how powerful Bill was, but I was past caring.

The rest of the day flew by. The other memorable event was Simon's squawked bum note during "A View to a Kill." In hindsight, it's possible his voice wasn't fully trained at the time because he'd been off the road for so long, but I wasn't too bothered by that either. Back at the hotel that evening I crashed into bed after partying with Ronnie Wood and Jimmy Page. The shenanigans were still going strong downstairs, but when a knock at the door came from one of the crew inviting me back out I couldn't take it.

This time the party really was over.

THE following day I gave up drinking. I got up and went to lunch with Danny Goldberg and explained the way I was feeling.

"You know, I need to get out of this," I said.

"Everything?" he replied.

"Well, I need to get out of the lifestyle, at least," I said.

Danny was a very intelligent guy. He helped me to unravel things and he gave me a lot of advice. He'd been Led Zeppelin's publicist for many years and he had traveled with them, so he was a seasoned old pro (he went on to represent Kurt Cobain). Danny was currently managing Don Johnson and Michael Des Barres. Don was very clean-living and he knew Steve Jones. Steve, my Sex Pistols pal from LA, had now decided to quit the bottle.

"Talk to Michael and Don," advised Danny.

From that point on, Danny helped me with lawyers and everything that I needed to extricate myself from Duran Duran. Of course, as far as the rest of the world were concerned, Duran Duran were still a group and we were at the height of our success, but behind the scenes things were now too badly fractured for the five of us to carry on together. John and I were still in the middle of the Power Station tour (we'd had to cancel a couple of gigs at a cost of around $250,000 in order to do Live Aid), so I still had a bit of time on the road ahead of me before I could go to LA to sort things out with Danny. It felt strange to be sober and on tour. Up until now John and I had been living on a diet of Jack Daniel's, cocaine, and fast food. I'd become cut off from the real world, and I had very little idea of current affairs or even about what was going on in the world of football back home, which was previously something I'd always kept in touch with. Being in Duran Duran had become like being sucked into some weird alternative reality in *The Lion, the Witch, and the Wardrobe*.

I was getting ready to go and do a sound check for a Power Station gig in the States when I turned on the TV news in my hotel and got a bizarre shock. There on the screen in front of me was footage of a yacht floating upside down in the sea.

"*. . . And once again the latest shocking news . . . A yacht belonging to Duran Duran singer Simon Le Bon has capsized in rough seas. The singer is believed to have been on board.*"

At first I was a bit numb. *This isn't real: that can't be Simon's boat,* I thought. I rang John in his room.

"Put the television on," I said.

The news bulletin didn't have any more details. Was Simon still alive? Was he still missing or had he been rescued? Who else was on board the *Drum* when it turned over? A million questions were going through my head, and any differences between Simon and me were

obviously forgotten at this moment in time. The sea looked dangerous and stormy in the grainy television images, and I knew from my
background in a fishing village that nobody could survive for very
long in seas like that. Our staff began calling Europe to try and get
more information, and we began to make plans to cancel that night's
show. Hell, if Simon was dead we'd cancel the whole tour and be on
the first flight back to the UK. Fortunately, news reached us fairly
quickly that he had been rescued. *You were stupid to go out to sea,
Simon, but thank God you are safe*, I thought.

In a funny sort of way the *Drum* incident was just another example of how the lifestyle threatened to destroy all of us. In fact, I
was convinced that someone would end up dead if we all continued
the way we were going. Another one of our nine lives had been used
up. After the tour ended, I told John how I felt while we were in a
car together in LA.

"You know, one of us is going to die," I said quietly.

"What are you talking about?" said John.

"If we keep going like this we are going to die. It could be a drug
thing, it could be an alcohol thing, or it could be something else.
Simon nearly killed himself on a fucking boat."

John didn't seem to grasp what I was saying.

"Look at us," I said. "We've been living on a diet of cocaine and
Big Macs. You should quit this lifestyle and be an actor. It doesn't
agree with you."

"What the fuck do you mean, I should be an actor?"

"You should give up being in Duran Duran and be an actor—
it's what you are good at. How many more times does something bad
have to happen? Car crashes, bad drug comedowns, arguments,
drunken bust-ups . . . How many more do you need before one of
us goes all the way?"

When you are sober, you come out of denial, and I knew that
we were close to losing everything. It wasn't just people in the band
who were living on the edge, it was those around us. Sooner or later
someone was going to pay the ultimate price. It could have been

Nick's wife falling off a balcony, or it could have been my wife through postnatal depression. Or what would have happened if the next time there was a stabbing at a party the knife went through someone's heart or lungs? What if one of us got alcohol poisoning or ran out of luck the next time we were racing to a gig and a tire blew? Up until now the booze and drugs had prevented me from seeing any of this, but we'd reached a crossroads and it was time to change direction. Simon nearly proved my point a few months later when he crashed his motorbike and spent six days in the hospital with bruised testicles. Ouch. Yet *another* one of our nine lives gone.

Roger, meanwhile, seemed to have reached a similar conclusion to mine near the end of the year. EMI had been anxious to keep a lid on things, so officially all five us were still in Duran Duran, but in December Roger announced he was quitting. He was suffering from severe anxiety and, unbeknownst to the rest of the band, he had become very ill. He was just burned out by the whole thing and he was later quoted in the *New York Times* as saying "I'd been on a thousand airplanes, but I didn't know how to get on one as an individual. I had to relearn life."

Only Simon and Nick seemed to want to soldier on. As well as Roger quitting, the other major event in December of that year was that Simon married Yasmin. As far as the press were concerned it was a marriage made in Heaven: the pop star and the gorgeous Persian model. I think his newfound love probably saved Simon from the sort of demons that the rest of us were facing. He'd always stayed positive, and in Yasmin he'd found a very smart girl. Years later (after we patched things up) I became friends with Yaz, and Simon won't mind me telling you that she's the one with the balls in the Le Bon household. She's super-intelligent and always argues her corner very well if you're debating something with her. Simon was later quoted as saying that he first spotted Yasmin's photograph when he was flicking through a model agency book with John. He was besotted from the moment he saw her and later managed to track her down and ask her for a date. He chose very well because as well as being a famous supermodel, she is sharp, witty . . . and a great cook. Their ceremony was a grand affair and it was nice to be going to Simon's wedding when we could so easily have all been going to his funeral. Simon told us how he'd feared his oxygen would run out while he was trapped in the upside-down hull of *The Drum* with his brother Jonathan, who is a very fit lad and a strong swimmer. Jonathan volunteered to swim underwater through all of the oil, shit, and ropes that were thrashing about in the sea in order to get help.

"I had to watch my brother go, knowing that I might not see him again. I also knew that if I didn't see him again I would be dead," confided Simon.

Thankfully, Jonathan had made it, and he'd been able to help rescuers pinpoint exactly which part of the hull Simon had been trapped in. Unfortunately, just like *The Drum*, Duran Duran was now almost beyond salvage.

We made one last attempt to find a way forward. I had to go to London to sort out some business and the four of us—Simon, Nick, John, and I—all met at a loft flat I owned in Wanstead. There had been a lot of legal wrangling and I had disingenuously given the others the impression that I was willing to carry on because I couldn't be bothered to have it out with them. I wanted to avoid a confrontation, but I knew it was very unlikely we would work something out.

It was a fairly friendly meeting, but we were just propping things up. Simon and Nick wanted to carry on with plans for a new album, but I argued we should take a rest. In my mind, I ran through where each of us was in life. Nick was locked in an unhappy marriage (given that he later divorced) and his long-term finances were far from healthy due to his lavish lifestyle. In 1994, the mansion he shared with Julie Anne in South Kensington was repossessed by Coutts bank. Meanwhile, I'd been close to a nervous breakdown and had nearly lost my wife. John was in danger of slowly killing himself through drugs, and Roger was no longer there. Only Simon seemed unscathed, thanks to the renewed vigor he'd been given by Yasmin, but even he seemed to have a death wish for crashing boats and motorbikes. I thought to myself that the band had only existed over the last year for the purpose of propping up Simon's boats, propping up Nick's new debts, and propping up John and me with drink and drugs.

Despite my feelings, the meeting ended amicably, but things were still unresolved. Eventually, Simon and Nick called in Nile Rodgers to play on the new Duran Duran album, *Notorious*. There was talk of legal action against me if I refused to also take part and eventually I agreed to come to the studio and play on a few tracks to make the transition a bit smoother.

When I arrived at the studio on a Saturday morning, as arranged, there was no one there apart from a French sound engineer.

"Where is everyone?" I asked.

"Oh, it was Grace Jones's birthday party last night so they are probably still sleeping it off."

Great. I go to the trouble to come here and help out against my will, and no one can even be bothered to turn up because they are all out partying with Grace Jones (who was the girl of the moment after starring in *A View to a Kill*).

I opened up a guitar case in the studio and out fell a bag of cocaine.

That just about sums things up, I thought. I plugged in my guitar, played a few tracks with the French engineer in order to honor my contractual obligations, and then I left to phone my lawyer.

It was over.

So what was it that caused Duran Duran to split in 1986? Booze and drugs? Creative tension and personality clashes? Legal arguments with the Berrows over cash? Our relentless schedule and the pressures of twenty-four-hour attention? All of these played a part, but in the end it boiled down to two things: we had stopped communicating with each other and we were exhausted.

Our dissolution wasn't caused by people. It was caused by the circumstances that we found ourselves in.

CHAPTER THIRTEEN

Beyond the Power Station: The LA Years—*Ooh La La*

TRACEY and I moved to a beautiful little house in Los Angeles, and it felt like we were slowly letting out the air that we'd been bottling up over the previous two years. It was our way of making peace with ourselves after all the stresses and mayhem of having to hustle through crowds of camera crews and screaming fans every time we went out in public. Of course, I was still recognized everywhere we went, but I soon discovered that in LA you can find a man to solve any problem. In a town full of Hollywood stars there's always someone to talk to who understands your needs and who has probably been through similar experiences to your own.

I was out walking one day when I found this wonderful wooden house in Malibu on the top of a hill, facing out across the ocean. It was a beaten-up old property that would need a lot of love and attention, but the view was exquisite. As I sat there, on the top of the hill looking out across the beautiful blue waves of the Pacific, I thought: *Wow—this is perfect.*

Tracey and I had a child to think about now as well as ourselves, and I sensed that living in the United States would give us the breathing space that we needed. We'd been grateful for the help and support of Tracey's family back in the Midlands in the UK, but if you're trying to cope with being trapped in the glare of the international spotlight, there aren't many people who can advise about that sort of thing in Wolverhampton. America was the natural choice for us to make.

I'd taken Danny Goldberg's advice to speak to Don Johnson and Michael Des Barres about how to take stock of things, and they both helped me throughout this period in my life. Don was a very interesting guy and I learned a lot from him. He was by far the biggest TV star in America at the time due to his role as gun-toting cop Sonny Crockett in *Miami Vice,* but he seemed to just naturally cope with all the attention that he created, and he accepted it all with good grace. Don was a little bit older and wiser when it came to taking things in his stride. He was fascinated by the music industry and we became good friends.

Later on, Don took me down to Miami, and it was like hanging out with a king because everyone in the city respected him so much. I can remember stopping at some traffic lights with him there while he was driving an open-topped Beemer. Suddenly, all the cars around us started to sound their horns in order to say hello: *beep, beep, beep!* We were quickly surrounded by well-wishers . . . but nobody banged on the car or tried to ransack the vehicle, like they'd done when Tracey was in a car at Heathrow. Instead, it was just hilarious. Everywhere we went there were cries of, "Hey—it's Sonny Crockett!" I thought I'd experienced it large up until now, but this took things to a whole new level. What was all the more amazing was that Don didn't always have twenty-four-hour security around him. Often he just dealt with it on his own. Of course, he was sober and together enough to be driving and looking after himself—something which I hadn't been for quite a while. At times in Duran Duran I'd have struggled to remember my car keys, let alone be in a fit state to drive—had I ever learned to drive in the first place!

Don did everything he could to accommodate me. He and I spent a lot of time talking about music because he was keen to learn how things worked in the industry.

"Andy, I am interested in how you approach making an album," he told me.

"Well, that's good, because I am interested in how you cope with things so well," I joked.

I soon discovered that Don was planning a solo record of his own and that he actually had a very good singing voice. Later on I did a bit of guitar playing for him on his album, but for now the immediate concern for Tracey and me was to set up our new home together. After completing the Power Station tour in LA, I had arranged for an extension to my visa in order to stay on in the States. Prior to finding the house in Malibu, Tracey and I stayed with her mum at the Chateau Marmont, where we had previously gotten married. We then moved into the Beverly Hills Hotel for a couple of months. During this time there was no booze, no drugs, and no need for things like the vitamin boost jabs that had helped to keep me going while I was on the road. Instead of bingeing on cocaine and Big Macs, I was living on salad, soup, and chocolate pudding, surrounded by a strange quorum of friends who formed a sober triangle, consisting of Don, Michael Des Barres, and Steve Jones (although it wouldn't last for long). It was around this time that I found the little wooden house in Malibu while Tracey was temporarily back in the UK to visit friends. When she got back to the States I couldn't wait to show it to her. At first she hated it!

"I don't like this, it's horrible—look at the state of it," she said.

Tracey had a point. The house had been built in the fifties and it looked like it hadn't been decorated ever since.

"Don't worry about that," I reassured her. "I am sure we could find the right decorators to help us to make it exactly how you want."

Although it would eventually take a small army of workers to achieve this, Tracey agreed to give it a go. Sure enough, we found some designers to help us fix up the place. They charged me the earth, $200,000—but it was worth it because in the space of about ten days we transformed the house so that it felt like the biggest hotel suite in Malibu. We had parts of it rebuilt, and by the time it was finished it had everything, including our own private pool looking out across the Pacific Ocean.

We'd bought our freedom.

We discovered that just up the road from us in Malibu there was a little fish-and-chips shop. I realized I hadn't done anything as normal as eat fish and chips, or even been around a chip shop, for five or six years. It's still there to this day and it serves excellent grub.

The sense of freedom was enormous. There was no Duran Duran to worry about, just Tracey, Andy Jr., myself, and our plethora of new friends. I realized that life in a band, the thing that had once been so special in my life, had turned into something that I didn't enjoy as the business side overrode the creative. That was the dilemma: you have Music and then the Music Business. It's a slimy old game, so the job that I loved had become something that I resented. Quite frankly, some of the people you have to deal with you wouldn't piss on if they were on fire. There's very little by way of example to guide you, and no university where you can study dodgy rock-and-roll economics or how to spot a scallywag in business. No, you have to pick it up as you go and take the blows on the way. It can sometimes be a very corrupt business, but it's the only one we have (barely).

So, taking a break was exactly what I needed. Tracey and I shared a lot of laughter as we immersed ourselves in our new world. For the first time in ages we could go out in a car and look in the rearview mirror and see nobody was following us home, so there was no more need for crazy maneuvering tactics to shake off a bunch of cars, fans, or paparazzi. The police in Malibu were great, and an officer popped round to greet us soon after we moved in.

"If you've ever gotta shoot an intruder, Andy, make sure it's inside the house, 'cause it's legal if they are inside the house and you kill them," an officer advised me.

He makes it sound so easy, I mused. "I haven't got a gun, never owned one," I said.

"You don't have a gun? I can tell you how to go and get one," he offered.

I decided I'd make do with an alarm system in the house instead, although we did arrange for a security company to provide an armed guard to patrol outside twenty-four hours a day. Thankfully he was never needed (although on one occasion we were awoken by a gunshot in the middle of the night when he shot a prowling hyena). Life was very comfortable, and we began to appreciate that America has a great service ethic—particularly in LA, where there was a great restaurant scene (unlike London, which hadn't had its social makeover at this point). We soon settled into a little routine of eating at our favorite hangouts, and I found that I was tremendously well received everywhere we went.

I can remember Tracey and me being round at Don Johnson's house on Thanksgiving Day with Don and Michael, their wives, and the actor Philip Thomas, who played Don's partner in *Miami Vice*. Michael, whom I obviously knew from the Power Station, was a lovely guy and he was also a bit of a thespian himself. We ate a traditional American turkey dinner together, drinking Pepsi and Diet Coke like a normal family. I had never been in such a conservative environment before, so it took a bit of adjusting to get used to this "well-behaved" scene. But it was good for me to be around intelligent, sober people for a change, and I am still very grateful for all the support they gave me at this time.

There was a different set of social rules in LA. It was the first place I'd lived in where it was simply not cool to get smashed out of your head every night. As a major city, LA probably has the biggest concentration of reformed drinkers in the world, due to the dominance of the movie industry. Film and TV shoots are very expensive things, and they require people to be up early in the morning. Hollywood is full of tales about actors who have turned up late with a sore head and it has cost them dearly. It was against this background that the modern culture of going into rehab grew, although I always maintained that I didn't need to go into rehab. I just needed to go home, preferably to my wife!

I didn't have very much contact with the other members of Duran Duran during this period in my life. It was like a clean break, but the funny thing was that none of us ever said good-bye. Roger was completely off the scene, trying to cope with the agoraphobia he'd developed, and John was in a different place for most of the time through booze and drugs. Nick and I had never really been close and had drifted totally apart, although he did come to my twenty-fifth birthday party, and somehow we'd managed to remain on civil terms. Simon and I never really stopped being friends, but the bitterness caused by our rows over the Berrows continued to linger between us.

After I departed from Duran Duran in 1986, the Berrows sold their share of our publishing rights to a newly formed subsidiary of EMI called Gloucester Place Music. I was furious that they hadn't offered the rights to us, as I'd found a backer to buy them out and I'd been intending to approach them. It meant that to this day we still do not technically own all the rights to our music; we are entitled to a share of earnings from it, but only after Gloucester Place has taken a cut.

Simon and I eventually found ourselves engaged in a stupid and nasty public slanging match. I picked up the *News of the World Sunday Magazine* one morning to see the headline: HOW ANDY TAYLOR LET ME DOWN, BY SIMON LE BON. Beneath it was a long first-person article by Simon in which he accused me of using Roger's illness as an excuse to back out of Duran Duran.

"What Andy always really wanted was to be the centre-of-stage guitarist. He was bored—or not satisfied—being the guitarist in Duran Duran," Simon wrote.

This was pretty dumb, I thought, considering that I had already formed the Power Station with another singer and was still happy to be playing guitar, stage left. But in my view Le Bon does have a habit of acting like a politician when being interviewed, playing to the crowd

226   **WILD BOY**

of the moment, whatever gets you off the hook at the time. It's also a little rich for any one member to so ferociously grab all the credit, even if it was predominantly from misguided boating trips at that time.

The article went into detail about some of our arguments and even mentioned the evening when we met at my flat in London to try and patch things up. I'd previously admitted in an interview that I'd been very unhappy toward the end of my time in Duran Duran, and Simon had clearly taken it the wrong way. He accused me of being "like a slippery fish"—*wasn't he the one nearly sleeping with the fishes?* I thought. Then he had the gall to criticize me for getting lawyers involved in my split from the band. He obviously forgot that I had to deal with the Berrows.

"There was me, Nick, and John on one side, and Andy on the other," Simon continued in the magazine article. He then proceeded to claim that everything about me—my looks, my clothes, my hair—were all just part of an image and he claimed the bottom line was that he felt I just didn't want to be in the band anymore.

I was flabbergasted. And from a man who pissed off on a boat for a year without any regard for the others; surely that was a very strong signal that *he* didn't want to be in the band at that time? I certainly did not agree to his ill-fated attempts at sailing for a whole year.

It was so out of character for Simon to get involved in something like that, and I foolishly decided to hit back. The following month I did an interview with the same magazine, in which I addressed some of Simon's points, including why I had not been keen to play on Duran's *Notorious* album.

"Two fingers to him," I blasted back. I couldn't stand the fucking coke and bullshit in the studio, and the erratic time-keeping that had become part of our existence.

"I hope this article comes out on the day they start touring," I was quoted as saying.

I got out of Duran Duran because I was fed up, fucked up, and fucked off with the attitude of the management primarily, and in case no one noticed the band was in terminal decline and Roger was gone.

Simon knew we needed to sort the management out. He may not have realized it at the time, but he was too close to the management and therefore compromised the ability of the band to deal firmly with the Berrows. I felt that by going off around the world with the Berrows, Simon had unwittingly left the five of us unable to be together to make collective decisions.

"When all the lads wanted me to do the album *Notorious,* I didn't do it straightaway because I couldn't stand being shut in a room for three months just going through the same old drivel," I said in the article.

And the songs *were* suspect, relying heavily on Nile to come up with anything choppy—*choppy* being the operative word!!!

I made the point that we were all approaching thirty and it had been time for a change. In hindsight, both of us were a bit childish for what we said, and a lot of our comments about each other were taken out of context. People misinterpreted me as saying Simon was too old and fat to be a star, which wasn't the case either then or now. But in a funny sort of way, our public slanging match probably helped both of us to get things off our chests. We had no reason to speak for a long time afterward, but I'm glad that we eventually did get in touch with each other and we were able to become friends again. Simon can be infuriating—no doubt I can be, too—but he's a decent person at heart, and I've always respected him for that and for his strong family roots.

LIFE in America was a whole new learning curve for Tracey and me, and we soon found ourselves mixing with lots of the so-called Hollywood A-list. For my twenty-fifth birthday we'd organized a huge party in a giant transparent marquee at the back of our house in Malibu. With Danny Goldberg's help I was in the process of negotiating a very generous solo deal with a major record label, so regardless of Duran's attempts to play legal hopscotch, money wasn't going to be a problem for us in the immediate future. I've always believed that if you are good enough it comes to you, and you don't need to run

around like a headless chicken chasing hits, doing dodgy promo tours or any of that "where are they now" stuff.

Since it was my twenty-fifth, we decided to really push the boat out and spent around £50,000 on the party. We invited everyone we could think of, including stars like Michael J. Fox, John McEnroe, and Tatum O'Neal. One of the reasons we spent so much was because my new management team were keen to use the party to help launch me as a solo artist—and in all there were about five hundred people on the guest list (of which I probably knew only about half!). When the day of the party arrived the heavens opened and there was torrential rain, which caused large stretches of the Pacific Coast Highway to be blocked by mudslides. As I watched the weather get worse I became increasingly concerned that some of the guests would be stranded, unable to get through the mud, so I phoned up the local sheriff's office for advice.

"No worry, Andy, we'll escort your guests to the party," they said.

What a town, I thought—only in LA!

It was one of the best parties I've ever been to. I remember standing there at the end of the evening with Tony Thompson and thinking how much fun it had all been. I had actually enjoyed being at a party again. After that, bumping into the famous and curious became a regular occurrence, and there are some people you meet who still leave you starstruck. For example, I was out on the town with Michael Des Barres one evening when he organized a surprise.

"Come with me," he said. "We're going to see Jack because I know you've always wanted to meet him."

"Jack who, Michael?"

"Jack fuckin' Nicholson, dude, who do ya think I meant, the Ripper? Ha ha . . ." Michael has an infectious way of laughing at himself.

"Excellent."

"That's right, he's in town tonight," said Michael, grinning broadly.

He took me to the Roxy, which was ironically the place where I had fled to when the cops had busted our crew at the Hyatt all those years earlier. We went to the upstairs lounge, which was deserted, apart from Jack Nicholson sitting alone at the bar with his shades on.

"Hey, Mikey," he said in that familiar drawl, the corner of his mouth turning up in a smile.

"Hey, Jack. This is Andy."

Michael knew I was a big fan of Jack's films, so it was a lovely gesture on his behalf. We only stayed for one drink together, but it was enough. I was happy to meet someone whom I admired so much without having to take things any further than that. It's usually the best way—trust me.

Like Jagger, Jack was the same person in private as he was in public. He had a special veneer around him, which I also experienced a few years later when I met Arnold Schwarzenegger. I worked on the musical score for Arnie's film *Commando,* and recorded the title song for the end of the movie. We were introduced so that we could watch the final edit together. He came in with a big cigar and greeted me like an old friend in his booming Austrian accent.

"Hi, Andy, how are you doing?"

We sat down and watched the credits roll together.

"Oh yeah. I like it, I like it," he said in his deep, sincere voice, and nodded.

It was enjoyable rubbing shoulders with Hollywood's finest, because I had the chance to play a creative part in their work. I also discovered that despite the conservative nature of life in LA, not everyone always conformed to the rules. I went to one party which the boys from Mötley Crüe attended, and they seemed to be intent on having as wild a time as possible, including sexually—and they didn't seem to give a toss who watched.

It was on the day of the Super Bowl at the home of a very Bohemian record-industry figure. After George Martin, he was without doubt one of the greatest British record producers, and he and I knew each other well. His home was palatial. It had a great big pool with fountains that flowed down into another pool on a lower level. At the party, waiters walked around holding up trays of delicacies. The whole thing was like a scene from a movie. Mötley Crüe were quite enamored with the whole Duran Duran scene, because although they were heavy rockers they wore makeup and they were quite into the glam scene. I knew Tommy Lee, who was a really nice kid, through Tony Thompson. Tommy was a lively character, very vivacious and easy to talk to; he was also a brilliant drummer and he really held the band together, so we had a kind of mutual respect for each other. This was before the whole Pamela Anderson saga, but even then he was famous for having the biggest appendage in town—and it was at the party that I discovered this unsavory fact. He was in the hot tub with some of the other Mötley Crüe guys and a more-than-willing group of girls. One could say that they were all hard at it (and I don't mean that they were beating the drums). It was like a vivid porno movie except it wasn't on a TV screen; it was going on live in front of anyone who cared to walk up to the top pool. Duran Duran had hardly been a bunch of prudes sexually, particularly during our Rum Runner days, but I've never been the sort of guy who wants to get naked in a hot tub with a bunch of other guys, and I must admit I found it all a bit intimidating (anybody would with their todgers out next to Tommy!).

But hey, they're Mötley Crüe, I thought. Aren't they supposed to do that? I didn't know it at the time, but some of them were heavily into heroin; and this was the eighties, so things could still be *very* decadent compared to today.

Of course, being sober didn't always ensure you kept totally out of trouble, as my newly reformed friend Steve Jones soon found out. Steve had been through the music industry mangle himself during his time in the Sex Pistols. Michael and Don had told me that Jonesy had been going through a tough time. He had problems with booze and drugs, and in addition his immigration status in the US was unclear. He'd started attending AA, and by the time I arrived in LA I knew he was out on a limb. I was anxious to make a record that could be understood as a guitar record for my first solo album, so who better to work with than a guitarist like Steve Jones? The Pistols had been famous for Johnny Rotten and his lyrics, but in my mind Jones and his guitar had also been priceless. Steve was down on his luck and I had just signed a $2 million contract, so I knew he'd appreciate the chance to work on something that had a chance of being a commercial success, and he loved his money. He was off booze and drugs; therefore, I guessed his head needed something to focus on while his body recovered. I thought this was the full circle from the Chic guys to the Pistols.

Steve agreed and soon we were having a lot of writing sessions together. I can remember meeting him at Tramps in LA one evening when he turned up grinning from ear to ear and flicking a coin in the air.

"Look, Taylor, I've got my one-month coin," he said. He explained that it was a gift from AA to mark his first month sober. "You know, you should come to AA, too," he said.

"Thanks, but I haven't had a drink for a while myself and I think I'm doing okay," I explained. We sat together drinking cranberry juice. Steve was a right old charmer, but being teetotal didn't prevent him from chatting up the ladies as they went past, and he was never short of female company.

I loaned Steve £50,000 against my record advance. We did a lot of good work in the studio together, then a few weeks later I got a phone call from one of my bodyguards. He told me Steve had gone out and bought a Harley Davidson with some of the money, and had been arrested by the cops for speeding on Sunset Strip in Hollywood.

"We have Mr. Jones here and we are holding him while we clarify his immigration status. We believe he has no license to ride and he has no insurance," the police had told our office.

I called my lawyer, Robert Shapiro (who later successfully defended O. J. Simpson), who resolved the matter, and Jonesey was back at the studio by teatime. It was a funny episode that, booze or no booze, proved that you could take the boy out of the Sex Pistols but you couldn't take the Sex Pistol out of the boy. Steve, who wore his hair very long at this point in time, had gone out and splashed $10,000 on the biggest Harley he could find, then deliberately burned up and down Sunset with his great mane of hair blowing behind him. I was Steve's way of saying, *Am I tamed after a month and a bit sober? Bollocks!* The one thing you could say for sure about Jonesy was that he always had a great attitude. He's still a bit of a cunt!

I managed to stay comparatively sober in LA. As I said previously, I quit booze altogether for several months in LA and it did me a world of good because I'd definitely been drinking too much. But slowly I started to drink again from time to time, although in a much calmer way (at least at first!). Over the years my drinking has gone back to being pretty epic on occasions, but it never became as destructive as it had been previously. I'm not going to pretend I've never since dabbled in other substances either, but I no longer take cocaine. I've learned a lot of lessons the hard way but I'm not going to sit back and preach about drugs—you can read this book and make up your own mind. What I will say is that I can't recall any occasion on which it affected my performance on stage. I once did a gig opening up for the Psychedelic Furs which turned into a bit of a fracas, but it was nothing to do with booze. It was because my set overran and the Furs' roadies turned on the lights while I was still onstage, and it led to a heated exchange with my own crew.

My solo album sold well (about 300,000 copies) and it made number one on the MTV chart. I also worked with many serious musicians in the States, but the one person who really stands out in my mind as being the funniest person to be around is Rod Stewart. My decision to be teetotal lasted until I started hanging out with Rod—and then we went into the studio, which soon felt as if it had become Rod and Andy's 6 p.m. Drinking Club. "We never close," was our motto.

I'd first met Rod a few years earlier when I was in a pub with Simon, and we'd gotten to chatting about songwriting (how bloody boring). Rod was a childhood hero of mine, someone whose voice I really loved, and I very much admired his songs from both the Faces and his solo career. Rod had been intrigued by the fact that we'd written all our own songs, and he'd become very inquisitive after he'd gotten a few beers down his neck. After I parted from Duran Duran we eventually shared the same management, so we agreed to meet up one night. We arranged to have dinner and talk about what we might be able to do together musically. He then asked who would be accompanying me.

"Just me," I replied.

"What, with no birds?" he replied in his wonderfully gravelly voice.

"Well, no. Tracey's back in England for a while, and I haven't got a reserve booked," I joked.

"What, no birds, no?" he repeated, disappointed. Rod had been divorced from Alana Hamilton for only a couple of years, and he was clearly still in the mood to enjoy his newfound freedom.

"No, we'll just sit and talk," I insisted.

When we met, I discovered that Rod could drink like a fish—or at least that was the impression he liked to give.

"We'll have one of them, and then afterward we'll have one of these," he said, eyeing up the drinks menu. Pretty soon the cocktails were having the desired effect, and I was beginning to feel a wee bit light-headed. What I didn't know at the time was that Rod was secretly tipping his own drinks into a plant pot, crafty old fox, or he'd wait for me to go to the toilet and then order the waiter to take only his own glass away.

"Come on, son, drink up," he'd say when I got back from taking a leak.

Then he'd act a bit drunk and lull me into a false sense of security about the fact that I was feeling so sozzled myself. He told me some hilarious anecdotes about the Faces in the seventies, all very funny stuff, and how Woody's departure was all Jagger's fault and he "nicked Woody even though he promised me he wouldn't." Anyhow, before I

WILD BOY

knew it I was pretty drunk. The next morning he phoned me up, and bugger me, he gave me total recall of the evening. *How can he remember all this if he drank the same amount as me?* I thought.

"You know that you were throwing ice at a bird's cleavage in the restaurant?" he asked.

"Was I—did I hit the spot?"

"Yeah, in more ways than one, and when we got back to Spunk Towers [his affectionate term for his residence] you drank a bottle of Lillet and scratched my records."

"Sorry about the records, chap, shall we go and have a drink?"

"No, Andy, I am going to the suntan parlor this morning."

"Bollocks to that, I am going back to bed."

I later realized that he doesn't actually drink it all, which a member of his staff later confirmed to me. So is that how he survives? I inquired. *The sly bastard,* I thought (but in a good way!).

"You didn't fall for that one, did you, Andy—did you really?" Randy Philips, our manager, just laughed. "You English, where do you put it?"

I said, "Practice, my little Californian friend, years of practice."

But there were plenty of times when Rod *did* knock it back, and we agreed to make an album together on the understanding that it would involve drinking plenty of his favorite cocktail, which was called a mudslide (there's even a song about it). This consisted of vodka and a mixture of liqueurs that included Bailey's and ice, all mixed together in a blender. It had been Rod's favorite party drink ever since he'd been served it on one of his birthdays. It's very drinkable and it absolutely hammers you. I agreed that the mudslides sounded like a great idea, but on our first afternoon I wanted to sit and rehearse together first, to see if we could get any decent tunes going. We decided that we'd go to a rehearsal studio that was well away from the main bustle of Hollywood, so that it didn't attract any attention. The last thing we wanted was to be surrounded by music biz big shots at one of the better known venues.

"I'll leave you to book the rehearsal room," I said.

When I got there Rod had chosen this tatty little place right at the back of a valley across the road from a strip club. I noticed that inside the studio everyone addressed Rod as Mr. Stewart, whereas I was referred to as plain old Andy. I later found out that Rod had a man who went around beforehand telling everybody what to call him. Naturally, I'd assumed we would get straight down to work, but Rod had other ideas.

"I've got this bag of crisps here," he said. "Shall we go and have some beer to go with the crisps?" That was the best excuse to go for a drink I had heard for ages—these crisps need some beer!

I discovered that Rod, not unlike myself, always had an excuse to go for a drink, so before I knew it we were across the road, standing at the bar in this seedy little strip club, surrounded by afternoon perverts.

"Hey, it's you guys! Awesome—How ya doing?" squealed the barmaid, who clearly hadn't been expecting Rod Stewart to pop in for a lunchtime pint with a former member of Duran Duran and a bag of crisps.

"No, shhh. Nobody is meant to recognize us," said Rod, winking conspiratorially.

Quite how Rod thought he would manage to remain incognito was beyond me, because with his shaggy blond hair, extended nasal features, and $10,000 suits, he's possibly one of the most recognizable people on the planet. Because he is always beautifully attired, his impeccable dress sense just made him look even more out of place in our sleazy surroundings. But we drank a few beers (to go with the crisps) at the bar, while the strippers performed elsewhere in the club, before we eventually staggered back to the studio.

Amazingly, Rod's warm-up technique of going to the bar seemed to have worked a treat, and that afternoon we wrote three cool songs, and it was only our first day. All three made the album we were recording (if you're interested, the tracks were called "Dynamite," "Lethal Dose of Love," and "The Wild Horse"). I remember thinking, *Well, whatever we did—it all worked out!*

WILD BOY

After that, Rod and I shared a host of alcoholic antics and I had a seriously good time with him. I can't remember us ever having a cross word, despite getting into some compromising situations. We shared a similar sense of humor. Rod was very impressed when I told him about the time I had sabotaged the toilets at the Carlyle Hotel by drawing rude pictures on the toilet paper rolls for the next guests to see when they unfurled them.

"That's funny because I used to do that, too," said Rod. "I was staying in the Presidential Suite there once and I discovered that the Queen was due to stay there next, so I drew a big picture of a cock and bollocks on the bog roll!"

It was typical of Rod's sense of mischief, and I can only hope Her Majesty didn't get too much of a shock when she came to sit on the throne! Because of the drinking antics, sometimes things would really go too far, so much so that we eventually got banned from Cherokee Studios in Hollywood because of all the mayhem we caused. I was awoken by a telephone call from our management one morning after a particularly heavy session.

"Can you remember what you did with Rod last night?" they asked.

"Er, no—not exactly. Did I lose him somewhere?" I said, struggling to recall anything through my throbbing head.

"You got thrown out of the recording studio and you are banned from going there again."

"Why?" I gasped.

"Because at one point you were pissing in a bucket."

"A bucket of what?"

"The bucket that holds the wastepaper basket and which is supposed to serve as a bin."

"Oh God," I groaned, realizing that there was more to come.

"And somebody has scribbled crude drawings all over the mixing desk in indelible ink, and then for good measure they have carved things on it."

Oh, no, Rod's been drawing pictures of cocks on things again, I thought. Then it all came flooding back: I'd been drinking Bacardi 151 (which gets its name from the fact it is 151 proof), then I'd thrown up in the wastepaper bin before relieving myself in it. After that, Rod and I had defaced the studio with marker pens. We fully deserved to get banned, which was a bit of a problem for Rod because he used to do all his best work there. I don't think it bothered him too much, though, because he later gave me a credit on the album sleeve, billing me as his best drinking partner this side of the Pennines.

In hindsight, it may have been very troubling for the management, and they used to work overtime to stop me getting him pissed and out on the raz, but what a bloody laugh we had. Sorry, Randy and Arnold, it wasn't all so bad!

CHAPTER FOURTEEN

Life Forces: Idols & Influences

IT always amazes me that nobody in Duran Duran ended up dead. It's not just the drink and drugs that can be your downfall. There are so many things that you do at such an incredible pace that you never really stop to take account of the damage it might cause to you or your loved ones. The history of rock and roll is littered with too many names of great and talented people who weren't as lucky at surviving as we were. John Bonham, the Led Zeppelin drummer who started the day with sixteen shots of vodka for breakfast, tragically drank himself to death at the age of thirty-two. Keith Moon of the Who died from an overdose at thirty-one. John Lennon was only forty when an assassin's bullet claimed his life in 1980. Kurt Cobain killed himself at just twenty-seven . . . the list goes on and on. Some of these were people who greatly influenced me, but I never wanted to pay for my success with my life. When I spoke to John in that car in LA back in 1986, I genuinely feared that sooner or later one of us would die unless we changed our ways. When I think of how many dangerous incidents we survived between us, I still think we really were blessed with having nine lives.

Sadly, not everyone who worked with Duran Duran was as fortunate. When I look back over the years at all the great times we had, it's with mixed emotions because there are so many absent friends who are no longer with us today. Among them are Colin Thurston and Alex Sadkin, the two producers who helped Duran Duran to achieve our greatest successes. It also seems unbelievable that John Taylor and I are now the only surviving members from the original lineup of the Power Station. Bernard Edwards, Robert Palmer, and Tony Thompson all died long before they deserved to.

Bernard was the first to leave us, passing away on April 18, 1996, at the age of just forty-three. He died in Japan shortly after coming offstage from doing the thing he loved most, playing rock and roll. Nile Rodgers was with him when he was taken ill shortly before the show that evening, and he begged him to postpone the gig. Bernard insisted on playing, even though he had to be helped while onstage during the performance. Nile found him dead in his hotel room a few hours later. The cause of death was pneumonia: he'd given everything he could to the job he loved.

Robert Palmer died from a heart attack in Paris in 2003 at the age of fifty-four. The last time I saw him alive was at the Grand Hyatt Hotel at Roppongi Hills in Tokyo about three weeks before his death. Duran Duran had just re-formed (which is a whole story in itself that I'll tell you in the next chapter) and Robert and I celebrated by sharing a wild weekend together when we met up by chance while we were both performing in Japan.

It wasn't the first time we'd spent a lost weekend together. Robert was a connoisseur of everything liquid. His partying was very enjoyable and used to happen in spurts lasting days—it was the going home afterward that was always the difficult bit! He once invited me on the spur of the moment to join him and his girlfriend, Mary, for a weekend at his château in the mountains above Lausanne in Switzerland.

We'd been working together in 1997 to promote our ill-fated second Power Station album, which was a project that began full of hope but became beset by tragedy when Bernard died and John went into rehab. This left just Robert, Tony Thompson, and me as the only ones involved, but Robert didn't allow our depleted numbers to dampen his enthusiasm for life.

He'd been working with EMI for many years, so he had a very good relationship with them. This was at a time when money was still no object for a record company, and spending was something that Robert had down to a fine art. He wasn't exactly selling boat-loads of records at this particular stage, but he was determined to make sure the record company continued to look after him as if he was, and you had to admire his attitude. He was very gentlemanly about it all, but he would insist on staying at the very best hotels at EMI's expense while we promoted the album.

I agreed to let Robert make all the bookings because I knew EMI would be happy to do things on his terms, which suited me fine. We enjoyed a fabulous few days in Paris before moving to London, where we played a gig in a club and stayed at the sumptuous Landmark Hotel in Marylebone.

"Why don't you jump on the plane and join me in Switzerland for a few days?" Robert said to me as the week drew to a close. "We can write some songs together."

What the hell, I thought, *why not?* I rang Tracey and explained that I wouldn't be home for a couple more days, and before I knew it I was on a plane (with her blessing, I hasten to add). We took a commercial flight out of the UK, then changed at Geneva before catching a private plane for the short hop to a landing strip at Lausanne, which is a beautiful little French-speaking town on the northern shores of Lake Geneva. Lausanne is famous for its medieval cathedral, which is regarded as Switzerland's finest gothic building because of its elegant turrets and spires. It's very impressive, although at night I would imagine it must look just a tiny bit like a classic version of Frankenstein's castle.

We traveled by car for the rest of the journey up into the mountains to Robert's home, which could be reached only by a single road that crossed a gushing Alpine river. Robert, as you can imagine, was a fabulous host. We were joined by some friends of his who owned a restaurant nearby, and they'd arranged for a banquet of Michelin-quality dishes to be delivered—and, of course, Robert's wine cellar contained nothing but the finest vintages. His château was decorated in classic style with lots of dark oak, but the grand old bedrooms felt slightly austere when you pulled down the shutters to lock out the howling night. *Never mind Frankenstein*, I thought. "*Welcome to Dr. Palmer's Château: you can come on in for the weekend, but don't expect to get back your liver in one piece!*"

It was just as well Robert had laid on plenty of food, because shortly after we arrived the heavens opened and torrential rain flooded the river, which meant we were now cut off from the rest of the world. We needn't have worried. It turned out to be a wonderful weekend that consisted mainly of Robert and me discussing music and jamming together while slowly working our way through the contents of his wine cellar. Robert would have these intense periods when he would sit down and look at music, then play me what he'd recently written. Before I knew it he was blasting loads of material at me and then making notes as we went through things together and swapped ideas.

He had the most incredible record collection I have ever seen, which he kept down in the basement where he had a little studio where he loved to hang out. Every single one of his records was on vinyl and alphabetically ordered, and he always kept them in pristine condition (just like his suits). We spent a lot of time down in that studio, and we ended up jamming the blues together. He had a couple of old Fender guitars, which are great for making that sort of sound, although it surprised me because he'd always sworn to me that he'd never record a blues album. I think he must have enjoyed the weekend as much as I did, because later on he changed his mind and did in fact record a blues album—so maybe I helped turn his head a bit!

After Switzerland, our paths didn't cross again until six years later in Japan, where we had a great time boozing and laughing. We didn't know it then, but it was the last time we would be together before his death. I guess it was fate's way of allowing us to say good-bye to each other. Duran Duran were in Japan because we were due to perform our comeback shows at a grand old auditorium in Tokyo called the Budokan. Our reunion had caused a lot of excitement, so our concerts were all sold out. Everywhere we went we were followed by hundreds of Japanese fans; they trailed us from the bullet train station to our hotel, and as ever, they always seemed to know in advance where we were traveling to.

When we arrived in town we were delighted to discover that Robert was due to play a midnight show at a nightclub on the same evening as us. I hadn't seen him for years, so I arranged to go and meet him after our sound check. Robert was as well groomed and as dapper as ever, impeccably dressed in his suit, and it wasn't long before he invited me to perform onstage with him that evening.

"There's a spare amp so get up and play if you want," he said.

I didn't need to think about it for long.

"Cool, what time is your set?" I inquired.

"Midnight."

"Midnight it is, then," I confirmed.

Later that evening Duran Duran performed in front of an ecstatic audience of 13,000 people. Then I rushed back to my hotel room for a steaming hot bath before going off to meet Robert. When I got there the place was heaving, and the crowds had been swelled by Duran fans who'd heard we'd be arriving. Robert explained that he had a young Japanese band who were backing him and that they'd perform three or four numbers before inviting me on. He also had four girls who were to join him onstage during "Addicted to Love"— nice work if you can get it!!! Robert had a tiny little dressing room, and when I joined him there I saw (for the first time) an unopened bottle of whiskey on the table. I knew that in the past Robert often liked a tipple before going onstage, and I was in the mood for a drink as I had done my "official duties" earlier in the evening.

"Right, let's be having one, then," I said, eyeing up the bottle.

"Nope—I don't anymore because I have got to watch the throat and I don't want to push it beforehand," replied Robert in his deep Mid-Atlantic/Yorkshire drawl.

Life Forces: Idols & Influences   243

"What, no schnifters before you sing?"

"No," he reaffirmed.

"What—not even one little livener, with your old Geordie mate . . . ?"

"Just can't anymore."

Bugger me, even Robert's slowed down now! Never mind, I thought, *there'll be plenty of time later. But does he mean his voice is getting shot?* I needn't have worried, because when we got onstage his voice was as deep and powerful as ever (Old Leather Throat was my nickname for him). In fact it was so loud at times that it was almost scary. He had a full rock tenor voice, and even without a microphone he had the ability to sound like a booming sergeant major. We played a tremendous gig and when we came off it was time for the whiskey, which we then consumed, with honor. After that we went from one set of bars and clubs to the next, drinking merrily to make up for lost time. Before I knew it, it was ten thirty in the morning and I was standing in Robert's hotel room. We'd been drinking all night without a break.

"Bloody hell, it's ten thirty—I've got to be onstage in six hours," I slurred, as the sun blazed down through the hotel room window.

I was due to be back at the Budokan for a televised show that afternoon and I needed to get it together. I always wear dark glasses during the day, and at times like this they are worth their weight in gold! It was a boiling hot day and the show was very early at four thirty, so it would take a real effort that afternoon. The air-conditioning in old buildings like the Budokan isn't always as effective as it is in some of the modern venues. Consequently, I was sweating like a pig onstage, feverishly gulping pint after pint of water to stay hydrated. It was so fucking hot . . . eventually it got to a point where a roadie told me I'd had eight pints of fluid and therefore couldn't drink anymore for risk of water poisoning. *Bloody hell,* I thought, *I better not have another late night with Robert Palmer,* as the temperature in the venue exceeded 105 degrees. Ironically, in Japan sweating is considered honorable, and drinking excessive amounts of whiskey is also socially acceptable. After the gig I met Robert in the greenroom (where

WILD BOY

artists and their guests relax after a show) and he seemed completely unruffled.

"Fucking hell, chap. That was a long night," I complained.

"What the fook are you moanin' about?" he said. "You never dropped a beat."

That was Robert all over: no fuss, just get on with it. But he didn't stand on ceremony; if I had messed up the show he would have been the first to tell me in the bluntest of terms. That evening we all went back to the Hyatt in Roppongi, which is one of the most modern and high-tech hotels in the world. It's also got one of the most fabulous wine cellars in the world, which suited Robert's palate perfectly, and around thirty of us had dinner together there. After a wonderful meal we all went off to a hip-hop club, where Le Bon got up in the middle of the dance floor for most of the evening while Robert and I and his girlfriend, Mary, chatted together. (Simon loves to get up on the dance floor at every opportunity, and God bless him for it, because he'll always be a front man at heart.) I finished the evening chatting with Robert over a gin and tonic in his hotel room at 3 a.m. It had been another long night, but this time both of us were still relatively sober and we spent the evening reminiscing about all the good times we'd shared. That was the last time I saw him—at 3 a.m. with a gin and tonic in his hand and a twinkle in his eye.

I was in Ibiza three weeks later, sitting on a rooftop terrace with some friends, when I got a phone call from someone in our office.

"Sit down, it's bad news. Robert has been found dead in Paris."

It was a terrible blow, but in a strange sort of way I was grateful for the time we had enjoyed in Tokyo. *Is this what they mean when they say something is spiritual?* I thought. *At least we said good-bye.* Soon after I received the news of his death I started to deal with media calls. It was no secret that Robert liked to drink a lot, and he had died of a heart attack, so his lifestyle was an obvious angle for the news networks to take. But he deserved to be remembered for so much more than that, so I went live on ITN and Sky TV and I spoke of how fundamentally important he had been to British rock music, one of the few UK singers to ever achieve that level of success in the United States. He was a singer's singer and a very competent musician with a huge amount of natural ability; he could noodle about on keyboards and guitars and create his own music without having to rely on a whole band to bring his work alive. Singer . . . writer . . . musician . . . he was one of the rare breed that could do all three.

I can remember looking up at the night sky later that evening and thinking about all the good times we had shared over the years, all the work we had created and sold; and stupid shit like the time we got drunk and dared each other to walk through Central Park in New York at night just for the sheer hell of it (neither of us did it in the end). Or the first man to drink three martinis (one for each shoulder, then the third hits your head), or his Top Five Restaurants (that one was always changing as he globe-trotted). He was very much an alpha male, but he was also a gentleman and he was great with kids. I remember when my son Andy was about ten years old, Robert sat down and spoke to him for hours and hours about music and this and that—he was very engaging with children. Meeting people like Robert is one of the great perks of working in the music industry. You might have thought we wouldn't have got on so naturally, as we both had a habit of being pretty blunt about things, but we were good friends. It was a pleasure to meet someone like Robert, not just because of who he was and what he achieved, but because underneath I always felt he was just a Northern boy like me who worked very hard.

Most of all, Robert loved his work and would sleep with a Dictaphone next to his bed in case a new song popped into his head during the night. Yet he never let his work get in the way of his zest for life. I can still remember his words when Bernard died and I asked him if he was going to the funeral.

"No, I don't think so. He was just a workmate," he said.

Robert wasn't being disrespectful. He was just trying to say that life was for the living and it was better to leave Bernard's family to grieve in peace. He never liked to be around any fuss. Sadly, I never made it to Robert's funeral due to work commitments. But I didn't need to—we'd made our peace in Tokyo.

TONY Thompson's death was less sudden than Robert Palmer's but it was every bit as tragic. Tony died a few months after Robert on November 12, 2003, from kidney cancer. He was age forty-eight, and his demise probably hit me harder than I realized at the time. We'd been out of touch for a few years when I received a phone call from his partner telling me about the cancer. There was a complication with his insurance, which meant he was unable to afford proper treatment in the States, so John and I phoned around to everyone we knew in the music industry and suggested that we all make a substantial donation to a treatment fund. But it was too late—a few days later his partner phoned back and told us he was dead. If only he had told us sooner. Why didn't we know how far his condition had deteriorated? There are a thousand questions you ask yourself over and over again. But quite simply, that wonderful, gifted, funny man—who had kept our spirits so high during the Power Station—had been too damn proud to ask. One thing we did discover was that he had recently married and for the first time in his life had found true happiness, but I still miss him dearly.

Another friend of Duran Duran's who died at a young age was Michael Hutchence, who was found hanging in tragic circumstances on November 22, 1997. His death hit Simon particularly hard, and he later wrote a very moving song about it called "Michael, You've Got a Lot to Answer For." Simon and Michael had been close friends ever since they'd met as young men during our first tour of Australia. Michael was thirty-seven.

The loss of all these people made me realize what a high price can be paid if you live life at such a fast pace. After all, you can't ignore issues about lifestyle when your friends are dying from it, and I am thankful that I slowed down when I did in 1986.

THE first time I'd met Bernard Edwards was in New York City. As I explained earlier in this book, in Duran Duran we were all in awe of the Chic guys. They exuded a certain confidence that was as natural as their seemingly endless string of hits. In fact, I believe that Bernard Edwards, Tony Thompson, and Nile Rodgers were a serious little trio who changed the sound of modern record production in their time. It would take a whole book to explore all the contributory factors, but for the purposes of this writing I'd like to tell you a little bit more about what they were like as people.

Getting to know these guys gave me a very unique experience of New York. It was their town, and they had a network of great musicians, sound engineers, studio owners, and nightclub bosses. Among the three of them there wasn't anything that they could not specialize in. Amid all the heat and frenzy of New York, they created more great music than Timbaland or Dr. Dre. Bernard always remained the anchor. He had an exceptional gift for organizing music; he could take apart an idea and strip it down to its essential elements, rearrange the tune, and then figure out what part everybody else would play in it. You always had to be at the top of your game to work with him, but he never gloated about his gift or rubbed it in on those who were less talented. He just gave it to you straight and he always respected the artists (well, at least to their faces!).

As well as being a great musician himself, he truly understood that the role of being a great music producer was to support others to help them do better things. I enjoyed working with Bernard because his watertight attitude suited me perfectly. In music, you often find that your best ideas come together within the first five minutes of trying something new, and he had an instinct for hearing quality straightaway within something that you were trying to shape. He also had the ability to dig you out of a creative hole on the days when you were struggling.

I didn't realize how much I was learning subliminally at the time when I worked with him, but later in life, as I came to understand his methods I attempted to apply them in my own work. He wasn't easily intimidated and he never suffered fools gladly. I doubt we would have ever finished "A View to a Kill" if it wasn't for Bernard having a big enough heart and the right character to see it through.

I can always remember Rod Stewart's reaction when he first heard Bernard and Tony play together in the studio. I had invited them to LA to record an album with us called *Out of Order* in 1987. Rod just stood there, stunned.

"Fuck me, Andy. I didn't realize they were that good," he said, and Mr. Stewart isn't the easiest to please in that regard.

Between them, Bernard and Tony produced a body of work that defined the times they lived in. They dominated the music scene from 1977 to 1987 and beyond by constantly challenging themselves and pushing each other to the limit. Chic are now probably the most sampled disco act in house and dance mixes, and their collective hit machine runs into hundreds of millions of sales. The four major projects that I worked on with them ("A View to a Kill," the Power Station, Robert Palmer's *Addicted to Love/Riptide* album, and Rod's *Out of Order* album) collectively accounted for around 25 million albums, and as Rod once said, "What an awful lot of alcohol!" As well as working with Duran Duran, Bernard wrote, played, and produced records with Blondie, Bowie, Luther Vandross, Sister Sledge, Diana Ross, Madonna, the Isley Brothers, and Earth, Wind & Fire—all massive mainstream acts.

Bernard had an endearing quality of bringing you down to earth with a bump if ever you needed it. I recall that at one memorable session in LA, I arrived at the studio after getting trollied on booze the night before. I was convinced that despite my alcohol intake the previous evening, I had recorded what I thought was the mother of all guitar solos. I pushed up the volume and played back my work as loud as I could, trying to convince myself that it sounded fine. After it finished, Bernard's voice filled the studio.

"You call that a motherfuckin' guitar solo, Andy?"

Ouch!

As well as all of his achievements I have listed above, he was also in my opinion the greatest bass player ever, and that alone would have been enough to carry him to the top. I think the definition of *legend* is well served by this man's contribution to music.

In memory of Bernard Edwards, Robert Palmer, and Tony Thompson. Why did you have to go so soon?

I'VE been lucky enough to work with many great people in my career, and another one of those was Colin Thurston. He was Duran Duran's first producer and arguably the most instrumental. His contribution to Duran Duran was fundamental because he produced both our first album, *Duran Duran*, and *Rio*.

It was Colin who first opened my eyes to the potential of the recording studio and my potential within it. I was nineteen when I first met him; he had already worked with seminal artists such as David Bowie and the Human League. With Colin's help I recorded nearly all the guitar work on our first album during two evening sessions—all the parts for the entire album in two nights—and he made it sound great.

What I remember most about him was what a nice bloke he was: he was very clean-cut, he didn't drink, and he had very neat handwriting! I believe John Lennon once said that to succeed in the music business you have to be a bastard, and the Beatles were the biggest bastards on earth (or something like that!), but Colin was the exception. He made our early time in Duran Duran very fulfilling, which can't always have been easy. Sadly, he recently passed away. Thanks, Colin, because without such a solid, professional beginning . . . who knows?

TOP 'N TAILS: Tracey and me on our wedding day with Duran Duran. From left to right: Roger Taylor (looking shy and respectful); yours truly, with my beautiful bride; John Taylor (full of laughter); Simon Le Bon (looking suave and sophisticated); and Nick Rhodes (raising a toast).

POOLSIDE: Tracey, in a Duran top, around the time we married.

MUM TO BE: Tracey pregnant with our first child in 1984.

YOU NEED
HANDS to
hold a little
baby. Me with
Andy junior.

NAPPY POSE:
Tracey and me
with baby Andy
after Tracey
recovered from
her illness.

EYES RIGHT: Giovanna Cantone (left) stares toward Julie Anne Freidman at a dinner in the eighties. Roger Taylor is in the center.

HI! A fun shot of Simon Le Bon's ex-girlfriend Claire Stansfield.

DOTING DAD: Me with son Andy and daughters Bethany and Georgina in Marbella in 1998.

STAIRWAY: Me and my children enjoying ice lollies in Dorset in 1998. From left to right: Baby Isabelle, me, Bethany, Georgina, and Andy junior.

MODEL LOOKS:
Tracey (left) with
Yasmin Le Bon
(right).

THE NIGHT BEFORE: Me making plans to move to Ibiza in 2000. The day after this photo was taken I flew back to the UK, where John Taylor called me to explain Simon and Nick had agreed to a reunion. Later, after John's call, I also learned my father had cancer.

TOGETHER AGAIN: The original Duran Duran perform live together during one of many shows after we re-formed.
Photo by Tracey Taylor

VOCAL MOMENT: Simon (left) and me, singing together onstage.
Photo by Tracey Taylor

ACOUSTIC SET: (Left to right) John Taylor, Simon Le Bon, and me, performing with acoustic guitars at a radio station in San Diego.

THAT'S MY BOY: Me chilling out on our tour bus deep in the heart of Texas, while my son, Andy (now looking not-so-junior!), plays guitar.

BEACH SHOT: I pose with daughter Isabelle during a shoot for Duran Duran's "(Reach Up for the) Sunrise" video.

TENDER MOMENT: My daughter Isabelle comes onstage after Duran Duran perform in Kansas, summer 2005.

Photo by Tracey Taylor

STRUMMIN': Onstage
with Duran Duran
at Earls Court
in 2005.
Photo by Tracey Taylor

HAPPY!
Tracey and me
on our twentieth
wedding
anniversary
in Ibiza in 2002.

One thing that Colin must have been aware of was that although the five members of Duran Duran were all very different, we shared a set of common musical influences. Colin was the filter that allowed us to come together as a whole. Everyone in Duran Duran was born within a few years of each other, so we all went through school at the same time and we all listened to *Top of the Pops* and Radio One. We all read *New Musical Express* and *Sounds* and listened to the same concert tours as they went into either Newcastle, Birmingham, or London.

That's why I recognized the musical influences in the advert that the others placed in *Melody Maker* when they were looking for a guitarist. It listed Mick Ronson and Steve Jones, and I think the other person named was Dave Gilmour of Pink Floyd. I recognized what they were trying to say straightaway, so we connected through our idols and influences. Going to concerts as teenagers laid the foundation for how we understood each other. Nick and I were always the two who enjoyed being in the studio, and we worked well with Colin as teenagers. With his help, we recorded all our own beats on the first album—all our own chords, all our own melodies, and all our own lyrics.

When I look back, the thing I ask myself most is, "How did we do it all so young?" But it didn't seem like we were young at the time because, as I mentioned at the beginning of this book, we were in an age when you went out to work full-time at sixteen and you were married by twenty-one. We didn't feel like a *young* band, we felt like a young *man* band. Like all musicians, the way we learned was through listening and watching all the great artists who were our idols and influences.

I think if you are interested in music at a young age, then when you listen to records you start to take them apart in your mind to figure out how all the different sounds fit together. In those days, as far as I was concerned there was only one type of hero, and that was a guitar hero. So I'd watch *Top of the Pops* and try to work out where you needed to put your fingers on the fret board to make a certain sort of guitar sound. I'd get my chord books out and try to copy it, but there was no easy and simple solution to fixing it quick; the only way you could really see what a guitar player was doing was to go and watch him live. I developed a trainspotter-style fascination for watching their fingers.

One of the first things I discovered was the blues scale for playing lead guitar twelve-bar blues. I can remember watching Angus Young in concert with AC/DC and thinking, *Are his fingers doing that scale?* I realized that all the great guitar players, like Jeff Beck, Ronnie Wood, Keith Richards, and Pete Townsend, all played the blues, so I wanted to learn to do the same. I found that Jimi Hendrix's "Red House" was relatively easy to play, and I soon progressed from there. Once you discover you can conquer one bit of what a guitarist does you look further to the next level: chord structure and riffs . . . the movement of the guitar part. Soon I was aggravating the neighbors, playing along to the records, things like Deep Purple's "Smoke on the Water," over and over until I knew it by heart. After you get used to copying riffs you can start to twist them around and experiment on your own.

All the great guitarists in the world were at their prime during the late sixties and early seventies. People like Angus Young, Eddie Van Halen, Jimmy Page, Eric Clapton, and Gary Moore were all from the same golden age of guitar heroes. In fact, the last great guitar riffer, in my opinion, was Steve Jones, who could have played in any band, not just the Sex Pistols. He was a rock riffer, not just a punk riffer.

So, basically, I ended up learning to play lots of riffs—I had always said I wanted to be in a band like AC/DC, but fortunately I was either astute enough, or skint enough, to join Duran Duran! Originally, I had no desire to be in a band that seemed so light compared to the heavy rock of the seventies, but the times they were a'changing very quickly, then the eighties and technology arrived. Things moved on from the Pistols and evolved into a very austere electrosound that came from the likes of Kraftwerk. It was the beginning of New Romanticism, but it was still very cold and had yet to become hedonistic.

Suddenly guitar didn't seem so central, and electronic keyboards began to take a leading role in the emerging music scene.

As far as idols go, David Bowie was probably the artist whom we collectively admired the most. Had there been a Duran Duran maypole that we all danced around, David Bowie would have been the person tied to it. His *Ziggy Stardust* and *Hunky Dory* albums were hugely influential records that we all grew up listening to and admired, probably our first collective influences.

By the eighties, even though the guitar was less dominant, it was still a crucial component for writing songs. If you listen to a hit like "Save a Prayer," even though the keyboard line is more dominant, all the chords and the basic structure come from guitar. If we couldn't have sat down and strummed an acoustic guitar, that song couldn't have come to life. Similarly, without the synthesized keyboards that Nick brought to life so well, it would have sounded like a poor imitation of the Eagles.

Unlike a lot of other New Romantic bands, in Duran Duran we realized that even though things were changing rapidly, we didn't want to lose the ability to have the punch and the edge that guitar could give us. We wrote with guitar *and* keyboards—and that was a fundamental part of our success. Simon has the ability to sit with a guitar and find things because he has a great understanding of music (which he needed in order to deal with the other four of us!).

Along with keyboards, the other driving force of the times was disco. Everything started with the dance floor and the Studio 54 experience. The dance floor was very powerful in those days as a medium for records to break. And that was where Duran Duran came to life— the crossover between the Pistols and Chic: guitar music with a disco beat, which turned out to be an unstoppable hybrid. Even though I was more of an AC/DC fan, I could see the magical potential of Duran Duran because we weren't one-dimensional like a lot of our contemporaries.

A band like Duran Duran is a fusion of fashion, hedonism, and music. When you added the club scene at the Rum Runner to the vision that Nick and John had when they were kids at art college, which was influenced by Roxy Music and Brian Eno, it was a unique mix. The five of us just seemed to click, and we created the bones of our first album in the first six weeks that we were together. The guitar skills I had learned from watching my idols and from playing on the road in Germany allowed me to experiment in order to make my guitar work with Nick's keyboards. He was doing something that nobody could really read at that point because only he knew what he was trying to achieve—but we found a clever way of working together in order to create something special. It was hard work at times, because you can be sitting there scrunched in a room going over each component of a song again and again, hour after hour. People often assume that bands write their lyrics first and then build the music around the vocals. But in Duran Duran it was the opposite. Ninety-five percent of the time it was the other way round: the music provided the basis for us to collaborate with our fusion of different styles; this in turn allowed us to create a magic carpet of sound for Simon to lay his lyrics over—and I'm very proud that I was able to be at the heart of that creative process.

Today, if I had to choose five albums to take to a desert island, the Beatles would top the list. No chapter about idols would be complete without paying homage to the Fab Four. My love for their work goes right back to that early copy of *Sgt. Pepper* that I was given by my cousin, and my interest in their music has never waned. In fact, if I were on my imaginary desert island I would have to cheat a bit and make my first choice the Beatles' *Anthology*, because then I'd get everything!

Electric Ladyland by Jimi Hendrix would be on my list because all the great rock bands of the sixties and seventies, from the Rolling Stones onward, were in awe of Hendrix and influenced by the blues. The first Oasis album, *Definitely Maybe*, would be there—you can hear all the classic components of the Beatles et al. working below the surface; they make an incredible sound for one large eyebrow. I'd also choose *Hunky Dory* by David Bowie, because it was one of the first albums that fascinated me in the early seventies.

And my final choice would be *Ooh La La* by the Faces. They were huge in the seventies—they should have been bigger than the Stones, but Woody left. The fact that the composition of our first single, "Planet Earth," owes a tip of the hat to "Do Ya Think I'm Sexy" shows that Duran Duran were all fans of Rod Stewart and the Faces. (Nick even wore the tartan scarf when he was a wee laddie.)

The one thing I wouldn't take to my desert island would be any Duran songs. They're great pieces of music, but I don't know any artist who likes listening to his own work; it's probably because you've heard it a thousand times over in the studio! Having said that, "The Reflex" is probably my favorite piece of our pop music. However, "Planet Earth" and "Girls on Film" also gave me a lot of satisfaction because no one had ever sounded quite like that before, and it's satisfying to think that we may have contributed to things changing. Those records helped to define the eighties, and I like to think that in our own way, Duran Duran helped to nudge the satellite of music into a new orbit . . .

CHAPTER FIFTEEN

Duran Duran II: Roaring Back— Into the Tiger's Den

THEY say (whoever they are) that time is a great healer, and some-times it's true. Simon and I didn't have any contact with each other for six or seven years after the breakup of Duran Duran, and it wasn't until the early nineties that we even spoke to each other again. Things had gradually thawed between us, and as the new millennium ap-proached we were both older, wiser, and willing to let clear water flow under the bridge. To be fair to Simon, I'd fueled a lot of the public friction between us after we split in 1986, so it was only natural that sooner or later he would choose to react in print himself. But as the years had passed we'd tacitly agreed to let bygones be bygones.

I called Simon one afternoon in 1998 to let him know I'd be in London for a while over the summer. We'd moved back to the UK by now and were living in the Midlands. It was around the time of the World Cup Finals, and Scotland were due to play in the opening game against the holders, Brazil. As Simon and I both shared a pas-sion for watching international soccer, he invited me down to stay with him and Yasmin at their house in the Home Counties. I discov-ered that Yasmin was a great homemaker and a very good mother to their children. It was the first of several times that I stayed with them and at one point Yasmin put me on a weight-loss diet which consisted of lots of sweet potato and grilled tuna and it worked like a treat. Like Tracey, whom Yasmin had become friends with, she often needed to have the patience of a saint. I remember on one occasion Simon tried to put together a chair he'd bought from IKEA or somewhere. He glued all the parts together in the wrong way and then stomped about in a fury when he couldn't rectify it. It was hilarious, but Yasmin would react to anything like that simply by raising an eyebrow!

It was a very different London to the one that had been our playground while we were recording *Rio* during the early eighties. The Embassy Club was still going strong, but the new in place where most of the young showbiz crowd liked to be seen was the Met Bar at the Metropolitan Hotel in Park Lane.

The night before the Scotland game, Simon and I decided to go out on the town and get off our trolleys for old times' sake. Simon wanted to go to the Met Bar, but I was a bit worried that I'd be like a fish out of water, because all the Brit Pop crowd liked to hang out there and I didn't know any of them. Crowded clubs and bars were never my favorite hang. It had almost been impossible at one point in the eighties to really do that sort of thing, and although the madness of the times had passed and it was now possible to move around in public without getting screamed at, I preferred the less "on show" places to get bladdered. I didn't want to be the bloke from the eighties trying to look young and hip again, but Simon was full of his usual enthusiasm.

"Come on, it'll be all right," he insisted. "It's better than those shitholes in LA you been hanging at."

We jumped into the sporty little VW that Simon used to get around town and he drove us to the Metropolitan, where he pulled up right outside the door. Simon plonked his car keys into a doorman's hand and asked him to park it somewhere overnight. I'd never been inside the Met Bar before, but I soon discovered that it's a curious little place, very small and dark, and the toilets are located on the right-hand side as you enter it from the hotel's reception.

Duran Duran II: Roaring Back—Into the Tiger's Den   257

We were standing there by the entrance when Geri Halliwell from the Spice Girls came rushing over to say hello to Simon. Hot on the heels of Geri was Victoria Beckham (who was still known as Victoria Adams, as it was about a year before she married David). Geri was very bubbly and excited, and I really wanted to meet her because she seemed like a really ballsy chick, more like Boss Spice. But Posh had other ideas. Victoria came over to us with a very stern face and pulled Geri away. *No way are we talking to you,* was the polite way of saying what her face showed; and *whoosh,* they disappeared off into the toilets. (Why do all girls head for the toilet when there's something going down?)

"What the fuck was all that about?" I said to Simon.

"Ah, well . . . ," replied Simon, looking slightly impish. "I think it might be because of something that I said to Victoria when I last met her."

"Tell me more."

What had happened was that Simon confided to Posh while they were chatting that he'd had a very vivid dream about her the night before. I presume that at first Posh was quite flattered, until Simon added that the dream had actually involved him having a perfect view up her skirt while she was wearing no knickers! Victoria was horrified, especially as Simon used a *very* unchaplike word to describe a certain part of her anatomy. She took great exception, and I think she ended up giving Simon a good slap in return. Don't get me wrong, there's no suggestion that Simon was trying to chat her up or anything like that, it was just his weird sense of humor coming out.

The whole thing had become something of a talking point in the showbiz world. In fact, an article about it appeared in the *Daily Mirror* a few months after we spoke, when Simon later alluded to the incident on the *Jo Whiley Show* on Channel Four. LE BON SO SORRY OVER POSH GAFFE, said the newspaper's headline.

"Simon Le Bon has written a grovelling letter of apology for disgracing himself in front of her," said the article. (*Fuckin' legend,* I thought, *that's sorted the men from the boys then!*) "Details of the Duran Duran star's embarrassing behaviour remain sketchy. But it appears he was less than a gentleman to poor Victoria when he met her at the Brits awards ceremony earlier this year."

I must admit I roared with laughter when he told me about it in the Met Bar, although I can see why Victoria was offended, as it's not really the best line to say to a girl, is it? *Great*, I thought. *We've been snubbed by Posh Spice because of Old Spice!*

But then that's what helps to make Simon so unique: he might have a very suave and sophisticated exterior, but deep down inside he can sometimes be a bit of a lovable slob just like the rest of us. He's been very misinterpreted over the years by the media, who often mistake his confidence and optimism for arrogance. He's taken a lot of stick for it, and as a result he's grown a very thick skin and learned not to react when people take the piss out of him. Actually, most people whom I've introduced him to are pleasantly surprised and end up saying what a nice fella he is. Often, however, strangers will come up and pick on him for no reason in public, presumably out of jealousy.

THE day after our brief run-in with Victoria Beckham at the Met Bar, Simon and I watched the Scotland match together at his home and chatted about the possibility of a reunion. Duran Duran's back catalogue of music was doing well, and we'd had one or two early approaches to see whether or not we wanted to do something for the turn of the millennium in 2000. Simon and Nick had carried on together in a watered-down version of Duran Duran during the nineties with guitarist Warren Cuccurullo, but the view seemed to be that if the original five were to reform it would create a lot of interest.

"Shall we do some millennium deal then?" I asked Simon as we sat watching Scotland lose 2–1 to Brazil.

"No, because everyone is going to be doing shows around that time. Let's wait for it to pass and then see where we are at," he replied.

"Okay." *Good*, I thought, *the millennium stuff's going to be well overdone.*

"How's Nick anyway?" I rasped in a thick Brummie drawl.

"Well, you know. Nick is Nick," said Simon pleasantly. "Getting divorced soon."

"Yeah, well, that's why I was asking. Is he still the same old Nick?" I persisted, but Simon was too much of a diplomat to be drawn out any further.

I had a few similar conversations about the possible reunion with Roger, but nothing came of them. Roger had pretty much dropped out of the public eye altogether and was still married to Giovanna. (They divorced later.) John, meanwhile, had finally confronted his demons in 1995, eventually going into rehab for his drug and alcohol addictions following a failed marriage to Amanda de Cadenet. I can remember very clearly the day he told me. We had arranged to work on a new Power Station album together when he suddenly called me out of the blue.

"I'm over," he said.

"Over what?" I asked.

"I'm gone. I can't do it anymore and I think you know why."

John explained his position and said he couldn't do the album. I could tell from his voice that he was serious about cleaning up his act. He told me he was going away and later claimed that it was because of Robert Palmer. I was surprised because he seemed quite lucid when we'd met to arrange Power Station II in LA, where he was living with Amanda. He was drinking carrot juice and told me he was off the drugs, but he must have relapsed or something because the following year he went into recovery and split from Amanda at around the same time, which was all covered by the press. I'd lost touch with him since then, but by the time the talk of a reunion came around he was leading a completely sober lifestyle.

After the start of the new millennium passed, there was talk of a possible Duran Duran supershow in 2000 featuring the original five of us along with Warren Cuccurullo and some of the other guys that Simon and Nick had worked with. But it all sounded a bit naff, and the idea was soon put on ice.

Meanwhile, after spending years in LA, the Midlands, and Marbella, Tracey and I were making plans to start a new life together in Ibiza. It's a beautiful, warm, friendly island—the ideal place to continue to raise our growing family. We had four children by then: Andrew, born August 1984; my eldest daughter, Georgina, born August 1987; Bethany, born June 1991; and Isabelle, born May 1996.

I'd just come back from making arrangements in Ibiza in the summer of 2000 when the phone rang. It was John. This was the first time I had spoken to him for years.

"Hi, Andy, what are you doing these days?"

Moving to the perfect sunset soon, I thought. I guessed straightaway that John was calling me about the reunion, because there was no other reason to contact me these days, unless something sad had happened.

"I'm okay," I replied. "I'm making plans with Tracey to move to Ibiza. What about you?"

John explained that he was calling from LA, where he had been spending some time with Simon and Nick. All three of them had agreed the time was finally right for a reunion. *Already making plans,* I thought.

"Simon is here now, he really wants to do it. I've spoken to Nick yesterday and he is coming around again to discuss it."

The first thing I said was, "Are you sure about all this, JT, are you ready for it all again?"

"Yeah, I think it is probably the case that if we don't do it now it will never happen because we are all either forty or well on our way to being forty."

John was right and in his mind it was a fait accompli. I wasn't so sure it would be that simple, but it was nice to hear from him and he sounded very positive about it. So I phoned Roger and asked him what he thought.

"Well, is it going to be a problem for you and Nick to work together again?" he asked.

"You know it's going to be a problem. Will he be capable of responding in an environment of five players and relinquish his hold?" I said. "Because attempting to reinvent the wheel will be a disaster, and who's going to produce things, Rog? I wouldn't relish that task if it were the last band ever . . . because we always need a producer when recording, or more like a bloody referee . . ."

Roger and I decided to see how things unraveled, and after a few more conversations we arranged a meeting of all five of us in a lawyer's office in London. One thing I was slightly uneasy about was that Nick and Simon were insisting that Roger and I should be on a smaller percentage share of earnings than the other members of the band. They argued that they'd kept things going while we were away and so they were entitled to a greater cut. I could see their logic, so I agreed to take a smaller share, but on the understanding that if things took off we'd eventually return to splitting things five ways like we had in the eighties.

It was the first time I had been in a room with Nick for a long time, but it was fine. He hadn't changed much, but at least we didn't argue. The main difference between now and the last time we had all met was the transformation in John. He had a new light in his eyes and he was clearheaded. John hadn't really spent any time with me since he had sobered up and come to terms with his demons. I sensed he was still carrying a few battle scars, but it was good to see him looking so well. John later confided to me that he couldn't remember a lot of the things that had happened during his time in the band all those years ago. His way of describing it was that when you're caned you tend not to take part, but this time around he wanted to take part fully in everything.

The five of us discussed the fact that we'd had a few tour offers from America, but for once Nick and I shared the same view about something: neither of us thought that touring was the best way to go about a reunion. Our motivation for getting back together was partly about empowerment. It's very rewarding to be doing what you love in a successful lineup like we had during the eighties. Later on the motivation also became financial.

"What's the future if we just go out on the road and do a tour? Simon and I have been doing that anyway. What's the big deal?" reasoned Nick. "So we'll tour with the original band and that will be okay for a while, but then what? How do you sustain it?"

"That's a fair point," I said. "The only way you sustain it in my view is that we actually do what we're supposed to do, which is be a complete band and make a record."

"Exactly," said Nick. "We have to make a record."

I think everybody else in the room was shocked, not because of what we were proposing but because Nick and I were in such close agreement on something. The looks on the faces of Simon, John, and Roger seemed to say, *Fuck! Those two are agreeing, they are going to talk the rest of us into actually doing this.* Nick and I had never really been close since our epic fallouts over my feelings about Julie Anne, and my mind had been busy unpicking the past. Of course I had apprehensions, but these were outweighed by the potential benefits of a reunion and I reasoned that being older it would be easier to deal with all the baggage that goes along with being in a high-profile band. But I sensed that John seemed to be uneasy, so I suggested the two of us go outside for a chat in private.

"Look, what's the problem? We'll make an album and we'll reach out to people, that way we won't just be cashing in on the past," I said.

I argued that touring would be good—and it would make us plenty of money—but in my view we also needed a new record to give us an edge and to build a bit of excitement. John, however, was less convinced and kept saying it would be difficult. He'd assumed we'd just go on the road together and hadn't anticipated going into the studio.

"It won't be like it used to be, Andy," he argued. "Trust me, it's not the same. A lot has changed in fourteen years."

"Well, it'll be the five of us again, so what we'll be able to do,

John, is something that none of us have been able to do for years. We'll be able to plug in and see if we can still play and write songs and make something come out of the speakers that sounds good enough to make us all go, 'Oh shit, that's all right.' We need to start at a place with which we are all familiar, and that's each other . . . not Madison Square Garden."

John nodded: I'd won him over. We shared a smoke and rejoined the meeting.

JOHN and Nick went head-to-head with each other almost straightaway, posturing about who was in control. I was with John when he rang Nick soon after the meeting in London to start making plans, and they began to bicker on the phone, just like a pair of siblings. *Oh well,* I mused, *it's business as usual, did you expect anything less?* I'd never expected any of us to behave like vicars, but at least it was less toxic this time around. Nick made a few condescending asides about John, saying that he hoped he wouldn't hang around the studio because he was never there the first time, apart from to turn up and play his bass.

At first things progressed very slowly—John, Roger, and I suspected that Simon and Nick were deliberately dragging their heels. So the three of us—"the Three Taylors"—booked a studio in Monmouth, Wales, without them, just to see if we could still play together. We spent about ten days breaking the ice. It felt good to be together, being creative and surrounded by the solitude of the countryside.

As summer 2001 approached, Nick and Simon finally cleared their diaries, and the five of us arranged to go into a studio together in the south of France. We all agreed that we would try to do things economically this time around, but the first thing we did was to go out and rent a huge house in St. Tropez for a whopping £15,000 a week. It had beautiful gardens with sweeping views of the mountains on one side and a private infinity pool on the other (it was landscaped to give the optical illusion that the waters of the pool merged with the infinity of the Mediterranean). There were two Michelin chefs to cater for us, so despite our vow to keep an eye on spiraling costs we'd gone back to our old ways almost straightaway.

As soon as the five of us arrived we decided to go into St. Tropez for a long lunch at the local yacht club. We had a liquid lunchtime, knocking back the wine until we finally went back to the studio to do some jamming together—before later going off to a restaurant and club in the evening.

The next day we went down to a trendy beach restaurant and bumped into Flavio Briatore, the Formula One mogul and acquaintance of Le Bon's. He invited us for some pasta on his private yacht that night, but then failed to turn up because something came up. Anyway what the fuck, Nick had arranged for us to go on board yet another huge boat that night, which was owned by an Australian tycoon whom he knew. *Here we go,* I thought, *boats, clubs . . . it's like the eighties all over again.*

Incidentally, over the first day or two we managed to write three of the songs that were to eventually appear on our *Astronaut* album, so despite all the partying it was still a fairly productive time.

Unfortunately, it didn't take much longer than that for Nick and me to have our first big fallout—and when it came, it was as if years of pent-up tension came flooding out. We'd had many rows in the past, starting with the so-called pork pie incident all those years ago when we threw food at each other in our tour van. But this time it was much worse—and given our surroundings we'll call this one the l'escargot incident.

We'd all been to a nightclub, and Nick and I were both fairly drunk when we returned to the house in St. Tropez. For some reason the mood had turned nasty on the way back—probably due to an excess of booze—and Nick started to accuse me of being an embarrassment in the nightclub.

"You fell asleep in the club," he moaned. Ever the Head Boy.

"Well, you were drunk and made a twat of yourself also," I hit back. "You know you can't fuckin' dance, and even if I did fall off the table, at least it was in time to the beat, pal." I probably sounded like a proper smart arse, but my attitude was *Fuck you, you Revlon-wearing tosser.*

Suddenly we were in a heated argument as each of us continued to accuse the other of being out of order.

"Don't talk to me like that, Nick," I said. "I didn't fall asleep."

"You fell asleep," he insisted, squaring up to me aggressively.

I thought, *Does he seriously want a fuckin' slap?*

"Nick, don't wind me up or I'll fuckin' whack you, and you are drunk," I snarled back, and then I physically pushed him out of the way. We were now close to coming to blows and Nick shouted something back along the lines of if he'd had a baseball bat handy he'd have been willing to hit me with it. *Ooh* I was racked with fear—not. I knew he would never break a nail, and I told him where I would firmly insert the bat if he ever tried something like that. In truth, I wanted to break his bloody nose, but I restrained myself, because I didn't have the heart to hurt him. He had never learned where the line was when he was a younger man. In real life he would have been decked on a regular basis had he spoken to the average bloke in that way. Well, at least we now knew where each of us stood, even if it had taken twenty-one years to come out. The others could see we'd both lost our tempers, and they quickly intervened to calm things down.

Things were a bit delicate the next morning, as you can imagine. I knew we'd both been drunk and we were both out of order, so let's move on, I thought. It was a Sunday and there wasn't much planned for the rest of the day, so Roger and I went down to the studio and played some music together. I thought about Nick and I wondered if the reason he was so uptight was because he'd been getting his own way for so many years while I wasn't around—whereas now that John, Roger, and I were all back, things had changed. Simon, as usual, tried to act as a peacemaker between us, and I remember talking to him about the incident later that night. Simon pleaded with me to try and work things out with Nick, and I got the impression he felt that matters might quickly implode.

Thankfully things calmed down after that, but I knew that

there would be very little chance of Nick and me ever seeing eye to eye about anything from that point onward.

IT took nearly three years to get most of our material together for a new album, during which time there was no money coming from our activities in the band. We spent most of the summer of 2001 in France. Simon then needed a month off due to a death in his family, while the rest of us used the time to reorganize our management structure by bringing in some new faces. I'd put all my other business commitments on hold for Duran Duran, committed all my time and energy, even though I'd just shelled out for a load of new studio equipment for the move to Ibiza, which was now redundant. Despite our pledge to do things economically, our lavish spending on the reunion had left all of us with a bit of a cash flow problem by 2003.

I was with Simon in London one afternoon when we went to the bank, where he put his card into the ATM only to discover it didn't work. I tried mine and it also didn't work.

"Oh fuck. Well I better just transfer some money from another account into this one and it will be okay," said Simon.

Unfortunately, he discovered there was no money in his other account either.

Join the club, I thought.

So here we were, two members of the world's most successful pop band of the eighties, and neither of us had enough ready cash in the bank for our cards to work. To add to our problems, EMI had turned us down for a new record deal. The record industry itself was teetering on the edge, due to falling sales and revenue lost through illegal downloads. In total, we had spent around £600,000 over the last three years, and our funds had dwindled. Something needed to be done.

Soon afterward we attended a publicity shoot for the Red Bar at Sketch, a trendy new restaurant in London. Luckily the restaurant gave us complimentary memberships or it could have set us back a further £500 a head for lunch! Over lunch, at the most expensive restaurant in the world, I raised the prospect with our management of doing some live shows very, very soon.

"We have no option but to get this band out on the road," I said. "We've got to do some gigs because guess what? We've run out of money, so unless you have a brighter idea, that needs to be the next call."

The stark reality was that we no longer had a choice about holding off from touring until we had an album deal. We needed to go back on the road out of financial necessity. It became a magical turning point. We announced that to mark our twenty-fifth anniversary we'd be playing a series of gigs in Japan, including two shows at the Budokan auditorium in Tokyo.

I was at home in Ibiza on the Saturday that the tickets went on sale and I awoke to find an e-mail on my computer which was short and sweet.

MESSAGE: SOLD OUT IN 20 MINUTES.
CALL US—THE OFFICE.

"Do you want to do some more dates?" they asked when I called.

Stupid question. Of course we did! We announced some shows in the States and discovered that the demand for tickets was so great that we sold 4,000 in about six seconds, and the whole lot were gone within two minutes. At one point it swamped Ticketmaster's servers. The reaction from our fans was truly astonishing, and we soon arranged a fully fledged Twenty-fifth Anniversary Tour. Between the Japanese dates and the early American shows we managed to pull in around $1.1 million in ticket advances in the space of a week. We shared some of it between us and the rest went toward paying back some of what we all owed to Simon, who'd pumped around £300,000 of his own money into the band's reunion. In effect, he'd been lending us money to keep us afloat, which was something that I had felt

WILD BOY

uncomfortable about as matters unfolded. John's new wife, Gela Nash, co-owner of the Juicy Couture fashion line, had also been giving sponsorship money. We'd basically been robbing Peter to pay Paul, but as soon as we went on the road it was obvious that our financial fortunes were turning.

The warmth that we were greeted with at every show was amazing. Our audience were there for us when we needed them most. We owe them a very big thank-you, because without them the new album might never have materialized. Without the incredible turnout for the live shows we were scuppered. However, I was happy that our ability to be a real band had pulled us from the brink once again. We now had some money to put back into the system, and we had lots and lots of new material that we could put into shows alongside all the old favorite numbers from the eighties. It felt as if we were doing a proper rock-and-roll job again instead of just being in the studio arguing with each other's alter ego. We still needed to rehearse a bit more in order to tighten up, but we had all the components in place for a proper comeback—we just needed a record label to partner with.

It felt great to be back on the road, and this time around I noted with approval that Nick and Simon insisted on taking a huge wine chest packed with the finest vintages everywhere we went. (It must have contained about two hundred bottles, and on a later tour I estimated that at one point, between us and our families and crew we were glugging our way through around £25,000 of wine a week.) I also noticed that this time around all the road crew seemed to refer to Simon as Charlie, the nickname I gave him way back in the eighties.

After the comeback shows in America, I went back to Ibiza and Simon joined me there for a holiday. We were sitting around enjoying the sunshine, when I got a call from a girl named Julie in our office in London.

"I know you and Simon have just got back there, but MTV have been in contact and they want you to go to the States to present an award to someone," she said.

Mmm, I mused. Overexposure before we even get a foothold,

presenting an award without a current record to promote. You don't want to create the perception that somebody has done you a favor just for the exposure. At first, both Simon and I were reluctant to go. We were with all our families and children enjoying the break. I recall we were in a fish restaurant and about to get into a huge plate of oysters when my mobile phone rang again.

"They want all five of you to present it. You really should go," insisted Julie from our office.

What Simon and I didn't know at the time was that MTV weren't actually interested in Duran Duran doing the presenting— they were secretly planning to *give* us the award, which explains why the $50,000 costs were covered without a quip.

"Can't the others go?" I asked. "We're on holiday, it's not like we have a record to promote, and it is going to be full of rappers— not our natural domain if you think about it."

"No they want all five of you, very seriously."

Grudgingly Simon and I agreed. We arranged to fly from Ibiza to Madrid and then go on to New York from there. We also agreed to play a gig at Webster Hall in New York the night before the MTV Awards, which again turned out to be a good move as we weren't just going to be present in New York as the "token eighties presenters."

The gig was excellent and we got a great review in the *New York Post* the next day.

"Welcome to the home of the second British invasion," Simon shouted to the crowd during the concert, and the *Post* loved every minute of it. The newspaper columnist praised our whole set, which included all our classic numbers along with some new material, and a cover version we did of Grandmaster Flash's "White Lines."

"Le Bon sounded a little more Justin Timberlake than Grandmaster, and Andy Taylor added a guitar solo worthy of any rock band," said the *Post*'s reviewer.

I was expecting that most of the MTV show would be geared toward a young rap audience. The date was August 28, 2003: *Will anyone even know who we are?* I wondered. When we arrived at the hotel there wasn't an awful lot to do because MTV kept putting our call time for the rehearsal back. I was worried we'd run out of time so I rang the control room to ask why.

"Oh, it's all right. You guys have done this sort of thing so many times that we know you can pull it off live from the script. We don't need a rehearsal."

Then they asked the five of us to pop down to the MTV stylists' room so they could check out our outfits. When we got there we were greeted by a small army of stylists who fussed over every aspect of our appearance. That's strange, I thought, why are they so worried about what we look like if all we are doing is presenting an award? Surely, all we've got to do is say a few lines and then get off? They kept us busy there for ages, which meant we didn't arrive at the venue until the last minute. We were shown into seats at the very front of the audience. The entire young urban music community seemed to be seated all around us. Eventually we were called backstage to go and present and, as is usual at these events, it seemed like chaos behind the scenes.

"Ah, Duran Duran. You are copresenting with Avril Lavigne and Kelly Osbourne," someone from MTV told us.

Eh? That's *seven* presenters for one award. They gave us a script that involved Kelly saying a few words, followed by John and Simon. While we waited to go onstage, I chatted to Kelly about her father's Brummie roots, any excuse to don a flat Brummie accent. When we finally arrived onstage Kelly grabbed the microphone and began to read the opening part of the script from a teleprompter in front of us. Suddenly the script stopped and the teleprompter went blank. That's when the penny finally dropped.

Kelly explained to the audience that the real reason we were onstage was because Duran Duran were being given a Lifetime Achievement Award. I turned around and saw a man walk onstage with an armful of MTV gongs. There were five of them: one for each of us. The crowd went wild, and it was a feeling none of us had experienced for well over a decade. It was a young hip-hop audience yet they all got up to applaud us—Brits meet Bling.

Afterward we had a few huge celebrations and we were treated to the full delights of New York. As we did a tour of the media tents outside, we could hear the crowds of people at the barriers, who were all cheering and whooping. Twenty-three years after we had first met, it was almost like a movie scene. On the way in we'd been greeted by a few claps, but the reception we were getting now after we had received the award was ecstatic. An MTV Award is probably the hippest thing you can achieve in the eyes of youth culture, and to have the American public cheering you is a wonderful feeling, particularly for a UK band.

We buggered off to the Bungalow 8 nightclub for a huge party, and stuck our awards on show behind the bar.

How come the hip-hop crowd got us? I wondered.

"Because they're just the same as you guys; they love the lifestyle—yachts, jets, and jewels and unlimited hedonism," explained someone. "It's still just rock and roll, Andy."

The club became a frequent haunt for Duran Duran while in New York. As we were beginning our sold-out US tour, we were getting merrily smashed on vodka when my attention was drawn to a very sanguine-looking Victoria Beckham sitting in the corner with her producer, Damon Dash. She didn't look very happy at all. She was polite and approachable this time, even said hello. No snub tonight. You would have needed very big golden balls to interrupt our posse that night, because we were completely unapproachable and lit up like Xmas trees.

Yeah baby, I thought, *we're called Duran Duran and we're back in the USA!*

CHAPTER SIXTEEN

Kings of the Brits

AT the end of the summer of 2000, my father had told me he had cancer. This was on the day that we had agreed to re-form Duran Duran. It's strange how fate can deal you such enormous blows just when you think you are about to fly so high. I hadn't long put the phone down from speaking to John in LA when my dad called me at the studio in the UK. My mind was still soaring from the initial news that Simon and Nick were seriously up for a full Duran Duran reunion, but something about my father's tone of voice immediately brought me down to earth.

"Sit down, son. I've got some news," he said.

Whenever he referred to me as "son," it was time for a serious chat. As soon as he opened his mouth, I knew something was badly wrong. He'd been diagnosed with cancer of the gullet, and it was very, very advanced. He said that he had a huge tumor, so large that they had to operate as soon as possible.

Tracey and I packed, numbed by the news, and the next day we drove from the Midlands up to Newcastle to be with him and the family. All I was concerned about was getting the necessary scans done as soon as possible. How could we speed up the treatment? What would the National Health Service lottery be like? I went to see a cancer specialist with my father, and the doctor explained to me that they would need him in very quickly to get the operation done. The odds were not good, but to their credit, the doctors didn't mess about. I can truly say that my father's NHS trust functioned in a very compassionate way for its patients, and I was very grateful to the staff for their unwavering care. I was feeling devastated and filled with dread, but my father was ever the optimist, and all he seemed to be concerned about was making sure that my stepmother, brother, and I were all mentally okay. We chatted together about the band while we were waiting in the hospital.

"You'll never guess who phoned me, Dad . . . John bloody Taylor."

"Oh, JT," he said. "I always liked John . . ."

I told him all about our plans to re-form Duran Duran, and I could see that even amid all the pain he was going through, he was extremely pleased for me. It was his brave way of telling me that life goes on and you have to focus on what's ahead of you, even if it's going to be somewhat of a rough ride. I knew that there were going to be a lot of difficult hurdles.

When the time came for the operation, we signed all the medical paperwork together in order to give the surgeons permission to do whatever was needed.

All I could do now was to wait and pray. He was only sixty-one years old at the time—surely still too young to say good-bye? The surgical procedure placed his body under enormous strain, on a similar scale to that of a heart bypass, but despite everything being stacked against him, my father pulled through. I was so relieved and grateful. The doctors had got the tumor out, and within six months they told us he was clear. It seemed like a miracle. The cancer was gone and surely lightning couldn't strike twice, could it?

AFTER the high of the MTV Awards, the rest of 2003 had flown by in spectacular fashion. Initially, there was no great master plan, but the phone didn't stop ringing and every show we booked sold out, often within hours or even minutes. Many of the concerts were large arena shows which were cosponsored by American radio stations, and the demand was still enormous. On September 20 we played in front of 57,000 people at the Hyundai Pavilion in San Bernardino, California. The Cure and several other eighties bands were on the same bill. We later spoke to the Cure about the possibility of touring with them, because the potential seemed astronomical.

A couple of weeks later we were sitting in the lobby of the Mercer Hotel in New York, when somebody pointed out that despite all the intense interest we'd created in America and Japan, we still hadn't played a single comeback gig in the UK. We really ought to organize something back home, we collectively reasoned, so let's put on a one-off show there—but without overegging it into a grandiose event. We decided to phone our old friend Rob Hallett in London, basically to ask his advice as we felt he was the only one who'd understand where we were coming from. At first we wanted to do the show in Birmingham, and we toyed with the idea of performing at the Hyatt Hotel, standing on our old roots where the Rum Runner used to be. But Rob, never one to mince his words, advised us to do it in London.

"At the end of the day most of your fans are going to be in the South, even if you are from Birmingham. Do it in the place where the most people are," he reasoned.

Rob suggested the Forum at Kentish Town in north London. It's an intimate venue with a perfect stage and a standing audience, ideal for our homecoming.

"When do you want to do it?" he asked.

"Within a week or so," we said.

Believe it or not, we organized it from New York in the space of about five days from start to finish.

The Forum was packed to the rafters with about 2,500 people on the floor and a further 500 on the guest list, which read like a Who's Who of the London showbiz world. For me, it was also a special gig because it was the first time any of my children came to see Duran Duran live—and they couldn't believe it. Most of the younger members of the cast of *EastEnders,* a popular British TV soap drama, were there, which impressed my family no end!

"Dad! They all came here to see you," was their initial reaction. I think it was all a little odd to them, and they were certainly not used to so much attention being directed at them.

When we went onstage we tore the place apart. The intensity of the reaction from our fans gave us a tumultuous high and it was without doubt the very best Duran Duran gig *ever.* I've performed at two Live Aid concerts, played live at Madison Square Garden, and performed at hundreds of arena concerts packed with tens of thousands of people. But nothing compared to this for sheer energy and straight-up fun. In hindsight, it's a shame we didn't film it for a DVD. We started our set with an album track, "Friends of Mine," which worked amazingly well as an opener. This was an audience of our most ardent fans and they greeted every number with enormous enthusiasm. A lot of our following were now grown-up women in their thirties, but they were acting like they were fifteen again, and it was amazing to see this new phenomenon. We closed the show with "Wild Boys" and then performed "Rio" as an encore . . . I guess some things will never change!

The reviews in the press the following morning were ecstatic, and word was starting to spread that we had finally got our act back together—all five of us. We got a similar, ecstatic reaction from fans in Philadelphia, where our tour bus was almost overturned by five hundred rampant mothers! It was nuts. There were crowds of mature women all behaving like teenagers, and they were rocking the vehicle. These were women, not girls, and the police had to clear the area with horses. (Don't get me wrong, ladies, we were secretly very, very flattered by the attention!)

Not long afterward, I had managed to snatch a few days' holiday in the Devonshire countryside with my family, when the telephone rang one Saturday morning. Would we be interested in touring Australia and New Zealand with Robbie Williams? I asked how big the shows would be and I was told we'd be performing in front of audiences of around 70,000. Of course we're interested! I was determined to say yes, but I was the only member of the band in favor of accepting the tour, so I had to talk the others into it. The promoter strongly urged us to go and argued that we would add 10,000 to 20,000 in ticket sales for each gig.

"Come on, guys," I argued. "We've never played in New Zealand, and it would be very cool to go back down to Australia." I guess I was also surprised by the initial negative resistance, but that's all part of a band's metabolism.

Eventually the others agreed and sure as sure can be, they were bloody huge gigs—*enormo-dome sized!* In Melbourne we broke the house record at the Telstra Dome for the biggest-ever gig, and it was overpowering. I've never seen so many people indoors before. There seemed to be tens of thousands of people, tier after tier, stacked to the ceiling. Robbie had this big walkway that extended out into the middle of the arena, and I realized that I hadn't done a gig that big since Live Aid. Robbie himself was very cool, friendly, well grounded, and very, very good live—he reminded me of a young Freddie Mercury onstage. Our own performances were also very energetic, and because Robbie had created such a huge stage, we'd cover a lot of ground during a show and it could be extremely tiring on the old legs.

I suspect that one or two of the other members of Duran Duran were secretly resentful of the fact that technically we were Robbie's support act, but I didn't feel that way. For me it was more like a festival arrangement, and professionally it was another important notch under our belts to appear alongside someone as current and as vibrant as Robbie Williams. When we were offstage, the tour was a very sober affair, although I admit that I was still physically shattered by the end of it!

On the way home from Australia we stopped off at Hong Kong, where we received a phone call offering us a further block of four to six shows in the UK. There had been around 200,000 applications to Ticketmaster for the Kentish Town gig, so it was a fair bet there would still be a lot of demand from people to see us live. We agreed and the tickets just kept selling, until we'd played a total of seventeen dates in the UK. This included breaking the house record at Wembley Arena for the most people at a single show, which was something that I got to announce to the audience—a little piece of Wembley history.

There was still no master plan, but our renewed success did mean that we were finally in a position to land what we needed the most: a record deal. It made sense for us to go with a US record company this time around, because a lot of our comeback activity had been based in the States. Sony, which is a predominantly American label, were keen to sign us, but Universal made us a better offer in the UK. There was a lot of debate about who to go with. There was something seductive about being with a British label again, but in the end we signed with Sony. I knew Donnie Ienner, who was president of the company, from my time in America, and we got on well because he was a bit of a rock fan and he loved acts in the mold of Bruce Springsteen. Donnie was a big, tall, Ivy League kind of guy who looked as if he could have been an American senator. He'd been in the business for twenty years and he could be a bit combative, but he liked to have a bit of a banter and he respected you if you held your own.

Donnie came to see us live at Wembley and he loved the show, so we did the deal with him instantly. Our ability to deliver live had served us well again. Intellectually, going with an American record label was the right thing to do, but with hindsight, and in my view, it was a fundamental mistake, because we later found ourselves under a lot of pressure to work with certain US producers who weren't all necessarily what Duran Duran needed. But for now, it looked like a great deal. We had Donnie on our side, and fans were packing every gig we played.

WE were in Houston to perform "Wild Boys" at a show that went out live on US network TV before the Super Bowl in February 2004,

WILD BOY

when I received a telephone call telling me that my father had cancer for the second time. It was a different type of the disease, completely unrelated to the gullet cancer he recently beat. My father had suffered prostate problems for several years, but it had now developed into fully blown cancer. The specialist said he could not have been more unlucky: to have beaten the gullet problems only to be diagnosed with an unconnected cancer was against all the odds, very unusual. Lightning had struck for the second time. It was as if the curse of Mr. Cancer had a personal vendetta against my dad. The disease had been rampant on my father's side of the family, something that deals unfathomable odds to you and your loved ones. I remember speaking to one of our bodyguards whose own father had died of cancer, and he told me that the second time around the disease doesn't want to let go. *It's going to get him,* I thought. From this point onward, the shadow of my father's cancer was always there lurking darkly in the background. All the feelings of apprehension and fear came back, and I knew the prognosis was not good.

Ironically, the news about my dad coincided with what should have been one of my happiest moments professionally, because it came just before we were due to receive an award for Outstanding Contribution to Music at the Brit Awards in London. It was well timed, because in early April we were due to start a fully fledged Duran Duran reunion tour of the UK. My father's diagnosis with prostate cancer had left me feeling shell-shocked, but as the Brits approached I tried to put on a brave face. We were due to perform "Wild Boys" and "Ordinary World" live at the awards, which were being held at Earl's Court in London. Nick had insisted on "Ordinary World" even though it was a song that had been recorded while Roger and I weren't in the band. I thought it would have made more sense to do "The Reflex" and "Wild Boys," but Nick got his way. (I wondered if secretly he liked the idea of grandstanding the one major hit that he and Simon had enjoyed *during the nineties* while Roger and I were out of the frame.) It was a strange choice, considering that two out of the five of us had nothing to do with creating it, but I didn't mind too much because it's a song that I love to perform—and it was an immensely popular song, as Nick never missed an opportunity to point out!

I'd only ever been to the Brits once before, in the nineties—Tracey and I had been guests of Rod Stewart when he collected an award with the Faces. That had been a hilarious evening. All the Faces were there, apart from the glorious Ronnie Lane. To me, they were all just the same as I remembered seeing them on TV, still all noses and hair, except they were a bit older. They all had a proper old drink together before going onstage and playing a fantastic set. Afterward we all went back to their dressing room, where they carried on drinking and cracking jokes (usually at some other poor bastard's expense!). Rod is one of the funniest guys you could ever meet, and watching him alongside the Faces was like an episode of *The Comedians* on TV. The Faces (formerly the Small Faces) were a quintessential bunch of Cockney lads who were determined to take the piss out of anyone and everyone they met, but all in the best possible taste of course.

Amid this hilarity, in walked Lenny Kravitz, who'd also been attending the awards. There was a pause in the merriment as the group eyed up their very tall, beautiful, and impeccably dressed visitor. Lenny was just about the biggest star in America at the time, so it was a very grand entrance he had acquired.

"Hey guys, I'm Lenny," he said,

"All right, Lenny," replied one of the Faces.

Each member of the band offered their individual greetings as Lenny went around the room.

"Hello, Lenny, son."

"Good to see yer, Lenny. Yeah."

"Nice one, Lenny."

Looking very pleased with this warm reception, Lenny then went off to continue his tour of the building and other artists' trailers. No sooner had he closed the door behind him, when there was a brief silence followed by the most English of put-downs: "Wanker!"

The entire trailer, guests et al., burst out laughing at the cruel assessment of Lenny. It was a very UK moment, and to me it summed up British rock-and-roll humor perfectly, and how not to take yourself too fucking seriously. It wasn't that the boys wanted to be nasty to Lenny; they were basically taking the piss out of themselves for exuding so much fake charm when they'd been introduced to him. It was also their way of saying, *You might be a big international star, but you're not in Kansas now, Toto!* The other thing I remember from that night is how the Faces constantly joked with each other by repeating over and over again the choice phrase, "Bollocks, you cunt!" (And to think they wrote some of the sweetest lyrics of the times!)

So it was with fond memories that I attended the Brits with Duran Duran on February 17, 2004. We arrived at Earl's Court in a single limousine, containing all five members of the band and two bodyguards. Also on the bill that night were 50 Cent, the Darkness, Dido, and the Black Eyed Peas. While we were getting out of our limo, a huge convoy of black vehicles pulled up containing 50 Cent and his enormous entourage. We watched in amazement as a seemingly endless stream of bodyguards climbed out of the stretched cars before finally the man himself emerged. I didn't have the heart, or the balls, to tell him that we don't pack heat in quite the same way over here in the UK, but who would?

When we got inside I found myself chatting with Justin Hawkins, the lead singer of the Darkness. He was a very nice bloke, very personable. However, the conversation was somewhat surreal, because he was wearing a huge set of feathered wings on his back. The bizarre outfit was part of his costume for his performance later that evening—meanwhile, he was passing the time before going onstage by playing table tennis. Just at that moment 50 Cent and entourage walked by and Hawkins squealed out a very enthusiastic greeting.

"Hey 50, man, wanna come and play table tennis with me?"

Big mistake, Justin, I thought, *big mistake. You're dressed like a chicken and he hasn't got a clue who you are, save that you want to play him at table tennis. To add to this, he has about thirty blokes on his side.*

Now, a game of basketball would have been more of a cultural exchange, but an offer from a chicken-winged, androgynous rock singer to play Ping-Pong didn't strike me as 50's definition of urban cool. Although Justin was wearing wings, I figured this probably wouldn't fly and if the rapper dude took it as a public put-down then . . . aren't they supposed to shoot you at that point? The rapper stared wide-eyed at Hawkins and then walked off, saying, "Weird, man—fuckin' weird!" It was another very English moment during an evening when Duran Duran took center stage and held it effortlessly, and we felt like kings of the Brits. I was very chuffed that my kids and family got to see the good side of our endeavors, and I was also pleased that we, as five guys all aged forty-plus, could still hack it live on national TV at the most prestigious event on the UK music calendar.

Later, at the aftershow, I chatted to Justin Timberlake, who presented us with the award. We talked about the possibility of working together at some point and he said it would be an interesting proposition. He was very into music and he'd been doing it a very long time for such a young man.

IT was a great evening at the Brits but the euphoria soon began to wear off as the impact of my father's illness sank in. Some of the shows that we performed on our tour were fantastic and got great reviews, so my dad was still smiling on his daily trip to the paper shop, but deep down inside I knew he was living on borrowed time. I did what I could to help and offered to pay for him to have treatment in the States, but he insisted on staying close to home. I felt uneasy that my commitments in Duran Duran meant I had to be away from him so much, and at times it felt like I was living in a Bermuda Triangle as I tried to juggle between spending time either with him or my own family or with the band. One small blessing was that Duran Duran played in a gig in Newcastle for the first time in twenty-three years, which was excellent because it meant my dad could come and see the band perform live in our hometown. It was an unforgettable evening and it lifted my spirits enormously to be on home turf.

Meanwhile, Sony were eager to get their hands on our comeback album, which we'd decided to title *Astronaut*. We planned to make it an out-and-out pop record. The problem was that we found ourselves in the crazy position of touring, doing promotional work, and trying to finish the album all at the same time. The pressure began to build, and Nick and Simon soon started to argue incessantly about lyrics. Nick had reappointed himself head of the Lyric Police, and he seemed to be always on Simon's back, and they bickered so often that some of the crew nicknamed them Hinge and Brackett after the two old women characters in the famous TV drag act of the same name.

Their rowing had started in the south of France, when we first began to work on the new album, and it got worse. On one occasion Nick pinged off an e-mail having a go at Simon about this lyric or that lyric, and he copied it to everybody else. *Who made you the boss, Nick?* I thought. In my opinion it showed that he still didn't have much respect for the rest of us to take it upon himself to fire off such an e-mail on his own. I felt that this was particularly harsh on Simon, who seemed to be going through a patch that many songwriters experience, wherein it suddenly becomes much harder to keep churning out the material because you literally run out of words.

I'd witnessed a similar thing with other singers. Rod Stewart had been very open with me about this and explained that sometimes it's possible to go through periods in which you don't always enjoy it so much. With us, it got to the point where Nick seemed to be threatening to write the lyrics himself. I was utterly against this, because Simon had always been the only lyricist we needed, and you can't replace the uniqueness of originality. But Simon couldn't seem to get his lyrics to where he was happy with them, and he didn't seem to want to take on board any comments from the rest of us when we tried to help.

I suddenly realized why John had initially been so against recording a new album. He'd been around Simon and Nick more than

I during the late eighties and nineties, and maybe he accepted that their creative relationship was badly fractured.

I spoke to Nick about it in the hope that I might be able to help; in situations like this it's often useful to have someone other than the singer throw in their ideas in order to get things flowing. I said something along the lines of, "I know I can work with Simon." I hadn't spent the wilderness years of the nineties with him, so we weren't worn out creatively. But my efforts proved to be mainly unproductive because I felt, rightly or not, that every time I offered any constructive criticism Simon seemed to take it the wrong way. If we'd been able to communicate healthily, then the input I was offering would have been taken in good spirit, but I think it was often perceived as an attempt to rip him apart. Was I expecting the old bugger to be up to more than he really was? I wondered. Whatever the answer, it definitely wasn't happening. I've thought a lot about why Simon was like that: maybe it was because he'd taken such a battering from Nick over the years or maybe that he simply couldn't take anyone else's input anymore. Or perhaps he'd been trying for commercial success for so long that he just couldn't see things with a fresh head or notice the wood for the trees.

Whatever the cause, it was very frustrating for all involved. Our management team had constant behind-the-scenes conversations regarding the problem but offered little by way of a solution. We must have recorded twenty or thirty songs that I could play you now, but they were never fully finished. Frustratingly, we all spent a lot of time and energy working on material that was not completed, either because Simon didn't write the lyrics or because Nick didn't like the way they were going or he had other things to attend to. It was as if the intensity of their focus seemed to have faded, although they still remained very close socially. Perhaps that's what Duran Duran was now, I wondered—a musical social club with an overpriced transport plan.

The difficulties started to cause new tensions between Simon and myself, and there also seemed to be growing friction between Roger and Simon, which was something that had never surfaced before.

Roger and I were still on a slightly reduced percentage of the band's earnings than Simon, Nick, and John, and it was beginning to irritate me. In my view, our live shows had been the major driving force behind Duran Duran's comeback, and I felt we had both made a huge contribution in helping to drive the energy and vigor of that. The problem was that every time I raised the issue, something would come up to put it off, and the matter was never given any proper airtime.

The friction over lyrics came to a head in the form of a blazing row between Simon and me during a session one Saturday afternoon when I suggested he try to sing a line to song called "Want You More" in a certain way.

"Why don't you do it like this, take the line and stick it here?" I suggested. His angry response was not in character.

"No. Don't be pompous with me," he snapped back.

Pompous! Why is he mad with me? I wondered.

"Don't call me fucking pompous," I countered. "When you write songs together, try living on a two-way street, then perhaps you won't feel like you are constantly driving in the wrong fucking direction year after year. You weren't like this when we were younger."

And neither, I thought, *was I.*

"I'm just saying change that line and put it somewhere different and you are flatly saying no?" I asked.

Simon stood his ground, taking as hostile my attempts to be constructive, and before I knew it we were in an angry screaming match. *I am out of here,* I thought. What concerned me the most was that his reaction was totally out of character. Did he harbor some deep resentment from all the troubles of the eighties? Pissed off, I slipped out of the studio and caught the first British Airways flight back from Gatwick to Ibiza. I stopped for a long overdue vindaloo en route to the airport, and like any Englishman with a belly full of curry, I then drank a lot of plonk in the departure lounge—so by the time I was boarding the plane I felt wobbly and full of anger and chillies.

When I arrived home my temper overheated and I threw a full bottle of beer across the courtyard of our villa, watching it shatter against the old walls. It was the first time in my life that I'd ever thrown something like that in anger and Tracey could see that I was close to the edge—it felt like we were back in Germany in 1982. She was right: I began to question in my mind whether my row with Simon was the beginning of something bleak and irreversible.

With the fact that we'd now been working on the album for three years and it was hardly flowing like a river, I realized that touring with Duran Duran was also becoming less and less fun. It was still exciting to receive so much attention, but we no longer had any sense of togetherness when we came offstage. We were all different people now (not to mention much older) and we didn't go off to clubs to drink together after our shows like we did in the old days. None of us were doing drugs this time around, nor were we sharing much else in common. We were five separate individuals, and it felt to me as if the band didn't seem to have any collective soul of its own. Even all the fine wine we carried around with us tended to be consumed away from each other with our respective friends or family when they visited us on the road. I felt that the only bit that was really enjoyable was the part where we were playing together onstage.

We carried on recording but it continued to be laborious work. Some of it was done in London and then the rest was completed while we were in the States doing promotion for the forthcoming but as yet unfinished album. Talk about putting the cart before the horse. I was getting the distinct impression that we were not getting the benefit of much good advice from our recently appointed New York–based management.

All the time we were doing promotional interviews on the radio I could tell the record wasn't really kicking in: it was just spin, spin, spin—but with no real substance. One of the things you learn very quickly in music is that you can't win by cheating—you can't fake inspiration or great songs. Just simply seeing how it's done isn't enough; there are some fundamental skills and instincts beyond basic PR. I began to wonder whether or not we should wait until the New Year to give us more time to get it right, but Sony were keen to go ahead.

Eventually, our new album *Astronaut* went on sale in late October 2004. I was happy enough with the music itself. I'd written a very large amount of the material myself and, despite all the ups and downs, I had worked very closely with Simon, but I didn't like the way we had mixed and finished it. We'd had no time to sit on it and tweak it for even a couple of weeks, which is often necessary in order to clear your ears and listen to it with a fresh perspective for one last time. I can never understand the almost hormonal rush for attention and cash flow that occurs with a record release.

We got the American chart result for the first week of *Astronaut* on the same day we appeared on the Ellen DeGeneres show in the States. Ellen was a great host, a really fabulous woman, but despite the pleasant experience of going on her show, no sooner had we blasted off when our sales figures soon brought us down to earth later that day. *Astronaut* sold 51,000 albums; it went in at number fifteen in the US chart and it made number three in the UK chart. It was a respectable start but hardly the huge comeback fanfare we'd been working for. Our management tried to put a positive gloss on it, but I wasn't willing to be fooled as the next week's shipping figures were already down by 50 percent.

"We've sold eighty million records in the past," I said. "This is fifty thousand."

To create any real momentum we were hoping for 200,000, or at worst 150,000 as a start, but as November hit, the album was actually moving down the charts—in total *Astronaut* sold about a million copies worldwide. It was enough to ensure that we didn't lose any money, but it didn't really create enough of a buzz to give us any focus on the radio. We probably sold more concert tickets in most areas than we did albums. Yes, there was still plenty of demand for nostalgia shows, but the album had been a laborious plod commercially.

To be fair to the others, I probably wasn't always the easiest person to be around during this period, and I can remember some ridiculous rows between us. We were traveling in a car when I had a huge rant at some of the others when they proposed playing a gig in China. I gave them a twenty-minute lecture on why I didn't want to go there because of the political situation. I began to enjoy winding them up. It was my way of intimidating the others to drop the illusion that we'd made the best of our collective endeavors.

One other very important fact was that I was on the way to suffering from depression. I lost my rag with Nick while we were in a car together in Europe doing some promotional work. We didn't have any security with us, and there'd been a few crowds that had jostled us for autographs as we went in and out of hotels. I'm normally happy to sign things for fans, but I was starting to feel twinges of the agoraphobia that I'd experienced twenty-five years ago. I was also quite snappy with people over our overexposure; some band members thought we were U2 and attempted to emulate them. Nick was sitting in the car with me droning on about something or other when I suddenly snapped.

"Shut the fuck up!" I screamed at him. "This is the real world, Nick, there are so many real things in life that are more important than what you are going on about."

We continued the rest of the journey in silence. I think some of the others could see I was under strain, because afterward John and Roger came and sat down with me in a room and we talked about it. Roger had made no secret of the fact that he'd found things mentally tough in the past and John, having been in and out of rehab, had also struggled with many demons. John knew what it felt like to come up against a big hump in the road that you can't seem to get around, which was the way I was beginning to feel. I explained that I'd never been one who liked struggling through crowds, and maybe the fact that the album had flopped had taken a bit of a toll on me, compounded by my father's illness.

"We need to start taking good care of ourselves," I said. "We shouldn't be at a boiling point all the time."

I think Roger and John sort of understood, and I was grateful to them for listening. Like I've said before, over the years being in

Duran Duran had given us enormous highs, but it sometimes took an unforgiving toll on all of us.

AS I jetted back to Ibiza toward the end of 2004, it was as if my own personal dark cloud was still gathering above me. The fact that my dad was battling cancer was still weighing heavily on my mind. The news of his illness had come off the back of Robert Palmer and Tony Thompson passing away the previous year. I'd been enormously close to both of them. Tony was in his forties, Robert in his fifties, and my dad was in his sixties. Suddenly death was within the range of my life force, and there were some big empty chairs in the musical family.

I used my time in Ibiza to spend a few quiet days with my family before I was due to travel to the States to do some more promotional work. I got up on the morning I was due to depart, with the intention of catching a plane to London in order to travel on to the States to do a TV appearance and a radio interview. At about 5:30 a.m. I went into the kitchen to have a cup of tea and a smoke—then a weird thing happened. I lay down on a big wooden bench as the kettle was boiling. Then the whistle went off, but I just couldn't get up or move from the bench. It felt as if someone was pushing me back down, physically pinning me to the wood. Suddenly I felt uncontrollably emotional and all heavy—what I envisage drowning must be like. I wasn't exactly having a panic attack, but I just broke down and I couldn't get up.

Tracey found me in the kitchen. I guess she wasn't surprised, because I think she'd already noticed that something was out of kilter within me. My dad had terminal cancer and she was concerned that part of me was blaming myself for not spending enough time with him, always being away, feeling selfish. I recognized that the signs were not good: I felt as if I was on the edge of a nervous breakdown.

Tracey urged me not to go the States. She didn't meet any resistance and I agreed to stay at home.

We tried to explain things to the rest of the band—I am not really sure that all of them completely understood how low I was. Looking back, I'm glad I'd at least explained things to Roger and John as best as I could.

I took a few weeks off, and I saw a couple of different people with a lot of wisdom about this sort of matter. I've always had a practical approach to the unexplained. Let's begin to explain it and start figuring this shit out, I thought, not exactly realizing what "this shit" was. Thankfully, the rest and peacefulness of being with Tracey and my family helped to calm down and relax me, but deep inside I knew there was still more to come.

WE were playing at the Hard Rock Cafe in Las Vegas in March 2005 when I received a text message telling me I needed to return to England immediately: my father had fallen into a coma. I got the first flight that I could the next morning and traveled back to Newcastle alone, praying that I would make it in time. When I finally got there he was heavily sedated with morphine and he had been unconscious for almost seventy-two hours. I could see that the illness and the effects of the morphine had taken a heavy toll on him. I spoke to him softly, and when he heard my voice he woke up for the first time in three days. He could see me and he was awake for about ten minutes: it was as if he had been waiting for me.

He had just enough strength left to break through the morphine and whisper good-bye to me in a tiny voice. I could barely hear him. Then he closed his eyes and he never opened them again. There was no pain at the end. He had a dignified death.

I thought of all the things he had done for me when I was a child. How he raised my brother and me after our mother abandoned us. How he stood silently weeping alone in the kitchen on the day she moved out, and how he always held things together with that strange Northern resilience that kept him going. I thought about all the conversations we'd had about my life in the band over the years.

How I'd called him in excitement the first time we'd appeared on *Top of the Pops*. I recalled the quiet pride in his eyes when I helped him pay off his mortgage.

The cancer had finally claimed him and I was going to miss him.

It was the hardest good-bye.

I didn't grieve properly at first. There was a strike of council workers in the North East, so there was going to be a ten- or eleven-day delay before the funeral could take place. I went back to the States to continue with our tour in the meantime, but my heart wasn't in it. After an awful journey, which involved a very difficult transfer between Gatwick and Heathrow, I went back onstage with Duran Duran in Detroit. I wore my dark sunglasses onstage as normal, and after the show I received an e-mail from a fan who had seen the tears rolling down my cheeks under the shades. Duran Duran later played a gig at Boston University while I was back in England for the funeral, and Simon dedicated his rendition of "Ordinary World" on stage to "absent friends!"

It was a very sad time.

CHAPTER SEVENTEEN

History Repeats: Why I Am No Longer in Duran Duran

I could feel the pressure building up in Duran Duran for a long time. I was tired of going over and over the same old creative difficulties and financial tensions, and I was fed up with having blazing rows with our management over what I perceived to be our lack of clear direction. But when things finally came to a head and we parted company, it was actually all over a simple travel visa.

I was getting ready to fly to New York to be with the rest of Duran Duran in September 2006 when I discovered our management had failed to organize a visa to allow me to enter the US to work during this time period. I suppose in the grand scale of things this might not seem like the end of the world, but as far as I was concerned it was the straw that broke the camel's back. After month upon month of arguing about money, and the implosion of our latest plans to record an album, what chance did we have of getting things right if our management couldn't even organize a simple visa? It meant I was stuck on my backside in Ibiza, while a very expensive session involving the rest of the band took place on the other side of the Atlantic. I was furious, and I fired off an angry e-mail to our management and copied it to Simon Le Bon.

"I'd rather not have to get into this with you, but I am fuckin' seriously unhappy," I told Simon in a covering note.

Within a few weeks the Duran Duran Web site announced that I would no longer be playing with the band when they appeared at a forthcoming gig in Hong Kong. So how had things become so bad that we had to go our separate ways?

I'D gone back on the road with Duran Duran in America after my father's funeral. For a while I thought that I'd dealt with the grief, and I hoped that I would put the disappointment of *Astronaut* behind me. The summer of 2005 saw our old friend Mr. Geldof organize Live 8. I was interested to see what the chemistry would be like between Geldof and Simon, because during the nineties there'd been some bad blood between them over Paula Yates's affair with Michael Hutchence. Geldof knew that Simon and Hutch had been good mates for years, and he phoned Simon up and furiously demanded to know whether or not Simon had known about Paula's affair while she was married to Bob. I wondered if there was any potential for further fireworks, but in the end we opted to play at the Rome leg of the show and I don't think they ever came face to face.

The day itself was a bit of a nightmare. Our management had a row with the promoter behind the scenes over something or other, and at one point we threatened to pull out. Our performance eventually went ahead but Live 8 felt strangely subdued compared to the original Live Aid in 1985. Afterward, we had to rush off to play at the Roskilde festival in Denmark the same evening, so the travel arrangements were very hectic. I nearly got stranded in Denmark thanks to a mix-up over the air tickets. Additionally there was a lot of fraying around the edges with other band members, and JT lost it after the Roskilde festival—totally lost it. The European tour had been up and down, which reflected in sales, and we had struggled to sell out certain markets, so I guess all this had taken its toll on John and he just erupted. He did the same song and dance I had run through in Germany the previous winter: he just lost his temper about nothing in particular, uncontrollably sober.

Even though our album sales had been a bit of a disappointment, we were still making reasonable money from touring. Donnie Ienner at Sony agreed to go ahead with a second album. I was surprised because he could easily have decided to walk away after *Astronaut;* nevertheless, he stood by us and repaid our faith in him. I was pleased, and despite the problems we'd been through I slowly started to feel positive about going into the recording studio again. *Perhaps we've turned the corner*, I thought, *and the cloud is lifting*. With every album you should get the opportunity to wipe the slate clean and start again (unless you're Duran Duran).

One of the highlights of the year came when we were invited on a private tour of the White House on the day we were due to play a gig in Washington. We'd never been particularly political as a band, so unlike a lot of other acts at the time we hadn't really spoken out about the war in Iraq. I think the military do a fantastic job, and hanging out with the forces in my younger days had given me respect and an insight into that life. Even though life on the road in a band can be cruel, it's nothing in comparison to what these boys and girls are asked to do. I felt they were given an impossible task in taming Iraq—but it was a viewpoint I kept to myself, as we never pontificated about politics in Duran Duran. We'd always stayed away from controversy in that respect, and I was delighted when we got a call from the White House inviting us up for a private tour.

Nick, Roger, and I accepted. In the morning the three of us went up to the White House, where we spent some of the most memorable hours of all my time in Duran Duran. The security, as you can imagine, was very impressive, but the Secret Service men were all incredibly polite and they showed us from room to room. President Bush was away at the time, but just to be able to walk around the famous old building was an honor. The three of us even posed together for a photograph at the White House podium, and it's now one of my favorite pictures. The American people always made us feel truly welcome whenever we were in the States, and the photo symbolizes that for me.

There was an embarrassing postscript to our White House visit.

When we performed that evening in Washington, for some reason Simon took it upon himself to break our silence about the war while he was onstage. Simon was normally devoid of any political opinion apart from the fact that he didn't like President Bush, and he chose the worst possible time to share it with the crowd. Scores of Secret Service men had come down to watch the concert after they'd made us feel so welcome at the White House, and here was Simon being disrespectful to their glorious leader. I think he said something along the lines of it being a shame that Bush was in the White House for another four years. He may have been correct, but he didn't stop to think where we were, in the most political environment in modern history—Bush's Washington. As soon as he started talking, I feared it would go down badly with the crowd, so I flicked my cigarette at him from across the stage to try and distract him, but it was too late. The crowd got riled, and in support of Bush they started chanting, "*Four more years! Four more years!*"

Aghh, Simon. Just fuckin' shut up and sing "Rio"! I thought to myself. He hadn't made a gaffe like that since we were young, but it made me laugh. I guess if you get a chance to piss in the Bushes' backyard, you may feel compelled to take it. And no, I didn't steal anything from the White House, not for the want of trying but because the Secret Service watch you like bloody hawks—they must have heard about thieving young Geordie lads!

WE played a lot of gigs and we made some good money that summer, but at times I felt as if we were just treading water after almost twenty-five years together. The old creative frictions within the band were still there, and it struck me that we'd never actually sat down together to lay to rest the problems and arguments that we'd had with each other for various reasons the first time around.

Meanwhile, I still had my own personal demons to deal with. Toward the end of the tour I'd started to enjoy rather more booze than was probably healthy, which wasn't difficult amid the abundant supply of fine wines and clarets. I'd opted to travel from gig to gig on my own tour bus so that I could be with my family rather than fly with the others. It meant that I had my loved ones around me, but also meant that I was increasingly distant from the rest of Duran Duran. As far as booze was concerned, I could feel some of my old habits returning, and I started reacting badly to a few people around me when perhaps I should have held my temper. I remember going back to the bus one evening and finding it was in darkness because the power had been switched off. I slipped on the stairs in the gloom and really whacked my shin, still bear the scar. I'm afraid I then went into a really aggressive rant I'm not very proud of, and even though there were children around I was very pissed off. I threw my mobile phone on the floor and petulantly stamped on it, then I demanded someone else's phone to make a call. I rang our tour manager and berated him for failing to make sure the electric stayed on. He said he tried to contact me to warn me. *Well, call me next time*, I thought, *but call me on what, now that I don't have a phone?*

The next morning, after I'd calmed down, he called me back on someone else's handset.

"I am not going to quit, because I know you are not normally a nasty fucker and you were drunk, but you know what? You scared me," he said.

It made me take a long hard look at myself. After our American tour ended I decided to dump the two bottles of wine nightly and opted for more sleep. We had about three weeks to rest and prepare before we were due to start recording the album, and once again I began to feel cautiously optimistic about the future. After the initial uncertainty about whether or not Sony would want to go ahead with another record, I felt we'd been given another great chance to shine. On *Astronaut* we'd been chasing our tails by trying to make an album that fitted the times, instead of leading the way by doing our own thing. This time around Sony said they wanted a rock album with some edge. Edge of where? I wondered. All our edges were now well rounded. I'd always favored a more rock-led approach, and I felt we were regarded as a serious rock band when we played live, but some people might feel that our recorded material gave less emphasis to rock.

John made it clear he wanted to play a big part in the production of the new album—initially he was obsessed about getting the *New Musical Express* onboard to support us. I wasn't so sure. I have a friend in Ibiza, Andy McKay, who runs an indie rock venue, Ibiza Rocks, which promotes the Who's Who of the *NME* indie world. Some of the best shows I've ever seen have been there, but I knew it would be a stretch for us to appeal to that audience, even for the most art-school version of Duran Duran.

"We'll never fit that format. Things have changed since you left the UK," I reminded John. "The *NME* never supported us before and they are even less likely to now."

JT was ever the romantic and still believed we could do it, but I balked at the thought of being labeled Old Romantics, which is probably how the *NME* would have perceived us. There's a big clue there in the name, John—*NME* stands for the *NEW Musical Express*! But if we made an edgy, alternative record and we went back to the root of where we came from, I was convinced it would be a cool place to start from. So initially, our second Sony album had nothing to do with the big commercial tricks that it later became associated with. The original plan was simply to make a record that would appeal to our fan base, something people would recognize for the songs and sounds associated with our original lineup. I reasoned that this could be the last record we would ever make, and we had a real opportunity to do something special. Eventually, we all agreed that going back to basics was our best course of action, so there was a positive quota of optimism as we prepared to commence recording. It later turned out to not be that simple because we made the classic mistake of trying to work without the balancing effect of a good producer, something we'd always had during the early eighties, throughout the period of all our best-selling records.

All we needed now was to decide on a venue for recording. Someone came up with a breathtaking plan (which was never fulfilled) to do it aboard a superyacht owned by Paul Allen, the cofounder of Microsoft. He had a $450 million vessel equipped with everything you could possibly want, including its own sound studio.

"You are welcome to use it and all you will have to pay for is your food and your catering," we were told.

We planned to pick up the yacht in Florida and then sail it down to Brazil in time for the carnival in Rio. Here we go again, I thought, yachts, fun . . . and parties! Everything was in place, and we even got the technical specifications of the studio sent over to us, but sadly the plan fell through at the last minute due to the boat becoming unavailable.

It didn't matter too much because we were soon offered an equally attractive alternative in the form of a $25 million mansion in San Francisco that belonged to Andre Agassi and Steffi Graf. The couple had asked us to appear at a charity event they were organizing in Las Vegas with Barbra Streisand, Robin Williams, and Celine Dion. We'd told them we didn't think we could make it because we were due to go into the recording studio, and we were once again thinking of renting a place in the south of France.

"Look no further," they responded. "You can use our home in San Francisco instead and turn that into a recording studio!"

It was an offer too good to refuse (along with being on the bill with Babs), so we accepted with the quid pro quo being that we agreed to attend the charity function in Vegas. Andre and Steffi weren't living at the house at the time, so there would be plenty of room for all our gear, and we were promised the complete run of the place for three weeks.

We were all looking forward to the trip, even though we only had a short break, but unfortunately the mood was soured when we had another row over money. Back in the eighties, anything we made after the Berrows had taken their cut had been split five equal ways, but now Nick and Simon argued that they were entitled to more because they had the most time served in the band. But did that "time served" really have such a positive effect on the Duran Duran legend? I tried to see their point, but it was always my understanding that I'd eventually be brought back up to parity. I had several blazing rows with our management about it. I felt that the input from Roger and me over the last five years had been crucial to help the band to the point where we were grossing millions of dollars on the road and Sony wanted to pick up a second album. At the same time, I was beginning to question what sort of percentage our management were taking from us, as I'd understood that the amount would be reduced after we'd grossed a certain amount of money from being on the road. So here we were, five years into our reunion, and still arguing about who got paid what.

WHEN we arrived in San Francisco we found the property we were staying at breathtaking. Andre and Steffi had clearly not spared a penny on the decor. The mansion was set in its own sumptuous grounds on a hillside across the bay from the Golden Gate Bridge. It was surrounded by some of the most expensive real estate in the world and it enjoyed sweeping views of Alcatraz down in the bay. I think it was a good job Andre and Steffi weren't around, because we soon turned the place into one big rock-and-roll recording party. We hired a professional chef and he turned out to be someone who had his own posse of mad friends from San Francisco. They all descended on the place on the first Sunday evening that we were there. The party just seems to find us!!!

Bloody hell, how are we going to get through this for the next three weeks? I asked myself.

There were CCTV cameras located throughout the grounds. I remember standing in the kitchen early one morning with John as we watched a hilarious scene unfold on a TV monitor that was trained on the gates. There were two women who'd been guests of our chef friend, and they'd clearly been partying through the night. I didn't think it was a good idea to give out the code to the gates to any of the guests, so they were in the process of climbing over the wall. Here we were in one of the most heavily policed parts of America, and there were guests clambering over the gates at 7 a.m. to leave the party! I'm sure Andre and Steffi would have been horrified, but thankfully none of the partygoers caused any damage, and we had cleaners who came up to the house each day to make sure we kept it shipshape.

We soon settled into a working pattern that was reasonably productive, although we could never quite finish what we were trying to do. In the past we'd had solid producers like Colin Thurston, Alex Sadkin, and Nile Rodgers, who'd helped to organize the band whenever we were recording, but on this occasion we were going it alone. In my opinion it was a mistake, because no matter how good an artist you are, you need the input of a producer because it's impossible to be objective about your own work.

Prior to leaving for San Francisco, I'd sat down and relistened to all the classic albums by David Bowie, because he'd been one of the roots of my inspiration when I was younger. I'd started writing material in different keys to what you'd normally use in order to make things sound a bit edgier. John, meanwhile, seemed determined to take center stage, and I noticed that he began to act more and more as if *he* was the producer by trying to coax the best out of Simon. Unfortunately, it didn't seem to be working, and the vocals refused to flow. We got bits and pieces in the bag, and I was heavily involved in writing a great deal of the material along with Simon. The creative process was something that the two of us had worked on together, but the guitar often sounded a bit too loud, and at times it seemed to overpower Simon. By the time our three weeks had passed we didn't have any songs completed, so we were supposed to meet up again in London soon afterward. I was disappointed as I felt we'd lost the momentum.

I spent the next few weeks with Tracey and our children revisiting some of our favorite haunts from when we'd previously lived in California. You could feel the conservative tide that had swept through America since our time there, but Tracey still regarded it as a home away from home. We looked up lots of old friends and it should have been a very nice time, but the problem was, *none* of it felt very nice to me. I'd stopped drinking and doing any of the things that affected me negatively, but I was still feeling very, very low. I still had trouble dealing with the loss of my father, and it struck me that most of my natural family back in Newcastle were now all dead, apart from one cousin. All my aunts and uncles who'd shared those long summer singsongs with my grandparents were all gone. Of course I had my own wonderful family now, but it still felt as if someone had cut the rope to my old life because there was nothing left back in Newcastle where I came from. It was a strange feeling, as if I was adrift six thousand miles away in California.

BY the time we prepared to reconvene in London, there had been no progress in the vocals department and it was now November. With hindsight it now seems obvious that we were heading for trouble. I was worried that we were moving too fast toward releasing the new album when we didn't have sufficient vocals in the bag. I poured out to everyone in the band. "Does anybody honestly think it's much fun having such an unplanned and incoherent schedule?" I asked.

Roger agreed that although the songs sounded great, it was very disappointing there had not been any progress with the vocals. Like me, he thought it was pointless to create any more backing tracks until Simon had nailed the existing tunes. There was also talk of trying to crank things up by tying the new album to a motion picture. I could see the potential in this, but I felt it was a very big idea to add to the proceedings at this stage. I again outlined to everyone my worries about our lack of direction and my fears that we were in danger of going ahead too early with the album. Looking at our recent record and ticket sales, I argued that we had to be realistic about the fact that we might not be able to shift anywhere near what we needed to ticket-wise if we went out too early.

I expressed my fears that the timeline being predicted for the release of the new album was not enough to accommodate our task. If we fucked up, we'd face an early bath, I warned. What we needed was finished songs, which we didn't have. Even Nick, so often my adversary, was willing to concede up to a degree that I had a point. He subsequently agreed we needed to be careful not to lose momentum or miss deadlines. Roger, shrewdly, added that until our existing material had reached its full vocal potential, if we did any more backing tracks all we would create was an "illusion of progress."

WE did some more recording in February 2006, and this time John seemed more determined than ever to take on the role of producer. It wasn't something that he articulated openly to us but he once again started taking center stage at every opportunity. I often wonder at what point in his day he decided to grab the bullshit by the horns. I agreed with his need to be positive, but it was overdone.

"Just drop that bit in here, Charlie, and do it like this," John would command Simon.

JT's enthusiasm was frightening at times, considering the quality of the material, and a more reluctant rather than petulant Le Bon would go with the flow. I guess working closer to John was some relief for Simon from me or Nick, however misguided it was. I think deep down John might have been trying to compensate for the fact that he'd missed out on a lot of the creative process in the eighties because he'd been so blitzed all the time. He was stone-cold sober now, but much as I love him to bits as a person, he's no producer. It was something that he'd never done before, and none of us seemed to be reacting positively to it. Nick has an ear for hearing when something is right and has a clinical way of getting things correct, but he seemed to have lost patience with Simon, and they no longer seemed to have a strong creative relationship.

So it was amid growing pressure that we found ourselves at Sphere Studios in London, which consisted of a big studio room, a drum room, and a lounge. By now I'd finished about twelve tracks as best as I could, but I felt there wasn't much melody to any of them. I was in the lounge watching the TV news when I realized I'd been sitting there for the last three days doing nothing apart from listening to John go over the same old things with Simon every time the studio door opened. It was costing us £3,000 a day in studio fees (even

302   **WILD BOY**

though by now I had my own studio in Ibiza) and yet they still seemed to be gardening up a hill. We'd spent £9,000 after three days and I was sitting around doing nothing hour after hour, having played enough guitar parts for about three albums. We needed a producer badly, and I wanted to stop the group from making a costly and irreversible mistake, as we were already heading well over our $450,000 budget to record the album.

"That's it. I'm out of here," I said.

"Finished for the day, AT?" I remember a sarcastic voice saying to me.

No, my friend, I am off back to a free bed and my family while you work this thing out. I don't and never have written lyrics. But I have a wife and four kids at home and they really do need babysitting, so that's where I will be. Additionally, you know that I have the studio at home where we can work for free at anytime, so let's cut the costs and get away from this very unproductive environment.

I had a bit of a row with Tracey that night because I was in such a foul mood, and the next day we flew back to Ibiza. I didn't know it then, but it was the last time I'd ever share a studio with the rest of the band, although I rejoined them as summer 2006 approached and we did a few more shows together. These were mainly corporate gigs designed to pay the staggering studio bills.

Despite my unhappiness in London, I still felt we had the makings of a good record. After all, I had written a large amount of the material myself and I had gone to great effort to make a success of things throughout the creative process with Simon. A lot of the basic structure of the unfinished tracks had been my work, so ultimately I wanted it to be a success. What we needed now, however, was someone to help us to filter and refine it. Two A & R guys from Sony came over to London in May 2006 to listen to the material and they gave us their verdict. Do not mix and deliver the record yet, it's not finished, they advised. It will only be rejected and you know you can do better with the right producer. A & R people don't always speak in such direct terms, but these guys were very concerned.

However, Nick, Simon, and John were determined to plow on with the mixing. Later that May they flew to New York to hand over the new material to Sony. Roger and I didn't go. We both felt the album needed more work.

"It just doesn't sound right, Andy," Roger told to me on the phone.

I was horrified with the mixes; they were undeliverable. The illusion of progress had taken over the process, and we were back to square one. Later I received a phone call from our management informing me that Sony had rejected the album. I could imagine Donnie Ienner sitting in his big office and listening to the album before saying bluntly, "Are you fucking kidding me?"

Surely, everyone would now accept that we needed to call in a producer to oversee the album? It was nothing to be ashamed of. Even the mighty Beatles would not have been the same without the genius of George Martin to guide them. However, I understood that our management were now hinting that Donnie, the president of the label, was the source of the problem!

What a fucked-up situation, I thought.

I expressed to our management my view that we'd progressed very little since San Francisco, particularly with regard to vocals. I told them in the strongest of terms that I felt it was outrageous that as a band we'd walked into a wall by presenting the album early, against the advice of the A & R team. I said it was a crass state of affairs and that we would never achieve anything collectively until we started to act collectively. It was my way of arguing to our management that we needed help. The way I saw it was that all the greatest records ever made had involved producers. No one is invincible.

Finally, after all this, the others eventually agreed to hire a producer. We were rehearsing for two corporate shows in June when we met with a well-known musical producer called Youth. He had a great track record. He'd just finished doing an album with Primal Scream, and I was intrigued by how he'd handled it. When we sat down with him I asked how they'd worked together and he said they'd done the whole thing in three weeks.

"We got up, we did the track, we did the vocals, we had dinner, and we finished it every day," he said.

In other words, you organized *the band and they respected you for it.* I felt he kind of understood what we needed. Everyone in the band was happy to work with Youth. We had a couple of gigs to play over the summer; one was a corporate gig for Deutsche Bank in Barcelona, and the other was a charity concert for the Royal Family in Monaco, after which we planned to begin working with Youth at his studio in Spain in September. I was confident he'd be able to listen to our sound and work out which bits were the most important and how to make all the various components work together as a whole. Sony were also very happy with this arrangement.

Around this time somebody came up with the idea that we could also do some work with the American producer, Timbaland. Although I was happy with Youth, I could see it made sense to look at this, as Timbaland was currently the top dog in the States, and producers can have a very positive effect on a record if their name is hot. *I don't have a problem with the proposal,* I thought, *as long as he just does one or two tracks with us and the whole thing doesn't turn into a million-dollar circus.* Later I got a phone call informing me that Timbaland needed to bring his session forward to September for scheduling reasons.

Although I didn't know it at the time, the show in Monaco was the last time I would ever perform live with Duran Duran.

I was tidying up a few bits and pieces in the garden at home when I received a phone call from someone in our office.

"How do you feel about working with Justin Timberlake?" they asked. I wondered what this added take on the Timbaland sessions was all about. Was this the reason they had been moved to September from October, forever looking for the Big Stunt? I remembered my conversation with Justin at the Brits, but I wasn't convinced he was the right solution to our problems. He's an accomplished and very successful artist, but we needed a strong producer, not a show business extravaganza.

History Repeats: Why I Am No Longer in Duran Duran   305

"Oh, but Justin is part of Timbaland's team," argued a member of our management.

"What fuckin' team? All we need is a producer," I said.

"Well, the Black Eyed Peas use a team."

I couldn't believe this. *We* are *the team,* I thought. *We just want an Alex Ferguson to coach us.* If, as I feared, marketing reasons were behind it then we were well and truly sunk. Either way, if it was destined to fail it wasn't for purely musical reasons. I just didn't get it. Maybe I was just not celebrity-oriented enough anymore?

IT was around this time that I looked at my passport and discovered that my American visa had expired four months previously. This sort of thing had always been handled by our US management company, so about three weeks before we were due to travel to the States to meet Timbaland I contacted our management in New York. Did I need a visa for this trip, I asked, and if so, were permits for all the band and crew in the process of being sorted out? Yes, it's all in hand, I was informed. Unfortunately, it turned out that my working visa *was* in hand, but only for the original October dates that we'd arranged with Timbaland (not the new September dates). It made me feel as if our management were now making the most basic of errors. The problem is that with today's security requirements you just can't blag your way into the USA like a naive English nanny. You must be legal and documented, and there is no slack allowed if you mess it up.

It was amid all this that life suddenly took an unexpected turn when I received the sort of phone call that every parent dreads.

"Hola, Señor Taylor?" asked the caller.

It was a doctor from the local hospital in Ibiza.

"I have your daughter, Georgie, here."

Zoom! A gazillion thoughts raced through my head.

"Is she okay? Why is she there?"

I listened as the doctor told me Georgie had been in a car accident while at the wheel at 5:20 p.m. She was badly shaken and had injured her leg, but fortunately she was sober and okay. She had been a very lucky girl. *Thank God*, I thought.

Georgie had an American passport because she was born in the USA, and the plan had been for her to come to America during the Timbaland trip to keep me company. I rushed down there to discover she'd damaged some ligaments in her leg and in her foot. It meant that she would need to be on crutches during the journey to the States, so I phoned the airline to make special arrangements. When we got to the airport a few days later I remembered that my visa situation still hadn't been resolved. It had been nagging away at me but because of all the last-minute disruption and panic caused by the accident I'd never got to the bottom of whether or not I could enter the US to work.

"Well I don't need a visa, Dad, because I've got a US passport," smiled Georgie at the airport.

As it transpired we couldn't have traveled to America that day anyway. Our flight to Madrid was postponed by three hours, and it meant we would miss our connecting flight to New York. A lot of rubbish was subsequently written about me later, claiming that I'd deliberately walked out on the band by refusing to go to New York, but that was never the case. The *Sunday Times* published a correction to this effect on May 4, 2008, which stated that I was "unable to get a US working visa to attend the New York recording session because of administrative failures by the band's management." I used the extra time we had in Ibiza due to the postponement to get onto the Internet and check out the exact situation regarding my visa, with a view to flying out the following day. I went ahead and confirmed the next day's flights along with wheelchair assistance for Georgie.

I then logged onto the Web site for the US Department of Homeland Security—and it confirmed my fears: it would be illegal for me to enter the States for work purposes without the appropriate visa. In the heated circumstances I was beyond angry with our management for letting the situation slide, and I tried to imagine what would have happened if I'd have arrived in New York without the correct paper-work. There was no way I'd be willing to lie and pretend I was not working. Logically, if any band members or any of their road crew had no work visas, then the sessions in September 2006 should never have been booked, period. In my view, there was just no excuse for not sorting this out and for allowing me to be put in this position.

I knew that after so much friction between me and some of the other members of the band over lyrics and money, they might interpret the fact that I couldn't travel as a sign that I no longer wanted to be in the band, but I felt I had no choice.

I later fired off the furious e-mail to our management that I copied to Simon, the one in which I said I was "fuckin' *seriously* unhappy." Unquestionably, everyone should now have been aware of the problem, or had at least been informed.

IN the days that followed there were several phone conversations between various parties on different sides of the Atlantic. I was still very angry and I could feel the weight of everything that had happened over the last year or so bearing down on me: my father's death, the constant arguments within the band—it felt as if I'd been trapped on a derailed runaway train. If I had believed I could legally travel to the States, then I would have already been in America, but the way things stood I no longer knew whether or not I wanted to continue in Duran Duran. It's one thing to deal with your brother's crap, but way too much of a stretch to accommodate management issues too. Once these start to interfere with the workings of the band it feels like they're trying to strap on some cheap new turbo to an old classic. If new parts aren't made with the same quality or class they will eventually fail.

The stress of everything was taking a heavy toll on me, just as it had done in 1985. I could feel that same weird sensation that I'd previously felt of being disconnected from the real world, and I remembered my recent conversation with Roger and John about how we all needed to take more care of ourselves.

Perhaps it was time to see a doctor, I thought. Part of me was thinking, *Don't be stupid, look at everything you have got. How can you be so down about things?* But life has its own way of unwinding and sometimes you have to adjust to it. So I saw a doctor and explained the way I felt and the context behind my circumstances. He sent me for a series of medical tests, including blood tests to check everything physical in case I had a thyroid problem or something of that order. The results came back clear and I was given a clean bill of physical health, apart from needing a small vitamin boost. Part of the problem was that my father's death was still taking a heavy toll on me.

"If you cannot control your grieving after a year then things have gone a bit further than they should have done," the doctor advised me. "The problem is that you haven't even stopped to think about it, you've just tried to carry on as if nothing has happened. You haven't taken any time to deal with this and it is having an adverse effect on you. Your work is unusual, and although many people suffer from problems at work, yours are of such a unique nature that you need to step back and address this with your business partners."

If only, I thought . . .

We had two concerts lined up for the near future, one of which was in Hong Kong. I understood that my lawyer had agreed with our management that I would not need to attend. I wrote a letter to the rest of the band, explaining that I wasn't feeling too great and that I'd been advised to take some time off, but that I was willing to attend our show in Warsaw. I suggested that I bring the doctor along and that he would be able to explain everything more fully to them, so I was offering to share some very private information with them.

I suspected I'd be able to gauge whether or not they wanted me to continue in Duran Duran by the tone of their response. The e-mail I got back from the rest of the band told me not to bother going to Warsaw and suggested that they come and see me instead. That wasn't the deal, I thought to myself. The e-mail read as if it had been written by the management rather than the band, and soon afterward my exit from the band became public.

"[Andy] has a virus and his doctor says he would be ill advised to travel," said a report that was posted on the Internet.

History Repeats: Why I Am No Longer in Duran Duran

There never was any virus—that information was false—but in the end, in late 2007, I *was* finally diagnosed as having suffered from clinical depression. The doctor suspected the root cause had been a delayed reaction to my father's death. I didn't take any medication, but the explanation made perfect sense. The stresses and strains had once again taken their toll.

AFTER parting from Duran Duran, I was now slowly starting to feel less depressed as I had the time and space to heal, although I can tell you that there were times when only a small part inside of me kept holding on, that tiny inner voice that reverberates to the famous chorus of *"Don't let the bastards grind you down!"*

I learned that depression is very common. It's not life threatening; it's something that given time you can get over. It's not something that I'm ashamed to admit to, because it can affect any and all of us, and it helped to explain why I'd been feeling so low at times. The one positive consequence is when you recover it makes you feel stronger inside and you find yourself running to places where you once feared to tread. You can take a battering in all different walks of life, and rock and roll is no different. So the doctor simply advised me to rest and he explained that the burnout I'd been through was mental and not physical. Ever wondered where you would be without your health? Well, now I know. Once again, it was time to slowly let out the air, just as I had done in 1986.

I guess the lifestyle we led in the band took its toll on all of us over the years in one way or another. For me that toll led to depression, John ended up in rehab, and Roger had his battles with exhaustion and agoraphobia. Nick got locked in what must have eventually been a troubled marriage to Julie Anne, given that they later divorced. Even Simon, who found so much happiness with Yasmin, didn't emerge unscathed, having been nearly killed on a yacht and landing himself in the hospital through a motorcycle crash. When people look at young stars today, like Britney Spears or Amy Winehouse, as they

310   **WILD BOY**

struggle to cope with life at the center of the circus, there's a temptation to think it's a new phenomenon. But we went through our own problems in Duran Duran—it's just that things weren't picked over in quite the same detail back in the eighties.

Shortly before we parted company in 2006, Nick had approached me one day at our rehearsals in June and he told me he thought he'd discovered a way of wrestling back ownership of all our early work from EMI's subsidiary company Gloucester Place Music (the company the Berrows sold out to in 1986). It could have involved taking legal action, but we never got around to discussing it further. It might have made a difference, because we'd have retained ownership of all of our work. Each one of us might be worth tens of millions of pounds today, and money might not have been such a sore point. Simon and I would certainly never have run out of money at the cash machine!

But you learn to take life as it comes and today I can look back on my time in Duran Duran with fresh eyes, and I realize that what we enjoyed together was something very special. I'm totally back to my old self now, and I can look out across the beautiful rolling hills of the Mediterranean and reflect upon why we couldn't make it work in 2006. I didn't listen to all of *Red Carpet Massacre,* the album that the rest of the band eventually released through Sony, but I heard a couple of the tracks. The title song "Red Carpet Massacre" was something that someone like me would have tried to avoid, because in my view it sounds like it was written in a hurry and the chorus is very repetitive.

People have wrongly assumed that I didn't want to be in the band, but the opposite is the truth. I always wanted to be in Duran Duran, but we'd ceased to function as a band; it was seriously *dysfunctional.* We'd returned to being five individuals pulling in different directions, just as we'd become in the eighties. When it came to sorting out our problems, just like before, we failed to connect. I don't have an answer for why that is—I guess we were all just coming from different places. In hindsight, that was our dilemma from day one: we were always five very different individuals, but it was that very diversity that drove our success. Despite all our arguments, Nick and I needed each other just as much as we needed every other member of the band. It meant we all had the capacity to do things which were incredibly original and successful, but we also had a huge mechanism for self-destruction. Perhaps things might have been different if we had all sat down together and discussed the tensions that tore us apart the first time around, but that never happened. In fact, I don't think I ever once went to dinner with Nick during the six years that we were back together. There was no cocaine the second time around, but in the end it was the similar tensions caused by internal disagreements that came bubbling back to the surface.

History really did repeat itself.

People sometimes ask me what was more fulfilling: Duran Duran during the eighties or our time together after our reunion? For me that's easy. The excitement of helping to invent something for the first time and breaking it in in the eighties will always remain our greatest achievement. We still lived in a much more naive world in the early eighties, and it felt like a much bigger prize to play for. But the second time around was also enjoyable for the recognition that it earned us via things like the Brits and the MTV Awards. When we were younger we got an enormous amount of success, but we didn't really get a lot of recognition from the music industry, at least not in the UK.

I will always remain incredibly proud of everything we achieved in Duran Duran.

But the one thing above all else that continues to make everything so worthwhile was the warm reaction of our wonderful fans both times around. I think they understand most of all that the secret of our success was our diversity. During the final stages of working on this book I received an e-mail from a woman who explained that Duran Duran fans love their roses and chocolates, but she said they also like steak and beer.

I guess that what she was trying to say was Simon and Nick were always very good at delivering roses and chocolate, but that I was the steak and the beer in Duran Duran.

I'm happy to settle for that.

EPILOGUE

Ibiza—2008

IT'S *a telling moment the first time that you hear recorded music in the control room of a newly installed sound studio. The acoustics of every room are different, and when all the work and the wiring are finally completed it's time to test everything and you know within the first few seconds whether or not you have it right. On the first day that I hooked up my equipment here in Ibiza, I grabbed the nearest mix CD to play on the studio speakers for the first time. It was a Trevor Nelson DJ set from Pacha in Ibiza, so I thought it would be funky and heavy on the bass, which are all good things to help judge the quality and resonance of the room. The CD had no track listing on it, so I skipped the first track, because on mix tapes the intro can go on for a long time, and I hit play on the second.*

Boom.

"I'm Coming Out," by Diana Ross, came on, which was produced, written, and performed by the late Bernard Edwards, Nile Rodgers, and the late Tony Thompson. Cool, and the room sounded good!!! The spirits are with me today, *I thought. Out of all the tracks I could have randomly played, it was that one. Still, I think we all agree that a person's influence*

can be as powerful in both life and death. The acoustics needed a tiny bit of fine-tuning, but since then I've never looked back. Many young bands have been out to Ibiza to record with me. Playing a great record is a very simple way to test a room, but I must confess that this particular experience was a bit more three-dimensional than usual and it still makes me wonder about things today.

As I stand on the balcony of our villa, looking out across the sun-drenched hills, Tracey is inside fixing up a cup of tea. We have four lovely children and a strong marriage that has survived twenty-five years of constant pressure. Below me is the courtyard where I smashed a beer bottle against the wall following my row with Simon Le Bon. Things are peaceful here now and I'm at peace with myself. So I'll return to the question I asked at the beginning of the book while I was tossing and turning in that sweaty hotel room after Live Aid. Was the roller-coaster ride all worth it? The answer is a resounding yes. Sure, there were plenty of lows (like the time I fell in that bloody lagoon) but life is a series of ups and downs and we all have to choose our paths as we see fit at the time. I don't hold any grudges against anyone in Duran Duran. Why should I? Maybe if there'd been fewer lows there wouldn't have been so many highs, so you learn to take the rough with the smooth. I can honestly say that even if I had to do it all over again I don't think I would change a thing.

Well, maybe next time I'll give a miss to swallowing all that elephants' piss . . .

INDEX

WILD BOY

Index

Who, the, 67, 74
Wickett, Andy, 41–42, 105
"Wild Boys," 184, 278–79
   video, 99–100, 111–12, 183–86
"Wild Horse, The," 236
Williams, Robbie, 276–77
Williams, Robin, 298
Wilson, Mitchell, 79, 82, 83
Wilson, Sean, 79, 82, 182–83
Wilson, Tracey. See Taylor, Tracey Wilson
Wolverhampton General Hospital, 86–87
Wonder, Stevie, 31
Wood, Ronnie, 6, 206–7, 214, 215

Wood, Roy, 44
workingmen's clubs, 10, 12, 29–30
World Cup Finals, 256–57
World War II, 11, 30
Worthington, Frank, 44
Wyman, Bill, 207

Yates, Paula, 136, 293
Young, Angus, 31, 252
Youth (musical producer), 304–5

Zachau, Eric, 23
Ziggy Stardust, 253